TRANSGRESSING BOUNDARIES
New directions in the
study of culture in Africa

Edited by
Brenda Cooper and Andrew Steyn

University of Cape Town Press
in association with the
Centre for African Studies

Ohio University Press, Athens

First published in 1996
UCT Press, University of Cape Town, Private Bag, 7700 Rondebosch, South Africa,
in association with the Centre for African Studies, University of Cape Town

ISBN 0–7992–1649–6

Published 1997 in the United States of America by Ohio University Press,
Scott Quadrangle, Athens, Ohio 45701

ISBN 0–8214–1183–7

Library of Congress Cataloging-in-Publication Data available

Text design and typesetting: birga thomas
Cover design: Kaleidesign
Cover illustration: Malcolm Payne
Illustrations on page 140: Figures 1 and 2 from South African National Gallery

Printed and bound by Creda Press, Cape Town

Table of contents

Notes on contributors

Colin Bundy is Director of the Institute for Historical Research at the University of the Western Cape, South Africa.

David Bunn is Professor of English at the University of the Western Cape, South Africa.

Laura Chrisman is Senior Lecturer in the School of African and Asian Studies at the University of Sussex, England.

Jean Comaroff is Professor of Anthropology at the University of Chicago, USA.

Brenda Cooper is Director of the Centre for African Studies at the University of Cape Town, South Africa.

David Coplan is Associate Professor in the Department of Anthropology at the University of Cape Town, South Africa.

Patricia Davison is Head of the Department of African Studies and Anthropology at the South African Museum.

Haile Gerima is a filmmaker and Professor of Radio, Television and Film at Howard University, USA.

Martin Hall is Professor of Archaeology at the University of Cape Town, South Africa.

Isabel Hofmeyr is Professor of African Literature at the University of the Witwatersrand, South Africa.

Terry Lovell is director of the recently established Centre for the Study of Women and Gender at the University of Warwick, England.

Obi Maduakor is Professor of English at the University of Nigeria.

Gary Minkley is Senior Lecturer in the Department of History at the University of the Western Cape, South Africa.

Malcolm Payne is a practising artist and Senior Lecturer in painting at the Michaelis School of Fine Art, University of Cape Town, South Africa.

Andrew Steyn is the Cultural Projects Co-ordinator in the Centre for African Studies at the University of Cape Town, South Africa.

C. Jane Taylor is a Senior Lecturer in the Department of English at the University of the Western Cape, South Africa.

Bridget Thompson is Director of *tomas films*, a film production services and education consultancy based in Cape Town, South Africa.

Introduction

Brenda Cooper and Andrew Steyn

In September 1993 the Centre for African Studies at the University of Cape Town ran a conference called "Appropriations: New directions in African cultural studies?" This book continues to ask that question. It repeats some of the debates that arose in and out of the conference, and it revises and modifies some of the issues that were aired there. It also includes new papers that we commissioned afterwards to take the discussion further.

In other words, this is not a collection of conference papers as such. The conference was a catalyst for us to produce a book centred on the question of the study of culture in Africa. What has been called African studies, including the study of culture, has in the South African context been largely restricted to studies of southern African issues. With the lifting of the cultural and academic boycotts in recent years, this tendency is rapidly changing, with greater engagement between South African and other African intellectuals now taking place.

Furthermore, neither African studies nor cultural studies exist in South Africa, either as concepts with a shared definition, nor in clearly identifiable and similar institutions across the country. These "studies" span centres, departments, institutes and campuses, and are located in disciplines as diverse as literature, anthropology, history, film, sociology, and so on. They are situated within diverse politics, language, theories and methodologies. We felt, therefore, that it was more correct to describe what follows as contributions to the questions of how, what and where cultural issues have been and are being studied in South Africa. This is to avoid the implication that a unified subject called African cultural studies is currently operative here.

The dominant themes of this publication of appropriations and transgressions of boundaries, have served to enable and focus debate on "new" emerging theoretical trends in a moment that has fundamentally challenged some of the established ways of thinking about our world(s). What are the new emerging intellectual lenses, and on what terms do we transgress now, as we create knowledge in radically changing times? Global events (the collapse of the Soviet Union, the hegemony of late capitalism, worldwide electronic communication, increasing poverty) and regional transformations (the collapse of apartheid hegemony, new nationalisms, shrinking university budgets, new political issues) intersect and challenge both traditional disciplinary discourses as well as interdisciplinary programmes. In a time of transformation and change politically and intellectually, where and how are new knowledges being created and what do they look like?

"Transgression" refers also to our sense that while we cannot pin the study of culture down institutionally, intellectually or politically, this study can be located at the "cutting edge" – disrespectful of the boundaries of disciplines, the turfs of departments, and the vested interests of institutions. It also refers most strongly to the fact that the study of culture is, by definition, multidisciplinary and covers a range of media. Culture is popular and intellectual, fine art, literature, music and film, as well as, more broadly, the values and ways of life of different groups in different places at different times.

Having said this, some of the chapters (Comaroff and Lovell) do advise caution in the too hasty overthrow of the disciplines and suggest that both boundaries as well as their infringement create the intellectual combustion necessary for highlighting new insights.

Lovell argues that, in fact, the disciplines have to some extent become less burdensome under the impact of the challenge that postmodernism has issued. There is also the reality that these once marginalised, vulnerable studies – of gender, culture and Africa – have "come in from the cold" and occupy much stronger, institutionalised positions of power, again with benefits and losses. This has resonance within a changing power balance here.

Also, and this point is critical, we recognise the danger of disrespect for some of the unique and particular demands of different branches of cultural endeavour, a point made very forcefully in Gerima's internal dialogue as a film-maker. We felt it was important at the conference to include work from different media. This is not to deny that a cultural class struggle exists, particularly on the university campus, where theoretical words are often conceptualised as the upper class and practising artists as the workers. We contest these boundaries in recognising theory as creative practice and the makers of art as pioneers in the construction of new languages of theory.

Be this as it may, the danger remains that when we contest boundaries, we collapse difference and thereby initiate a new kind of intellectual and cultural imperialism. The tension between transgression of boundaries and respect for difference remains a struggle and a debating point.

There are two types of contribution to this book, although there are substantial overlaps between them. There are, firstly, the highly theoretical essays, all of which tend, very helpfully, to try to map this vast field of the study of culture. They, between them, examine the relationship between Marxism and Postmodernism and attempt to pinpoint the current politics of culture (Lovell, Bundy and Comaroff). They look globally and make suggestions regarding what might fruitfully be appropriated from, say, Britain and from other studies, like woman's studies or the far more concrete cultural studies practiced in Britain (Lovell and Chrisman).

There are, secondly, the case studies and the responses to them, the bulk of which, however, are highly self-conscious, theoretically and methodologically. The three main case studies, which act to demonstrate, exemplify and highlight some of the theoretical debates and questions, are poison (Bunn, Taylor and Hofmeyr), the Lydenburg Heads (Hall, Payne and Davison) and slavery (Maduakor, Thompson, Coplan and Cooper).

The papers by Cooper and Steyn and Minkley also combine functions in the attempt specifically to help focus and pull together some of the theoretical issues raised in this book. They also make some suggestions as to the nature of the future directions that might emerge.

Underlying all of these contributions is the essential point that what is at stake is cultural politics; that African studies is what Lovell calls a standpoint knowledge, the wish to understand, in order to challenge, oppression.

Part One of this collection debates some of the macro-theoretical issues of the day. Terry Lovell's paper compares woman's studies, cultural studies and African studies from a number of different standpoints. She centres her argument on the British case, in which she works, and provides a basis for comparison and learning for us in South Africa. Lovell questions why, given that the existing disciplines did not have an appropriate language for the study of gender, women and the working class, were they not forced to transform themselves? Why did these studies have to develop beyond the disciplines? Like the disciplines, moreover, Marxism did not have a language that could speak the issues of gender. Lovell demonstrates how Marxism's inability to meet the needs of woman's studies, turned feminist theorists towards postmodernism with its abandonment of the dominant male narratives, of which Marxism was seen to be one. At the same time Lovell states that global developments cannot be understood without a theory of capitalism and it is still only Marxist-influenced theories which address these questions.

Bundy argues that the central challenge of Lovell's paper is its call for the reintegration of the issues of cultural and woman's studies with the explanatory force of Marxism. He responds with a much stronger and less ambiguous call for a revitalised Marxism. Bundy does not underestimate the enormity or complexity of that process of revitalisation where Marxism has to respond to the valid critiques of feminism and cultural studies. Marxism's tools will have to be sharpened and even overhauled. However, what survives as an immutable core is the totalising powers of Marxist analysis. Bundy concludes that, paradoxically, the most productive "new" direction for a radical African cultural studies may be to appropriate and borrow not only from the postmodernists, but from the Marxist armoury.

Jean Comaroff examines on a global scale what she describes as our current profoundly destabalised moment of late capitalism, a moment that has been called, among other things, postmodern or postcolonial. This crisis of naming, the proliferation of scare marks, is indicative of how many core assumptions are being called into question. This moment, described on a global scale, from a United States perspective in Part One of this book, has very interesting parallels with, and differences from, the equally unstable 'nineties in South Africa, as sketched by Steyn and Minkley in Part Three. Comaroff also struggles to define a desirable theoretical middle space – one that accepts the social and cultural determinations of Marxism, but at the same time understands that these determinations operate differently from the story that classical, universalist European narratives told. She argues that conceptions of power, agency, practice and meaning cannot be accounted for in the language of the old Masters, be they Marx or Weber.

We pointed out earlier on in the Introduction that the Centre for African Studies conference was merely a springboard for this book. This is reflected in the fact that while Lovell was the keynote speaker at the conference and Bundy was the respondent to her paper, Lovell has since re-worked her paper to include her response to Bundy's response, in true postmodern style. This explains why Lovell's paper precedes Bundy's and simultaneously refers to it. A month after the conference, Jean Comaroff visited the Centre for African Studies and made a presentation tackling many of the same issues rehearsed by Bundy and Lovell, and which she edited for inclusion in this book. Bundy spoke as a South African historian, Lovell as a British sociologist and pioneer of a new Centre for Woman's Studies and Comaroff as an ex-South African anthropologist based in Chicago.

Part Two is organised around the case studies of poison, the Lydenburg Heads and slavery, which are presented as illustrations of the power of multidisciplinary study of culture in Africa.

The thrust of both Bunn and Taylor's papers is the analysis of cultural forms as texts or discourses. They acknowledge some of the dangers of textualist analyses of culture. As Bunn realises, talking about poison is not simply a textual matter. Poison was a powerful tool in the arsenal of the indigenous population in its struggle against the settler. Its symbolic force derives from its material reality as superior and lethal local knowledge. Bunn examines South African texts in the eighteenth and early nineteenth centuries and Taylor considers metropolitan texts in the Victorian era. In this regard, Hofmeyr in responding to the papers, notes that they situate themselves at the boundary of local and imperial knowledge, within an interdisciplinary model.

Hofmeyr goes on to raise questions about the issue of what can and cannot be read from texts and to bemoan the general lack of interest in the complexities and specificities of local knowledge. Hofmeyr concludes with important comments regarding the necessary expansion of African cultural studies in South Africa, beyond our own borders.

The next case study relates to the Lydenburg Heads and their various representations and appropriations. Hall's paper negotiates that complex relationship between objects as material culture and texts as representations and interpretations of the past, always put to use in the present. He charts the various manifestations of the heads, ranging from diverse interpretations of their origins, to their transformation into an image for use as a logo for the Centre for African Studies, to their inspiration for the artist Malcolm Payne, to the Centre for African Studies' re-appropriation, now of Payne's image as logo for the conference and as cover for this book. In other words, during the course of his paper, Hall uncovers three overlapping sets of meanings acquired by the heads – the archaeological interpretations, the politics of symbolic meaning in their usage as logos and as inspiration for the artist who transforms them, politically and aesthetically.

Davison responds to Hall's paper with a plea for a greater concern with human agency in the theorisation of the object. She also insists that while the significance of the heads is open to many readings, there is also a degree of historical, factual knowledge about them that stabilises the range of meanings attributable to them.

The third case study is the representation of slavery. At the conference we hosted the South African premier of Haile Gerima's film about slavery, entitled *Sankofa*. Coplan and Thompson give very different interpretations of the politics of this film. Gerima himself very significantly takes a different angle in his discussion. He criticises the tendency to look at the contents of film and argues passionately that film requires to be understood in its own unique, cinematic terms. He shows how desperately impoverished the infrastructure is for those who wish to make African film in opposition to the values, money and power of Hollywood.

Maduakor looks at the representation of slavery in the imaginative fiction. He traces the history of this representation and is surprised that the consciousness of the slave past is so marginal to Nigerian writing.

Cooper concludes this part by trying to bring together some of the theoretical issues raised in Part One and to link and apply them to the case study of slavery in Part Two. Within the theoretical paradigm of the reconstituted Marxism, as proposed by Bundy, she attempts to analyse the representation of slavery in the fiction of a Sierra Leonian, Syl Cheney-Coker. This she does with a view to making some comments about possible desirable theoretical and methodological directions of

African studies at the University of Cape Town.

Part Three concludes the volume with theory linked to questions of the future of the study of culture in Africa, within a reconstituted South Africa. Chrisman, who summed up for us at the conference what she saw as having emerged by the end of it, later prepared this paper for this publication. She looks at the politics and history of the emergence of cultural studies in the U.K. with a view to suggesting what might be appropriated by us here and now.

Steyn and Minkley map this unique South African moment of the 'nineties in terms of both the past and the possible dominant directions of the future. Their paper functions also as a conclusion to the collection as a whole, given that the mapping process they undertake enables them to classify many of the contributions to this collection in the terms of their sub-title which questions whose are the "dominant voices" and where are the theoretical trends.

Part One

MAPPING THE FIELD

Marxism, Postmodernism, the Disciplines

and the Study of African Culture

The Burden of the Disciplines
African studies, women's studies, cultural studies

Terry Lovell

African studies, cultural studies, women's studies: three intellectual developments which are quite literally undisciplined. They cannot be contained within any single organising frame, neither have they developed into recognisable new disciplines. Rather each has remained a broad field of study which borrows across a diverse range of disciplines in a series of appropriations which have frequently been transformed by their new context. Often there has been an uncomfortable relationship to the "parent" disciplines, critical and sometimes abrasive. Women's studies, (British) cultural studies and a radicalised African studies from the 1960s are self-consciously "standpoint knowledges". Each erected their knowledge-claims from the standpoint of a subordinated and oppressed social category or grouping that had suffered what the French sociologist, Pierre Bourdieu, terms "symbolic violence", within structures of domination and subordination based on colonialism and "race", gender or class. Bearers of subjugated cultural formations (Foucault 1980) which had been disallowed or ignored within the dominant culture, these social groupings, in so far as they were recognised within the dominant disciplines of knowledge production at all, were objects rather than knowledge-producing subjects.

Of the three, only Africa was the object of systematic scrutiny. The colonial gaze generated a new discipline, anthropology, and new branches of study based on established areas of inquiry: African literature, African art, African languages, politics, history. Collectively these ventures founded African studies, one of a number of "area studies", many of them set up in the second half of the twentieth century in the wake of independence movements in colonial and postcolonial states.

Women, and the working class, putative knowing subjects of women's studies and (British) cultural studies respectively, were rarely deemed worthy of disciplined study, with the single exception of biology in the case of women. They were represented rather in the discourses of common sense, opinion, prejudice, popular iconography. They were produced as objects, idealised as often as they were execrated, of a broad range of cultural discourses. A mythologised image of the British working class, for example, has from time to time been drawn upon to figure a sentimentalised national identity:

> Its face stares at us from a thousand photographs and films. In popular representations the virtues are familiar: decency and common sense; community and a sense of everyone pulling together, everyone "doing their bit"; deference to one's betters and sympathy for the underdog; stoicism and resilience under duress; gruff fatalism and a philosophy of modest but legitimate expectations. (Eley 1)

Woman, the African, the worker: all produced in such cultural imaginings, but also, in parallel discourses, objects of fear, fascination, loathing.

Radical African studies evolved in a space which was already occupied and marked out by discourses and disciplines which frequently, if not uniformly or directly, serviced the intellectual needs of the colonial administration. Here, the relationship between knowledge and power was fairly transparent. By contrast the founders of (British) cultural studies were able to locate themselves within radical traditions from the start, for the proletariat is, of course, the prime object of studies which locate themselves within Marxist and socialist traditions of thought, putative knowing subjects of these investigations. Cultural studies made raids on literary criticism and cultural and sociological theory from a secure base in which the claims of the working class as subjects of knowledge were already established and acknowledged, even privileged: working class historiography, labour studies, adult education, Marxist and socialist theory.

Women's studies began with perhaps the fewest credentials, for it lacked legitimacy even within the radical discourses of labour history and Marxism. "Woman" was, as Virginia Woolf discovered on the visit to the British Museum described in *A Room of One's Own*, the object of prolix discourses:

> Have you any notion of how many books are written about women in the course of one year? Have you any notion how many are written by men? Are you aware that you are, perhaps, the most discussed animal in the universe? (Woolf 27)

Yet this discursive cacophony was in stark contrast to the near-silence about women and gender within academic disciplines such as sociology, history, literary criticism and theory, economics, political theory. These disciplines were constructed by and large as though the human world was genderless. The knowing subjects of the humanities and social sciences were men masquerading as the abstract individual inquiring subjects of Enlightenment philosophy, objective, disinterested and rational observers. The "humanity" studied had distinctly masculine traits.

I can match Woolf's anecdote with one of my own. In the early 1970s I was asked to give a talk on the education of girls in contemporary Britain. I visited the section of the library at Warwick which housed books on the sociology of education, to find what was known about the schooling of girls. I searched through the radical canon of texts deeply critical of educational practice and the ways in which it serviced capitalism in reproducing class relations of domination and subordination, which purported to be about the education of that genderless category, the child, but turned out to be exclusively about the education of boys. This neglect of women and girls within the literature of sociology was, paradoxically and with no sense of irony or apology, used in the early 1970s to try to block the development of courses on "women in society", "gender divisions", etc. on the grounds that the academic literature was too sparse. . . .

The major discipline which placed women under the microscope, was of course biology, and here gender-difference was produced as part of an unchanging natural world. Recent deconstructions of biological discourse, such as that of Emily Martin, describe the ways in which social stereotypes of gender were inscribed in the very terms used: in accounts of biological processes such as menstruation and conception. The ovum was personified as a passive, immobile, sleeping princess, who depended on the heroism of the active, probing, energetic sperm, hell-bent on rescue even at the cost of "his" own inevitable destruction, in the interest of awakening "her" to "her" biological destiny.

Feminists who wanted to make women the subjects, women and gender the objects of disciplinary interest, drew on the ephemera of the burgeoning women's movement, reached out and borrowed whatever was to hand and relevant: poetry and imaginative literature as well as more academic forms of writing. Radical texts from the Marxist and socialist canon were scrutinised in an effort to make them yield feminist knowledges. But working-class historiography and the new forums created for the study of working-class culture in the mid-1960s, proved every bit as male-orientated as the disciplines and histories they challenged so radically. Sally Alexander recalls

> . . . the gust of masculine laughter at the 1969 Ruskin History Workshop when a number of us women asked for a meeting of those present who might be interested in working on "Women's History". I do remember the bewilderment and indignation we felt as we walked away from the conference to plan another of our own. (Alexander 127)

All three infant fields of study, then, had to establish themselves in large part negatively, through extended critiques of literatures within which Africa, women, the working class, were invisible, marginalised, or (mis)represented, and then to produce the new field of study in positive terms. They drew upon and recovered subjugated cultures: African culture, working-class culture; women's culture, developing and transforming these to feed into counter-disciplines. All three were quickly constrained to develop a positive literature and a theoretical frame of reference with which to mark out their field. All three drew on many of the same theoretical resources in their projects: Marxism and the radical theory, still at that time owing allegiance to Marxism, which was being revitalised and transformed in Paris and elsewhere.

Interdisciplinarity

Women's studies and cultural studies developed as interdisciplinary studies. African studies, as was pointed out by my respondant Colin Bundy, was multidisciplinary, flowing along the lines marked out by the older disciplines.

Granted that the existing disciplines, as they were framed, could not readily accommodate the study of women and gender, or working-class culture, why did they develop across disciplinary boundaries, rather than forcing the transformation of those frames, or the staking out of new disciplines?

Disciplinarity, like formal organisation in political life, has after all distinct advantages. A discipline, with its theoretical and methodological paradigms, directs inquiry, defining the questions to which answers may be sought within its terms, and indicating how to go about searching for answers. A discipline demarcates a relevant literature, and I often think when attending such conferences as these, that what facilitates communication between participants is less a shared and rationally demarcated discipline than shared reading. While straying into other literatures is often serendipitous, with exciting recognitions of analogies and parallels or new ways of looking at familiar problems, the placing of limits upon what one needs to read and understand, before being able to make a contribution, is perhaps essential. Disciplines make intellectual inquiry and study orderly and manageable.

Why then the felt need for interdisciplinarity? Disciplines not only focus and direct inquiry; by the same token they make certain questions difficult if not impossible to ask; they close off certain lines of inquiry before they begin (Foucault 1970). To give just one example: Carol Cohn was a college teacher in the U.S. who seized the opportunity to spend a year at a university centre on defence technology and arms control. Her motivation was to try to understand the irrational "rationality" of the systems they explained and justified for dealing with the problems of nuclear weapons. The questions she wished to ask of the "defence intellectuals" with whom she was in daily contact were those she brought from her own feminist and pacifist politics. What she found was that the questions were not taken seriously because they were not posed within the terms of the discourse of defence technology and control. So she set about learning the language, and she describes the buzz of pleasure it gave her to become a competent user, to be listened to and taken seriously. But she also found that it was increasingly difficult to frame her questions within the terms of "clean bombs and clean language". "It is simply learning a new language, but by the time you are through, the content of what you can talk about is monumentally different, as is the perspective from which you speak." (Cohn 705)

Feminist intellectuals will be very familiar with this experience, whatever their discipline. Indeed we had the same difficulties when we attempted to make Marxism our own. We learned the language to enable us to master the *Capital* and then we tried to make our questions fit his answers (Graham 1983). The whole tortuous history of the infamous "domestic labour debate" graphically illustrates this process (Malos 1980). Such experiences do not encourage respect for boundaries, and the sanctioning of such disrespect by the discourses of postmodernity is, no doubt, one of the reasons why many feminists have been attracted to them.

Feminism, like postmodernism and like cultural studies, has been associated with the movement not only across disciplinary boundaries but between types of discourse. It has moved freely between imaginative literature and culture, and the academic disciplines. Feminists, like others working within cultural studies, have been greatly influenced by the work of Raymond Williams, despite the almost entire absence within his discursive writings of any direct discussion of gender. Anyone who wishes to extract Williams's understandings of gender will do well to turn to his novels. For the nature of this particular form is such that gender cannot be missing in quite the same way, and perhaps this is why feminists, since Mary Wollstonecraft, have experimented with different kinds of writing, especially fiction. For here is a discursive frame which centres gender.

I will argue that the movement across disciplines and discourses was doubly determined. Firstly, these interdisciplinary and multidisciplinary studies began not from any theory that marked out its proper object and domain, but from concrete political subjects, the oppressed groupings and categories whose standpoints they took. Secondly, by the fact that the theory which was drawn upon was increasingly what Edward Said has called "travelling theory".

Standpoint theory and politics

If women's studies, like cultural studies, has been interdisciplinary, it has nevertheless been governed by a discipline of sorts. The frame which set the questions, which Cohn wished to put to her defence intellectuals were political and moral. Those which governed women's studies as it negotiated its path through and across the disciplines was the urgent wish to understand, in order to challenge, the oppressions suffered by women. Women's studies, like African studies and studies of working-class culture, are standpoint knowledges. Women's studies took, consciously, the standpoint of women, and the shift in terminology from "women" to "gender" has occasioned passionate resistance on just this count.

In a sense, of course, all knowledges are standpoint knowledges – situated historically and socially, generated from within the world and not from some archimedian point outside. But they do not, typically, begin from the study of concrete categories of human beings. The objects studied are demarcated by the paradigms which govern theory and method within the field. Standpoint theories, armed with an epistemology which links knowledge to human interests, begins from those interests. But typically, these take the theorist across conventional demarcations of the disciplines within the social sciences and humanities, because all of these resources are required in order to understand and confront the multifarious forms and sites of that oppression. Furthermore, because that oppression is not produced and reproduced independently of these disciplines, but in part in and through them. Knowledge-production and the production and reproduction of structured inequalities were understood to be deeply implicated in one another. Standpoint knowledges were to be knowledges which would work for the excluded and dispossessed.

Feminist standpoint epistemology was modelled on the Marxist class-centred account of knowledge production. Where Marxism took the standpoint of a collective working-class subject, feminist standpoint epistemologists argued for the erection of feminist knowledge grounded on that of women (Hartsock 1983, Harding 1986, Harding 1989, Smith 1990). However, standpoint theory very quickly runs aground on some thorny problems. What does it mean to take the "standpoint" of women, Africans, the working class? For these are not unitary categories sharing a readily defined common set of interests and objectives. For a start, they are not mutually exclusive categories, and it is usually black women who are systematically occluded in each standpoint approach: "all the women are white, all the men are black" (Hull 1982).

Feminism was sharply critiqued by black women in Britain and the U.S., who pointed out the exclusionary practices and terms of much (white, middle-class) feminist politics and theory. Standpoint epistemologists such as Sandra Harding attempted to meet the challenge by ceding the diversity of feminist standpoints (Harding 1989). But the effect can be to drain feminism of any specific meanings or specific political commitments, as the proliferation of standpoints fragments and splinters any collective subject of political action. Once this happens, feminist interdisciplinary inquiry is in danger of losing its bearings entirely, as the very concept of feminism is deconstructed in its turn.

Marxism and its discontents

The theories on which women's studies and cultural studies have successively drawn, have travelled along a trajectory from Western Marxism to contemporary postmodernism. Travelling theory, too, travels across the boundaries of the disciplines. Many feminists have pulled up short on this journey with travelling theory. African studies in general and African cultural studies in particular, now face the question of whether to go the whole distance: hence the conference theme of "appropriations". What in the Marxist heritage is it vital to retain? How does it need to be transformed and reworked in the post-communist era? What appropriations is it necessary or useful to take from contemporary travelling theory?

In so far as they drew on Marxism, women's studies, African studies and cultural studies were all three, necessarily, "Marxists with problems". For while Marxism is a theory which takes the standpoint of the working-class movement, thus centring the working-class subject of (British) cultural studies at least, yet it was deeply problematic for the *cultural* aspect of cultural studies because of the inadequacies of its conceptualisation of language, art, literature. These were so frequently, within the orthodox Marxist canon, opposed along with "ideas", to "material life". Still, cultural studies could at least draw on the writings of Western Marxisms, which concentrated on so-called superstructural relations and processes – Lukacs, Gramsci, Sartre, and then in the 1960s, Althusser. And in Raymond Williams's "cultural materialism" cultural studies was offered a Marxism which comprehensively refused the distinction between base and superstructure, culture and material life (Williams 1977).

African studies may be multidisciplinary rather than interdisciplinary. But the difference is perhaps not as great as all that. Radical African studies drew above all on Marxism, but Marxism is not bounded by any single discipline. In principle, it is an overarching "grand narrative" within which the objects of all the social sciences and indeed of the social world may find themselves. Marxism disciplines, no doubt about it. But it does so through the rigour of its theory.

Classical Marxism has more to say about colonialism than about language and culture. But Africanists faced a difficulty, which may be seen in acute form in the case of the troubled history of the notorious "Asiatic mode of production". Marx was of most use when what he had written directly and immediately about colonialism was ignored. In his journalistic writings on India and China in the 1850s, Marx took a perverse pleasure in at once denouncing and exposing the moral perfidy of British and other imperialist powers, yet welcoming the functions of the Western despoiling of the East, which he saw as propelling stagnant, cyclical social formations into history:

England, it is true, in causing a social revolution in Hindostan, was actuated only by the vilest interests, and was stupid in her manner of enforcing them. But that is not the question. The question is, can mankind fulfill its destiny without a fundamental revolution of the social state of Asia? If not, whatever may have been the crimes of England she was the unconscious tool of history . . . (in Avineri 94)

These writings were not focused on Africa, but their tenor is as Orientalist as that of any of Said's imperialist apologists. The exponents of Afrocentrism will not find much ammunition in Marx, without some very fundamental reworking.

Radical feminism eschewed the attempt to forge Marxism into a theory for feminism. Marx and Engels were dismissed, alongside the whole gamut of contemporary and past theoretical gurus, left and right, as "malestream thinkers". Those of us who identified as Marxist or socialist feminists, struggled mightily with the *Capital*, and were eagerly drawn to visit and revisit the work of Engels on the family, in an attempt to make these texts deliver a Marxist feminist theory that could hold its own academically, winning the intellectual respect of our radical left colleagues at least, and forming the basis for left intellectual and political alliances and exchanges. But even feminists who wished to draw on Marxism might draw back on account of the inequality of the emerging relationship between the two. Heidi Hartmann drew attention to the problem in a striking analogy:

> The "marriage" of marxism and feminism has been like the marriage of husband and wife depicted in English common law: marxism and feminism are one, and that one is marxism. Recent attempts to integrate marxism and feminism are unsatisfactory to us as feminists because they subsume the feminist struggle into the "larger" struggle against capital. To continue our simile further, either we need a healthier marriage or we need a divorce. (in Sargent 2)

But there were more fundamental limitations to Marxism as a theoretical resource for feminism. Firstly, as Carolyn Steedman puts it:

> When the mental life of working-class women is entered into the realm of production, and their narrative is allowed to disrupt the monolithic story of wage-labour and capital, and when childhood and childhood learning are reckoned with, then what makes the old story unsatisfactory is not so much its granite-like *plot* built around exploiter and exploited, capital and proletariat, but rather its *timing*: the precise how and why of the development of class-consciousness. (Steedman 14)

Secondly, it was becoming clear that gender identities and attachments were not like restrictive corsets that might be discarded once their deforming effects were exposed. They were deeply implicated in the inner life of persons, inscribed in the very sense of who we are at a fundamental level. But Marxism did not theorise an interiorised sexed subjectivity and the development of the self. Feminists were obliged to seek elsewhere, and where else was there to begin the search but Freud, and after Freud, Lacan?

Thirdly, Marxism placed at the centre of the frame, as the prime mover of history, the social relations of production, and because women were marginalised in production, they were also marginalised within Marxist theory. As I wrote in an earlier piece, "Marxism permits feminist history, but without necessarily permitting it to *make a difference*. While psychoanalysis is every bit as male centred as Marxism, because it theorises sexual difference and sexed subjectivity, then feminist intervention here *must* make a difference. Sex and gender are quite crucially at stake in a way in which they need not be in Marxism." (Lovell 25).

I want to reiterate these points about the intellectual and explanatory inadequacies and limitations of Marxism in relation to feminism that made even Marxist feminists hold back, and search so urgently for another means of theorising "the sex-gender system". Feminism, like cultural studies, embarked along the road marked out by "travelling theory" because such theorising promised to deliver more adequate understandings of sexed subjectivity, language and culture. Moreover most of those Marxist feminists who took to the road with travelling theory did so on the understanding that they were developing a theory which complemented Marxism. Many, such as Juliet Mitchell, developed what became known as "dual systems theory", looking to Lacanian psychoanalysis to theorise the "sex-gender system" or "patriarchy", alongside the Marxist analysis of the capitalist mode of production (Mitchell 1974). It was only gradually that the extent of the move away from Marxism became apparent.

Travelling theory and the disciplines

Travelling theory was beginning to travel from the 1960s, then in directions which seemed to lead further and further away from Marxism. This trajectory was already in evidence in the heyday of campus radicalism. The new intellectuals of the Left Bank were developing ideas which, while often claiming to advance or build upon Marxism, were already more strictly post-Marxist: Foucault, Barthes, Levi-Strauss, Lacan, Derrida, Kristeva: This illustrious roll-call identifies the precursors and prophets of a postmodernism and poststructuralism, which have between them threatened to sweep the intellectual board in the late twentieth century. Under the auspices of postmodernism, the death of grand narratives and above all the master narrative of Marxism, was soon declared. Even Althusser, who wrote his texts "for Marx", founded his work in positions that some of us believed to be profoundly incompatible with Marxism. Edward Said's analysis of Orientalism in 1977 had an enormous impact, but his approach owes as much to Foucault as it does to Marx.

It was cultural studies above all that was heir to the revisionism of travelling theory, for such theory brought language, culture and subjectivity, crucial in the study of culture, from the marginal spaces they occupied within classical Marxism to the centre of both theory and analysis. This was their strength and their attraction. However, they also succeeded over time in marginalising what had been centred in classical Marxism: class, the economy, the modes and relations of production. Within the discourses of postmodernity it is rare to find the kind of integrated study of gender, subjectivity, African and working-class literature and culture, in a carefully delineated history of capitalism national and international, of the kind that we had sought within the early formation of cultural studies and women's studies. It is for this project that we need to seek new appropriations in African cultural studies.

Yet it was in a large part the unstitching of disciplinary boundaries under the impact across a broad range of disciplines of "travelling theory", that facilitated the founding of these radical interdisciplinary fields of study. The story of the Centre for Contemporary Cultural Studies (CCCS) in Birmingham has been told many times. It is a tale of a hostile and grudging process of accommodation, squeezed between the departments of English and sociology, denied full legitimacy by both. This hostility was perhaps prescient, for cultural studies challenged the boundaries and methods of both adjacent disciplines, creating in the process an intermediary resting place which facilitated the move back and forth between English and sociology: Stuart Hall began in English, became the second director of the CCCS, and then moved to the Open University as a professor of sociology. Simon Frith passed him moving in the opposite direction, from the sociology department at the University of Warwick, to the chair of English at Strathclyde.

We may add a little codicil to the story. For cultural studies has finally (or at least temporarily) come in from the cold. The ravages of Thatcherism and the reification of market principles in the academy has led to some unexpected windfalls. Numbers persuade at least as eloquently as scholarship. Effective demand commands resources. The Centre in Birmingham, now incorporating the rump of one of its old opponents, the department of sociology, launched an undergraduate degree two or three years ago. It attracted about 1 600 applicants for some 40 places. Intellectual credentials are no longer wont to be challenged openly in the face of such impressive evidence of student demand. You cannot buck the market, as they say. . . .

The story of disciplinary resuturing that I know best concerns sociology in Britain, under the impact of feminism, and of "travelling theory", and it is in itself an interesting sociological narrative. In 1963, when I was an undergraduate, women represented about 29 per cent of the student population in higher education in Britain. Today the numbers are approaching parity. During the 1960s higher education expanded rapidly, and new universities such as Warwick, Sussex and Kent were founded. The local authority sector, the erstwhile polytechnics, which have recently received university status, also expanded at an unprecedented rate.

Sociology itself grew from a minor discipline, which was professed in few places, and which had no A-level to feed into it from schools, into a major discipline within the social sciences. Seventeen new university departments of sociology were set up between 1960 and 1970. The number of degrees in sociology attained between 1962 and 1967 had increased by 389 per cent.

This exponential growth happened to coincide with the onset of the Women's Liberation Movement and the advance of contemporary feminism. Many more young women began to enter higher education, and they chose to study traditionally "feminine" subjects, including sociology (sociology attracts roughly the same proportion of female students as English – upwards of 70 per cent or more). Many of these women were active in the women's movement. They came through higher education at a time when, for a fleeting moment, it was easier to embark upon an academic career than it had ever been before or has been since. It was this generation of women who confronted sociology (and English) with feminism, and fought to establish women's studies courses within sociology and other degree courses, and later in specialist graduate studies programmes.

However, I do not believe that this could have happened had not the disciplinary certainties of sociology already been systematically eroded under the impact of travelling theory during the 1960s and 1970s, from sources that had little to do with feminism *per se*. Structural-functionalism, the dominant theoretical frame of reference within the discipline at the end of the 1950s, was in decline, and there was a search for alternative and more radical approaches in phenomenology, ethnomethodology and, above all, Marxism. The argument that there was no *sociological* literature on women and gender would perhaps have been decisive in a discipline which was more securely in command of its own paradigm. Feminism's impact on departments of politics or economics, and even, in Britain, in more orthodox history departments, has been later and less extensive. In sociology we were permitted to make shift with what was available without having to worry unduly about its academic credentials as sociology, until a sociological literature began to emerge from feminist research. Today there is a plenitude of such literature.

And so I would want to say, in considering the question of "the burden of the disciplines", that the relevant disciplines are no longer what they once were, and no longer so very burdensome. Many of the older established disciplines are on the defensive. English, for example, has a long-standing and acute sense of crisis, which is not unconnected with the development within its boundaries of feminist literary theory and criticism, cultural studies, postcolonial literary theory, deconstructionism, and so on (Bergonzi 1990). Indeed we might repeat what Stuart Hall has to say about the way he finds himself propelled from margin to centre in a "postmodern" world:

> One of the fascinating things about this discussion is to find myself centred at last. Now that, in the postmodern age, you all feel so dispersed I become centred. What I've thought of as dispersed and fragmented comes, paradoxically, to be the representative modern condition! This is coming home with a vengeance. (Hall 44)

It would be a gross exaggeration to claim that African studies, women's studies, cultural studies are the representative modern forms of intellectual investigation, the fractured subjects of postmodern inquiry. But it is hard to find any discipline in the humanities and social sciences, and even in the "softer" sciences, which has not begun to question and transgress its own boundaries under the influence of deconstruction, structuralism and poststructuralism, and postmodernism, as they cut broad swathes across disciplinary frontiers.

The disciplines have become less burdensome then, under the impact of radical "travelling theory" and student demand. In Britain at least, the times are not unpropitious for multidisciplinary and interdisciplinary studies. There is a generation of scholars in place in institutions of higher education and research centres, many in senior posts and well-placed to sponsor new developments in these areas. There is not the same concerted resistance from the older disciplines, which have had perforce to allow such developments to emerge from within their own ranks and may even welcome their externalisation in specialist programmes (Bergonzi 1990).

Today, cultural studies and women's studies programmes are springing up all over Britain, in a scramble to take advantage of buoyant student demand. Resistance may still be mounted successfully from the backwoodsmen, but one has the sense that their hearts are no longer in the fight. So far as women's studies goes, my own university, Warwick, established in 1993 a Centre for the Study of Women and Gender, with two new posts in the first instance, and the promise of more to follow as the Centre expands. The reason is abundantly clear. We attract highly qualified, highly motivated students in large numbers.

However, if the disciplines have changed, so has travelling theory, and so too have these new interdisciplinary studies which have drawn so heavily upon such theory. How radical have these developments remained in the face of incorporation, combined with the deracination of a great deal of travelling theory? It is notable that the students who are attracted to women's studies courses may no longer be assumed to be feminists, and often have no history (how could they have, the youngest among them?) of involvement in an active political women's movement. There is a noticeable split in each group that comes through our M.A. programme between intellectually very gifted young women whose interests are primarily philosophical and theoretical, and who do not identify feminism as first and foremost a *politics;* for whom Marxism and Marxist feminism belong, perhaps, in Jurassic Park; and those, often older, students who take the programmes on a part-time basis and who have employment or other experience, which brings them into day-to-day contact with grossly disadvantaged and oppressed women; whose interest in women's studies meshes feminist political and theoretical questions in the manner of an earlier generation.

Cultural studies, too, has travelled with travelling theory, away from the concern with working-class culture that has today become distinctly unfashionable, and into the higher reaches of often arcane and always difficult cultural theory. When I compiled a collection of articles on feminist cultural studies in 1992, one woman, who I approached for advice, asked me whether by "cultural studies" I referred to the British tradition, in which the link with working-class culture is still tenuously maintained through the study of popular culture, or the American, which she identified as "groovy theory". Of African studies I have no personal experience. However, the programme announcing this conference located its concerns in the context of the crisis of Marxism, the "master narrative" which has provided the intellectual lens for radical African studies, including African cultural studies.

What's left? Appropriations, retentions, syntheses

I want to argue then, against the burden of my title, that the disciplines are less burdensome than they once were; that interdisciplinarity carries its own burdens; and that the major intellectual problems facing women's studies, cultural studies and African studies, now that they have each become more or less accepted, concern the direction such studies should take in the face of the onslaught on Marxism and the rise of "successor theories". These successor theories have delivered a great deal; certainly they have transformed cultural studies in ways that are exhilarating and liberating. Both women's studies and African studies are implicated in the project of cultural studies, and women's studies especially has begun to buy into these successor theories in a major way. But these theories have, equally, provoked dismayed incomprehension, suspicion, reasoned rejection (Lovibond 1989, Soper 1991, Modleski 1992). African studies as it has been practiced at the Centre for African Studies at the University of Cape Town, host of this conference, has located itself in relation to both a Marxist-orientated historiography, and to feminism, and has insisted on the necessity of addressing African literature and art within the same frame as African history, economics, politics. It therefore faces the questions addressed in this paper in a particularly acute form.

What Marxism theorised above all was the capitalist mode of production. It identified conflict and contradiction as its historical motor: between forces and relations of production; between the classes that were its precipitates. What Marxism facilitated was the analysis of concrete historical social formations in a manner that would guide political intervention to hasten and aid the transition to socialism.

In principle, this architectonic structure of theory might include culture, language and gendered subjectivity. But it provided little by way of concepts and theory to guide these inclusions, and those who wished to place cultural studies within its frame worked with the concept of ideology as developed by Western Marxists, especially Gramsci and Althusser.

In a recent work, Michèle Barrett, one of the leading exponents of Marxist feminism in Britain during the 1970s and 1980s, identifies and critiques the various versions of ideology which Marxism generates, and finds them all wanting. She argues for the selective and critical appropriation of Foucault for the work of theorising subjectivity and culture. And she is surely right that Marxism has not been notably successful in incorporating these matters into its accounts of history and politics.

However, I am left with a problem in so far as her critique leaves untouched the question of whether these newer theories can in their turn address the areas of social life that Marxism centred in its analysis: capitalism and the social relations of production. Travelling theory has offered women's studies and cultural studies more satisfactory tools for analysis of phenomena absolutely central to their concerns. But it has given little place within its own theorising to the social relations of production, which have quietly absented themselves from the work within cultural and women's studies of theorists who have appropriated these newer approaches.

Meanwhile those left theorists, who are still centrally concerned with economic and political analysis, continue their work undisturbed by the questions which cultural studies, feminism and travelling theory have raised, untouched by any necessity to consider language, culture and gendered subjectivity as relevant to their enquiries.

The suffering and inequity which prompted the emancipatory projects with which African studies, cultural studies and women's studies associated themselves in erecting themselves as standpoint knowledges, are no less urgent today. In contemporary Britain there is a sharp and widening divide that separates those women who have benefited from two decades of access to higher education from the rest. Many young women now routinely expect to have careers as well as marriages and families; to remain single without stigma; to feel free to assert alternative sexualities. Women are beginning to gain ground in hierarchies within places of work, occupations, cultural production. The proportion of women in the workforce is rapidly approaching parity, and it is predicted that in the near future women will overtake men, so that the typical worker will be a woman.

In so far as she *is* typical she will of course be low paid, and may see stretching in front of her not the expanding opportunities of her well-heeled sisters, but a lifetime of inescapable poverty and disadvantage. An article in *The Independent on*

Sunday described working women as "the new proletariat" (Cohen and Borrill 1993), one which is without the institutional protection of the labour movement, and whose slender guarantees against superexploitation have been removed with the abolition of Wages Councils, whose brief was to monitor certain traditionally low-paid industries and to set minimum wages and conditions of work. This is a class divide between women that is subtly different from the earlier, more familiar one. Increasing numbers of women are gaining middle-class identities and life-styles, not through their personal relationships with men, but through their own independent occupational status. They are beneficiaries of the 1970s women's movement and wider access to higher education. They have learnt to be assertive. They may well have followed women's studies courses as part of their degree programmes. A deep gulf has opened up between these women and the new female proletariat.

Meanwhile domestic violence continues unabated; the poverty line finds women and children heavily over-represented among those who struggle to live their daily lives beneath it. And women of African-Caribbean and Asian descent are very much more likely to be unemployed and impoverished, to have open to them only the least attractive forms of employment, than are white women. There has been an escalating attack on single mothers, who are threatened with the withdrawal of welfare benefits. Racist attacks are increasing in frightening fashion. Our inner cities and the housing estates, in which the so-called underclass must pass their lives, are in decay and disorder.

The global perspective offers even worse prospects. The tragedy enacted in Bosnia is causing appalling suffering, not least to women and children. Rape is used as a weapon of war and of "ethnic cleansing". The breakup of the former Soviet Union has all of us holding our breath, for fear of what may yet transpire there. The planet itself is buckling under centuries of assault. The left has been obliged to contemplate a future socialism built not on plenty, on the accelerated exploitation of a nature whose bounty knew no limits, but on scarcity, and on the urgent need to place environmental issues high on the political agenda. And finally, here in South Africa, the long-awaited overthrow of one of the most evil forms of colonial domination in history is accompanied by desperate scenes of slaughter and destruction.

Can such developments be monitored and understood without a theory of capitalism, global and local? I very much doubt it. And it is still Marxist-influenced theories which address such questions. Those theorists who view structures as the illusory products of outmoded narratives do not on the whole address these phenomena. I have yet to see a postmodernist analysis of women's changing place in the workforce, for example, or of the new international division of labour.

Yet it is equally true that these same theories have been utilised by feminists to analyse phenomena that simply fall outside the purview of Marxism. Foucault has been appropriated by many feminists who have used his theories of discursive formations to analyse such diverse phenomena as sexual murder (Cameron and Frazer 1987), pornography and the law (Smart 1990), gendered subjectivities (Hollway 1984, Weedon 1987) and domestic woman in eighteenth-century literature (Armstrong 1990). Yet these, too, are sites of women's oppression which feminism must address.

Poststructuralism and forms of postmodernism have informed studies of postcolonialism in literature and social life. Black feminists such as Bell Hooks have begun to argue that we should use its resources to avoid the dead-end of essentialist identity-politics; of standpoint epistemologies that, with the endless proliferation of standpoints from which it is claimed our diverse knowledges and politics flow, leaves us all, finally, able to claim that we represent a minority of one (Hooks 1991). (At a recent dayschool on equal opportunities one young woman unveiled with pride her firm's new equal opportunities slogan: "What do all of us have in common? We are all different.")

Appropriations to the left; but one reason for the suspicion on the left of poststructuralist and postmodernist theory is that they seem to be as readily appropriable from all sides. While it is true that very powerful appropriations have been assayed from the left, it is clear that within the discourses of postmodernism and poststructuralism, left political stances become strictly optional. I am reminded of the story Terry Eagleton tells:

> I once had a conversation with a member of the "Yale School" about Derrida's politics, which ran slowly aground on my gathering recognition that, as far as my interlocutor was concerned, we might have been discussing Derrida's taste in antique snuffboxes. (87)

Although appropriations as opposed to strict orthodoxy has always had to be the name of the game in relation to Marxism so far as African studies, cultural studies and women's studies were concerned, it was a matter of principled appropriation within certain parameters. The political engagement was *not* optional, and could not be discarded. It is not so much the actual political commitments of this or that poststructuralist or postmodernist thinker that is disquieting: for every de Man there is a Spivak. Rather it lies in the fact that there is no necessary connection between the theory and the politics, and that the self-same theoretical stance may be as readily appropriated to the right as to the left.

The move away from Marxism is often portrayed as yet another instance of the betrayal of the intellectuals (Gross 1990). While I would fully endorse the view, expressed by Colin Bundy in his response to this paper, that ex-Marxists have ceded too much too soon, it is vital that we do not lose sight of the *intellectual* motivations behind the recourse to travelling theory. The unmasking and condemnation of political betrayals may have the effect of sweeping away from sight these very real intellectual difficulties. While the move from psychoanalysis and semiotics to structuralism, poststructuralism and postmodernism may have coincided with a move to the right, I do not believe that this rightward movement explains this intellectual development. Unless we engage very fully with the intellectual and theoretical arguments at stake here, we are in danger of losing the gains made in the course of this move into new forms of theorising, reinstating unreconstructed forms of Marxism (Gross 1990).

What we urgently require at the present time is neither to abandon Marxism, nor yet a return to Marxist fundamentalism, but the urgent and major reworking of Marxism in a spirit that is not overly reverential or too anxious about accusations of revisionism. It was asked in the conference discussion whether there were any components of Marxism that were "write-protected": not to be questioned or tampered with if the result is still to count as "Marxist". Perhaps it would be as well to accept for a period at least the suspension of all "write-protection". We should not worry unduly at this stage about the precise standing within the Marxist tradition of any emergent synthesis, nor about intellectual copyright, though I do believe we must strive for overall coherence and intellectual credibility, and not succumb to an unprincipled eclecticism or pragmatism.

My experience of this conference, and of the intellectual atmosphere that obtains in this my small sample of academic life here in South Africa, suggests a very different "structure of feeling" than any with which I am familiar. South African intellectual life still bears visible marks of the period in which the universities were important *loci* of resistance against apartheid. There is a strong and vibrant sense that is quite electrifying in comparison with anything that I have come across in Britain for over two decades, that cultural policy and intellectual work *matters*. Perhaps the southern African context is one of those, like Sartre's moment in Paris at the end of the war (Sartre 1988), in which literature, and intellectual work more generally, feels the absolute necessity of commitment and therefore of a very clearly politicised theory such as Marxism, and perhaps also one which has the strongest motivation to engage in the work of developing the type of synthesis that we all so urgently seek.

Sharing the Burden?
A response to Terry Lovell

Colin Bundy

Our keynote speaker has flown to Cape Town under the flag of travelling theory. She represents (she has today re-presented) British radical interdisciplinary studies: not as an ambassador, nothing so formal; but perhaps as an emissary, one with a message, and with the subsidiary hint of espionage that the term conveys. Terry Lovell joins us as a travelling theorist: not in the banal sense of having journeyed here to discuss theory, but having located her commentary within Said's concept. That is, she draws attention to the origins of theory; its transmission, its reception and impact, and its eventual incorporation.

It is not clear where this leaves a discussant. Is my role that of the immigration desk, checking the *curriculum visa* of our visitor and authorising her stay? Is it that of customs officer, scanning her intellectual baggage for contraband ideas? Or am I a tour guide, making sure she is comfortable and apologising for local hotels? Having checked with the conference organisers, I discover that what they expect the discussant to be is a porter. My role is to follow Terry Lovell, to pick up what she has brought with her – the paper – and to share its burden. But (it is hardly necessary to warn someone travelling theorist class) porters will sometimes rummage inside what they have been given to carry, even rifle its contents. This inhospitable act, pilferage masquerading as service, is yet another form of what this conference calls appropriations.

However, it is entirely unnecessary surreptitiously to purloin from the keynote paper, so generously does it hand out ideas, themes and problems that will engage participants for the duration of the conference. Let me identify a few of the issues it poses, none of which I shall have time to explore, but each of which deserves further consideration during the conference.

First, there is the whole question of disciplinarity: of how areas of formal study are defined, defended, breached, broken apart and bridged. Lovell suggests that women's studies, cultural studies and African studies are similar. Each appropriates from a diverse range of older disciplines; each is self-consciously a "standpoint knowledge"; and all share a disquieting, critical relationship with their parent disciplines *and* with their common paradigmatic godparent, Marxism. There is some tension in this taxonomy. Women's studies and cultural studies, quite clearly, were inter-disciplinary fields of inquiry: their locus was interstitial, their advances secured by hand-to-hand combat in the disciplinary marchlands.

In contrast, African studies (as Lovell notes) comprised a stable of existing disciplines: literature, art, history, languages, politics and latterly anthropology, sired by Colonial Office out of Law and Order. Although each of these area-specific disciplines was radicalised in comparable ways in the 1960s, and while there was a powerful cross-disciplinary thrust in scholarship on Africa, they were never inter-disciplinary in the same way as women's studies and cultural studies. Perhaps one of the tasks of this conference is to be precise about prefixes: to tease out the differences between inter-, multi-, supra- and contra-disciplinary approaches.

Secondly, Lovell also raises important questions concerning the penalties of success. Cultural studies and women's studies in Britain no longer fight for recognition. Driven by student demand, validated by institutional approval, these areas of study have shifted from the academic margins to somewhere nearer the centre. And, asks Lovell, how much has the erstwhile radicalism of these interdisciplinary studies been blunted by their incorporation? If they have largely been delinked from the social forces that once energised them, how has this affected their research agendas? Do structures of knowledge production appear somehow different when one is inside them, looking out? Lovell poses these questions, retrospectively, in the British case. The identical issues already confront us in South Africa, but, on all sorts of intellectual and institutional fronts, promise to become rapidly more urgent.

Thirdly, Lovell's paper emphasises the extent to which cultural studies and women's studies – originally "rooted in Marxism" – have travelled away from Marxism. This rerouting stemmed from a "growing recognition of the imitations of Marxism with respect to language, literature and culture, gender, subjectivity, 'race' and 'otherness'". More than that: "Under the auspices of postmodernism, the death of grand narratives, and above all the master narrative of Marxism" was soon declared. Lovell draws up a pretty conclusive balance sheet as to the contemporary standing of Marxism in British intellectual life: "Today, it is extremely difficult to found one's scholarship and research in Marxism"; "postmodernism and poststructuralism . . . between them have swept the intellectual board in the late twentieth century"; Marxism has been displaced on the shelves and reading lists, by the successor theories.

Lovell is torn by this. On the one hand, she identifies herself quite strongly with the criticisms that have been made of classical Marxism, its blind spots, its totalising narrative, its privileging of class over other social identities, and so on. On the other hand, she is also aware of the way in which the strengths of Marxism have been dissipated; she is concerned that cultural studies have lost sight of the social relations of production, effectively reinstating the distinction between culture and material life. She regrets that within postmodernity "there is no necessary connection between the theory and the political". There is an unmistakably wistful note to the conclusion of her first section.

> Within the discourses of postmodernity it is rare to find the kind of integrated study of gender, subjectivity, African and working-class literature and culture, in a carefully delineated history of capitalism national and international, of the kind that we had sought within the early formation of African studies, cultural studies, women's studies. It is for this project that we need to seek new appropriations.

This is arguably the central challenge of Lovell's paper: a call for an intellectual project that can reintegrate the subjects of cultural and women's studies – and their concern for liminality, diversity, multivalency – with the historical explanatory force of Marxism. It is not entirely clear how Lovell would advise us to meet this challenge. If radical feminist and African studies have called into question the ontological and epistemological bases of Western scholarship, including Marxism, then upon what terms is a reappropriation of the strengths of Marxism to take place? How ought – no, how *can* – the current generation of scholars reintroduce politics, or a critique of capitalism, or praxis to a discourse that not merely downplays but anathematises them? Presumably it involves more than an exercise of will and cannot be achieved by a kind of paradigmatic pardon? Crucially, we would need to consider what Said calls "conditions of acceptance or, as an inevitable part of acceptance, resistance" (227) which confront any travelling idea.

My response to Lovell's challenge is an oblique and tentative one. It does not pretend to solve the problem just mentioned; rather, it revisits the dilemma, reformulating it from the standpoint of a social scientist with some background in African studies. First, I would like to offer a different take on the "revisionism of travelling theory", focusing not upon its epistemology so much as its history and politics. Secondly, I would like to make a couple of comments on Africa and the development of African studies. Finally I will try to loop back to the question of Marxism, postmodernity and appropriation.

The dizzying story of intellectual ferment and innovation in post-war France has been extensively reviewed, and its broad outlines are familiar. In the early 1950s, existentialism, phenomenology and an orthodox Marxism held sway; Sartre tried, but failed, to reconstruct French Marxism, to make it intellectually less reductionist and politically less subservient to Stalinism. Instead, Levi-Strauss and Lacan seized the high ground with the linguistically-orientated discourse of structuralism. French structuralists accounted for social phenomena in terms of linguistic or semiotic structure, rules, systems and codes. Althusser attempted to graft the new vocabulary and concerns of structuralism to the body of Marxism, and create a more scientific materialist philosophy; but ultimately "cloistered knowledge within a wholly circular, self-validating conceptual realm" (Geras 18).

Scarcely had structuralism set out its stall when its assumptions and procedures were in turn assailed by the post-structuralists, led by Derrida, Foucault, Lyotard, Barthes and Kristeva. Critical of all universal or totalising explanations, insistent upon the instability and contingency of meaning, scornful of conventional representational models of knowledge, and alert to the myriad, dispersed sources of power and dominance, the post-structuralist project defined itself in opposition to rationalism, progress and humanism. It also broke decisively with Marxism, rejecting its monism, essentialism, reductionism and claims to epistemological superiority. In the 1970s, the post-structuralist critique fairly dominated French intellectual life.

These distinctively Gallic developments increasingly took on Anglo-Saxon accents; and they formed "part of the matrix of postmodern theory" (Best and Kellner 25). I have already committed more than enough violence to complex ideas by such brutal compression, and shrink from trying to define the theoretical and cultural concerns of postmodernity. Let me simply quote from Ihab Hassan's well-known and rather lyrical evocation of the broader pattern of postmodernism: its characteristics are

> indeterminacy and immanence; ubiquitous simulacra, pseudo-events; a conscious lack of mastery, lightness and evanescence everywhere; a new temporality, or rather intemporality, a polychronic sense of history; a patchwork or ludic, transgressive or deconstructive approach to knowledge and authority; an ironic, parodic, reflexive, fantastic awareness of the moment; a linguistic turn, semiotic imperative in culture; and in society generally the violence of local desires diffused into a terminology of seduction and force . . . a vast revisionary will in the Western world, unsettling-re-settling codes, canons, procedures, beliefs - intimating a post-humanism. (Hassan xvi)

Hassan also proposes, in an avalanche of alliteration, that the mode of enquiry of postmodernism proceeds by "decreation, disintegration, deconstruction, decentrement, displacement, difference, discontinuity, disjunction, disappearance, decomposition, dedefinition, demystification, detotalisation, delegitimation" (92).

But back to France. The sequence of intellectual shifts summarised a moment ago took place alongside, and articulated with, an equally momentous set of political developments: the eight years of war in Algeria; the grandeur of the de Gaulle era;

the headiness of 1968 – and the hangover that followed it. In three decades, from the mid-1950s to the early 1980s, France ceased to be the home of a coherent socialist and Marxist left; in 1984 Perry Anderson wrote "Paris is today the capital of European intellectual reaction" (32). In a fascinating essay, George Ross links the story of the intellectual shifts to an account and explanation of the restructuring of French politics (Ross 1990).

Ross' analysis operates at three levels: First, and familiarly, at the level of the intellectual titans – Sartre, Levi-Stráuss, Lacan, Derrida, Foucault, Barthes. His second layer is that of the "artisanal" political sociologists – the echelon of academic reading and teaching the new work. And thirdly he looks at successive generational cohorts of young French intellectuals: the whole new "middle stratum" of graduates produced by a rapidly expanding university system. He identifies an Algerian War generation, the May 1968 generation, or *soixante-huitard*, and the generation that came of age in the aftermath of '68, and which helped elect Mitterand in 1981. What he demonstrates is that the break with Marxism came at different times and for different reasons with each of these layers. But, by the mid-1970s, the younger intellectuals and by the early 1980s the academic artisans, had decisively broken with Marxist thought and politics.

Poststructuralism in France during the 1970s (concludes Ross) was a form of thought welcomed by the new middle-strata hostile to socialism and seeking an ideological hegemony of their own. It was appropriate to a generation deeply sceptical of politics, opposed to state intervention for public welfare, and imbued with a new individualism. French neo-liberalism in the 1980s, the "micro-waved reheating of John Locke and Alexis de Tocqueville" (Ross 221), marched in step with the politics of Thatcher, Kohl and Reagan.

I suspect that the next step of my argument is already evident, especially if we bear in mind Said's advice on how to track travelling theory: examine its point of origin, its passage through the pressure of various contexts to another time and place, and the reception, accommodation and transformation that ensues (Said 226–7). Poststructuralism and postmodernism crossed the English channel and the Atlantic Ocean with remarkable success. In America, most particularly, the dominant form of post-modern theorising accommodated itself most comfortably within the revivalist right-wing ethos of the 1980s. The decentred, playful, open-ended virtues sung by Hassan all too readily transposed into depoliticised, cynical and faddish disengagement.

The 1980s, remark Best and Kellner, "was an unparalleled era of corruption, cynicism, conservatism, superficiality and societal regression, and one could argue that postmodern theory expressed these trends". Post-modern discourse, they suggest, "offered solace for isolated and embittered intellectuals who gave up hope for social change" (297, 285). This pattern – of intellectuals despairing of radical change, abandoning macropolitics and finding justification in selected tenets of post-modernist thought – should provide food for thought for left academics in South Africa today. The shift here is still a shuffle rather than a stampede, but it is a move in the same direction. To historicise postmodernist thought in this way (especially when one is painting with such broad brush-strokes) is not to reject its insights, emphases, concepts and approaches *tout court*. It is a way of suggesting that some of the excesses, biases, tendencies and political implications of some poststructuralist and postmodernist analyses reflect larger political, cultural and historical developments.

France, Britain, America, South Africa: this may seem a rather circuitous journey for a conference on "New Directions for African Cultural Studies". But having arrived on this continent, I want to make some rather bald comments about the project of African cultural studies at a South African university. Firstly, it might be asked whether this conference is discussing African culture – the production and consumption of culture in Africa – or whether it is primarily concerned with how African culture is received, mediated and studied in the metropolis? How audible or silent here are some of the issues and debates that have engaged African scholars and intellectuals in recent decades? What echoes are there at this conference of specifically "African discourses on otherness and ideologies of alterity" (Mudimbe xi) – *negritude*, Diop's Black Personality and African philosophy? Of the perennial concern about importing western concepts and categories to represent African realities? Or of more limited exchanges like that between the Nigerian *Bolekaja* critics and Achebe and Soyinka? Of Ngugi wa Thiongo's radical proposals for "decolonisation of the mind"? (It is hard to resist mentioning that this conference is partly funded by a University of Cape Town fund called "Into Africa": Now *there's* a term fairly crying out for deconstruction! Into Africa *semper aliquid nova*?)

Secondly, in what kind of Africa is culture, and knowledge about culture, being produced? It is a continent growing poorer, weaker and more marginalised. Life for millions of its inhabitants is becoming harsher, more violent, less secure. During the second half of the 1980s per capita income fell, the number of people in employment declined and government expenditure shrank. Real wages in Africa declined by an average of 30 per cent in the 1980s. Famine is severe in six African countries and "serious" in ten others; wars have killed tens of thousands and turned millions into refugees; the Aids virus proliferates. Death, destruction, famine and pestilence: the grim horsemen ride roughshod in contemporary Africa.

The picture is equally bleak if one considers institutions and structures involved in the production of knowledge. The proportion of children in schools declines year by year; there has been a precipitous drop in university enrolments since 1987; African academics either shoulder on in grotesquely under-resourced universities, become part of the intensifying brain drain or leave academe. The collapse of African publishing houses since 1980 has been almost total.

The point behind all this is a pretty basic one. Any cultural studies in contemporary Africa not moored in these brute material facts is likely to become as arcane, self-isolating and arid as Lovell has indicated that some cultural studies is becoming in Britain. What is needed, in short, is that integrated study of literature and culture with a carefully delineated history of capitalism, whose possibility Lovell posed as a challenge. And, I am going to conclude by suggesting, a revitalised Marxism must remain a vital component of that project.

There can be little dispute over the contribution of Marxist scholarship to our understanding of Africa over the past thirty years. The radical paradigm in which much African social science was conducted forefronted "discussions of inequality, conflict, social class and unequal development of the world" (Jewsiewicki 30). Marxism, more successfully than any other approach, has since the 1960s traced the terms on which Africa was inserted into a capitalist world system; "the contentious organisation of and struggles of labour, in grand design and in everyday life", and "the integration of politics and consciousness into understandings of peasants as agents in history" (Stern 11).

Above all, as Colin Leys has written recently,

> What Marx's perspective on capitalism tells us is that what has happened in the world, and not least what happened in Africa in the 1980s, is not an accident. It is the effect of the operation of capitalism on these ex-colonial, semi-demi-transformed societies: the effects of capitalism's *natural* dynamics, its *inherent* tendencies . . . which it is the business of contemporary capitalist ideologists to make us forget. (173–4)

The "crisis in Marxism" was already acute when the events of 1989 intensified it – and for many scholars made it terminal. In Europe and in the United States, I would argue , ex-Marxists have ceded too much, too soon. They have leapt from political economy to textuality – with scarcely a footprint in the sand between. There is something exaggerated about their apostasy: It is as if they have thrown out the baby and drunk the bath water.

Marxist scholars – let there be absolutely no mistake about it – will have to respond directly and honestly to the valid critiques mounted *inter alias* by feminism and by cultural studies. To retain class as a central analytical category, Marxists will have to be equally curious about gender, ethnicity, generation and other social divisions. To sharpen the theoretical tools of Marxism, they must cease to regard them as infallible and immutable. If they insist that the basic categories for analysing human existence are themselves historically and socially constructed, they must accept that this is true of class and capital too: "problematising those categories – stripping them of their universalistic and mechanistic properties – is both threatening and revealing to Marxist analysis" (Cooper 193). If capitalism in its late, post-Fordist, multi-national phase places a strain on actually existing Marxist theory, then that theory must be overhauled. Yet even contemporary capitalism is an historical phenomenon; accumulation, the commoditisation of land, labour and culture, new forms of proletarianisation have to be grappled with. "The territory may need to be remapped", argues Fred Cooper, "but the problem which Marx made his life's work is not about to go away." (193).

In other words, Marxists need also to assert what is durable: they must not jettison the use-value of their paradigm. They should resist the "saturnalian subjectivism" of poststructuralism and should refuse to follow the logic of late Foucault, when "causality as an intelligible necessity of social relations of historical events disappears" (Anderson 51). They should be properly wary of the rampant relativism of much postmodernity which denies critical thought any ethical or political points of vantage.

Marxists should be prepared – let me take a deep breath here – to defend the totalising powers of Marxist analysis. "Totalising" not in the sense of claiming a monopoly of explanation, but in the sense of thinking holistically, of relating issues of consciousness and culture to a theory of capitalism and an analysis of the systemic relations between the different levels and institutions of the capitalist state. Jameson, most explicitly, has called for just such a totalising analysis of postmodern culture, which he calls "cognitive mapping". For Jameson – as for Lukacs before him – narratives "make connections between events and contextualise them within a larger milieu outside of which they are incomprehensible" (Best and Kellner 189). Narratives enable us, says Jameson, to grasp "the lost unity of social life, and [to] demonstrate that widely distant elements of the social totality are ultimately part of the same global historical process" (226).

I am arguing, I suppose, that radical scholars – and new directions in African cultural studies – may be able to appropriate more boldly, more confidently, than Terry Lovell seems to suggest. They must borrow from their critics; but must also be prepared to seize and deploy items from their own armoury, however tarnished it might appear in the false dawn of the end of history. Perhaps – just perhaps – travelling theory may have been issued with a return ticket. And, thus equipped, we may join Terry Lovell on Raymond Williams' "journey of hope".

Late 20th-Century Social Science:
A conversation

Jean Comaroff

It is a rare pleasure for me to participate in a forum such as this, and to engage in a dialogue with people at the centre of one of the most fascinating, frightening and challenging conjunctures in the current world. I will therefore say little about my own research, or about what I personally perceive to be going on in this country at present. I am here to learn more than to teach. But I will start the ball rolling by saying a few things about what I perceive to be common concerns among South African and American scholars at the current moment – especially among social scientists. I teach anthropology at the University of Chicago; ours is a large graduate department with many students from a variety of backgrounds, all trying in their own ways to grapple with the so-called "new world order". I sense that rather similar things are at issue here – notwithstanding real differences in social and historical conditions.

For unique as recent events here appear to be, they are obviously also part of a more universal conjuncture that must be viewed in global terms. In fact, parallels between events in South Africa and elsewhere are constantly being pressed on us; the media force a predictable set of metaphors – sometimes less than helpful ones – upon us. I have been struck by the recurrence, in local political discourse, of certain analogies now quite entrenched in comparable European and American contexts: the Bosnian analogy, Russian parallel, the comparison with the Middle East. These *are*, of course, similar situations in certain respects, also being particular expressions of the global moment in which we all participate. Exploring just how this moment has played into various localities is extremely important. But glib insistence on surface similarities can also be misleading – even dangerous. The extent to which, in the summer of 1993, the British press (from right to left) pushed the parallel between Bosnia and South Africa began to perturb some of us (to the extent that Shula Marks, for one, felt bound to make a public response). All too often, the comparison is used to circumvent more complex histories – and to underline what is taken to be the primordial power of ethnic identities to thwart the "progress to modernity" in benighted places.

What is more interesting to me than such putative primordialisms is the extent to which, on a global scale, we are experiencing a profound destabilisation of the modern world as we have known it. It is a moment that some have called postcolonial, some postmodern, some late capitalist, some pure fantasy. The variety of terms implies various theoretical understandings of its advent and meaning. But whatever one's preferred epithet, I think we would probably all agree that the recent past has called into question a number of the core assumptions comprising the intellectual capital on which many of us, at least in the West, have long lived comfortably. Whatever else we may feel about the recent past, it has been a time when many of the basic categories of modernism – and of our Eurocentric world – have been challenged. Whether we speak of persons, communities, cultures or states, we increasingly feel the need to do so with ironic detachment. When social scientists give talks these days, at least in America, every second word is placed in quotation marks to suggest a knowing distance. "God forbid you read me literally; I am not an essentialist." While my sense of this derives primarily from my situated perspective within anthropology, I think it indexes a sense of alienation felt much more generally within the human sciences. The legitimacy of our basic terms has been fundamentally questioned; so much so that even those of us who still defend the possibility of interrogating a world beyond our own subjectivity feel fainthearted. I would like to pursue a little further some of the manifestations of this moment in the academy in which I work. Then I would like to hear whether similar issues are of concern to you in your lives and work.

To some people in the United States, the late twentieth century has seen a kind of epistemic break with everything that has gone before: Their world is radically decentered and fundamentally altered, and the modern social sciences no longer seem viable. It is a world of fragmented subjects, floating signs, friable texts – choose your metaphors! Economies are highly flexible, meaning constantly shifting. For those who believe all this, it is a time of great trauma and moral impoverishment, a true exile and loss of meaning. Thick description, the kind of solid cultural ground that a modernist anthropology presupposed, appears something of the past. Contemporary social scientists are increasingly looking back even at things like the nation-state with a sense of nostalgia. We now all eat out of the same satellite dish; we all watch CNN; we all suffer from an incredible likeness of being. As global technologies and electronic media lift sound bites from context and flash signs around the world, we are all condemned to inhabit a virtual reality that touches no tangible base at all.

For others, this postmodern moment has a more positive gloss. It spells a world of flexibility, even opportunity. Precisely because all seems unfixed and decentred, it is a world of polymorphic perversity and playful possibility. Old dominant structures, we are told, have been dislodged, old master narratives no longer apply. And the division of labour has become so global that whole regions have become the wage slaves of others; to be sure, some national economies support hardly any primary production at home. "Offshore" manufacture in the United States may well take place in Sri Lanka or the Philippines – which is where you find the "American" working class. Is it surprising that, in the West, life is increasingly experienced in terms of shopping alone, as if goods sprung forth, fully formed, without actually having to be produced. Is it surprising that some perfectly serious theories posit a postmodern world whose basis lies not in production but in consumption? Or that strategies of resistance have recently argued the possibility of remaking oneself through the expressive power of commodities mobilised in performing one's gendered identity? I am not merely being facetious; views of this sort cannot be lightly discounted – notwithstanding the fact that, from here, they seem like an indulgence that we cannot quite understand.

But there *are* other worlds, different modernities. Many students who come to my university from places like Sri Lanka, South Africa, the Middle East, South Asia or even the South Side of Chicago find the preoccupation with flexibile realities and shifting meanings almost incomprehensible. These students reached maturity in places where the luxury of this kind of contemplation is almost inconceivable. In their lifeworlds, the structures of determination, of inequality, were all too predictable. Not for them the anxious burden of choice of identity. For them, identity and possible courses of action were often painfully constrained, meaning brutally fixed. To many of the less fortunate – East and West – social class is all too real and cultural hegemonies all too coherent; there is no possibility of dispensing with such "modernist" dualisms as domination and resistance. Their reaction to the self-indulgent nihilisms of postmodernism, or to the self-seeking separatism of certain identity politics, is typically one of extreme impatience; any dialogue with this kind of world-weary solipsism is, for them, a loss of political integrity and fidelity with history.

I would hazard the opinion that most of us, here, fall somewhere between these two poles. We are still contained within a discourse that, while constantly being renewed, was born of the European enlightenment. We seek to explain the world in terms that do not capitulate to its diversity, its unpredictability, its pure contingency. We still maintain that there are social and cultural determinations – though they might not be as coherent, or even as determining, as we once thought. But at the same time we are very aware that most of the classic, universalist European narratives are no longer viable. Our world gives little evidence of the neo-evolutionary logic of modernisation or secularisation theories, or of the homogenising forces that were meant to erode all local distinction. In fact, the assertion of difference, of cultural identity and of religious politics (what some call fundamentalism) is apparent everywhere. We have somehow to find the terms to account for this; conceptions of power, agency, practice and meaning are more complicated than those that came to us through the legacy of Durkheim, Marx, Weber, or through idealist theories of culture that many of us, at least in anthropology, were raised on. Nor, in my view, is the kind of theory staked out by the "posts" – by poststructuralism, post-Marxism, and the like – adequate for handling the complex convulsions of the late modern world.

How then to engage that middle ground, that space of argument, where modernism runs up against its own contradictions? This is the question that detains many of my students and colleagues in North America right now. In addressing it, we are also caught up in cross-cutting debates with non-European scholars and critics. One of the great omissions in the history the West tells of itself is the integral role of non-Western peoples and cultures in the making of modernity. The West produced itself in large part by appropriating the surplus value – the material and symbolic value – of its "others". As that submerged pole of the modern dialectic is made visible, the terms of the social sciences themselves have been deeply challenged. People like Said, Mudimbe, Chatterjee, and a host of postcolonial intellectuals and literary figures – many trained in the salons of Europe – have had a powerful impact on how we in the American academy think about theory, history, colonialism, the curriculum, and so on. In taking their often trenchant critiques to heart – to do so, and not fall prey to nihilism or unhelpfully paralysing guilt – is part of the current challenge. For the history of our world may indeed be multicentered, but it is not uncentred. And the European story may not be the only story, but it is a story, one with far-reaching consequences in making the modern world. In as much as that world was born of arguments and encounters of global scale, our analytical perspectives must be capable of capturing its formation (and, with it, the terms of modernity itself). To capitulate before our contemporary experiences of fragmentation, and to build theories on the appearances of the moment, is to confuse experience with explanation.

One solution to this conundrum now popular in America, following earlier developments in Britain, is the attempt to develop generic, transdisciplinary positions – like cultural studies or the history of consciousness. These gesture towards an embracing humanistic science capable of accommodating diversity within a single, general discourse. Such moves are, in many respects, the academic equivalent of multiculturalism. They express the same synthetic urge, and elevate its key concerns – "culture" and "identity" – into organising constructs. This has put disciplines like anthropology in a very difficult position; our distinctive concepts and methods ("culture" and "ethnography") have been purloined and put into mass circulation. This has had some beneficial effects. But it also carries certain dangers. Let me address them briefly, since they raise some more general, constitutive concerns.

Like most others, I have benefited from the permissive interdisciplinary climate of the moment. Yet I remain sceptical about a generic social science. It all too easily becomes a sort of smorgasboard of concepts plucked from their location in more complex theoretical arguments, conceptual frames and methods. While the recombinations achieved can be exciting, and point to inadequacies in existing perspectives, they are often also glib and superficial. Take, for example, what happened to the notion of "ritual" in the hands of some writers of the Birmingham School (Hall and Jefferson 1976), or the idea of "bricolage" (Hebdige 1979). These were efforts to historicise useful anthropological constructs. But, in the process, much of the subtlety and depth of the original formulations were lost. Lévi-Strauss and Althusser cannot be reconciled by putting their constructs on the same plate and serving them. These constructs are drawn from antithetical theoretical approaches and presuppose contrasting sets of related assumptions.

We still need a division of intellectual labour, one that recognises distinct, situated approaches to dimensions of the social world – some complementary, some fundamentally irreconcilable. But it has to be the kind of division of labour that encourages openness to multiple discourses. Let us engage and vex each other, avoiding either simple synthesis or plural cacophony. And let us try to build fields of coherent argument that enhance each other's understanding of a multifaceted, but interconnected, global reality.

One issue that anthropology has faced of late, for instance, has been the need to move not only into history, but away from small, peripheral, isolated societies. Increasingly, in Chicago, our students wish to study their own world. They want to work in America or Europe, and are doing so for a variety of reasons – some pragmatic, some in response to the critique that anthropology has fetishised others. This, in turn, has presented new possibilities and necessities. Suddenly, anthropologists are studying the state, "guest workers", ethnicity, diaspora cultures. And they do not have a clue how to set about it. How do you extend a face-to-face empirical method, derived from "participant observation", to a global canvas, without a loss of depth or explanatory possibility?

Many have looked to other, more large-scale disciplines for the answer. Some are becoming born-again political scientists or political economists; they study the state in abstract terms, devoid of grounded human activity, rather than devising a distinctly anthropological "take" on the phenomenon. Others look to literary criticism; right now American social scientists are increasingly studying texts, often without an adequate sense of the difference between them and the processes that generate them. This move has long been anticipated by the use of textual metaphors in American cultural anthropology; but, in the expanded horizons of a global ethnography, everything becomes a text. The relationship of texts to context, the question of who produces those texts, the political economy of their circulation and consumption, the culture of readership – the sorts of things with which thoughtful literary critics are now concerned – are often lost in their social science appropriations. On the other hand, a lot of social theory is currently being written by literary critics, and often they are not adequately equipped for this either. There are, I stress, fertile cross-overs, in which people like Giyatry Spivak, Homi Bhabha and Mary Louise Pratt are producing fascinating analyses with great appeal to social scientists concerned with colonialism, postcolonialism, diaspora cultures and the like. But where perspectives developed in the realm of textual representations are applied *too* easily to social relations and historical forces, they lead to banal generalisation and idealist simplifications of the workings of society and history. They also tend to reduce all socio-historical action to "representation", or to "speaking for" people, rather than understanding how their worlds are produced. Yet this interplay between literary criticism and socio-cultural analysis remains vital – as long as it is respectful of the difference (and relationship) between texts and contexts, representation and embodiment. This seems to me to be the challenge. And I do not think an answer will come from the kind of cultural studies or history of consciousness that takes ideas from a variety of contexts and makes a pastiche of them.

In short, I am still anxious, as an anthropologist, to preserve something of the special legacy of my discipline, even as I encourage my students to broaden their understanding of socio-cultural systems in time and space. One distinguishing perspective of anthropology is its groundedness in mundane practice, and this relates to calls made by certain scholars here, like Njabulo Ndebele, to rediscover the ordinary, to recognise, if you like, the "epiphany of the every day" (Frederiksen n.d.). Ethnography brings a degree of concreteness to the big abstractions of the modern world – like the state, nationalism, citizenship, identity and subjectivity. Anthropologists, I believe, ought to pursue these Big Issues in terms of their classic vocation: by investigating the dialogue between subjective experience and practice on the one hand, and broader, even global socio-material forces on the other.

One of the things that the "postpositions" have alerted us to is the necessity to understand subject positions, motivations, and agency. Yet *how* does one actually study agency empirically as an historian or anthropologist? How does one grasp the subject positions of, say, participants in a social movement and still not lose sight of the fact that people do not make history exactly as they please? How do the big abstractions – politics, society and culture – come to rest on human shoulders? To what degree can we explain events in terms of the forces that emanate from social and cultural regularities? These seem to be the interesting questions of the day. And anthropology is well placed to address them. But it must do so with an awareness of the complementary competences of other situated perspectives and approaches.

I have had some interesting discussions with students here about the possibilities of doing certain kinds of research in South Africa at present. We have to show a good deal of sensitivity as to where we can and cannot proceed with our projects and methods. But at the same time, the very problems of doing "research", the dialogue between modes of knowing the world and living in it, raise general questions about the politics of knowledge. This is exactly the sort of discussion we should be having. We discussed the difficulties of doing conventional anthropological field work here now, and how the current situation throws into relief wider political dimensions of privileged research methods. Our own practices are central to the world we inhabit and strive to understand; they should not be exempt from scrutiny. The "field" is not "out there". It is the ground on which we all stand. Recognising this precludes more indulgent forms of reflexive postmodernism, those that obsess about the way in which the world affects the individual researcher. Instead, we might examine the dialogue between research and its object in a particular historical situation.

Challenges to our projects and methods are real enough. But these confrontations are products of the very history that we are trying to comprehend. They help us to think through crucial questions: How do we analyse the emergence of modern social worlds and their current destabilisation without merely replicating modernist discourses, and without falling prey to postmodern nihilism? How do we discuss the politics of democracy in Africa, for instance, in terms that move beyond Eurocentric judgementalism, yet do not relapse into naive relativism or remove the possibility of political critique? Many of my students come back from Central and West Africa with vivid accounts of the significance of witchcraft and sorcery. What do we do with these things in the here and now? Why, at the same time that discourses of democracy and development flourish, that NGOs ply their "rational" trade up and down the continent, do we witness the effervescence of these kinds of nightmares? What do they say about the limits of the state and conventional politics; or about the difficulties that many scholars, African and European alike, have in dealing with these sorts of phenomena?

I think that we have to be imaginative and broad-minded in thinking about these questions: To me, for example, one of the most suggestive things that emerges out of discourses of sorcery in Cameroon or Niger is what they tell us about similar movements in the USA. I have recently written about child abuse in America, where the threat to the young has come to express a sense of loss and danger to local worlds, a sense that current global events have (literally) bought home to many ordinary communities. Why was it that one of the most potent issues in the last election was "family values"? Note that this discourse fetishised the domestic realm and eclipsed a whole variety of other political discourses about class, race and gender. The child, and increasingly the foetus, has been made alibi for a utopian world, a world ostensibly put at risk by unsavory forces – from aborting mothers and professional childminders to lascivious perverts. We hear of fanatical searches for satanic abusers in communities that are feeling the impact of global economic forces, of shifting patterns of immigration, and so on. Of course, children *are* molested in the world in which we live; these are not just paranoid fantasies. But there is a connection, in America, between the growing fear of child abuse, the politics of abortion and the demonising of certain categories of person (like unwed black mothers); the debate about the nature of the foetus, and foetal citizens as subjects with rights, are popular discourses about social reproduction, which outrun the imaginative and moral limits of established political or religious ideologies. And in their active mode – in the witchcraft-like search for abusers and perverts and monster citizens who seek to consume American "values" and "futures" – they provide powerful insight into the way in which the world is experienced in the late 20th century. In some cases, outbreaks of alleged child abuse and satanism link up with things going on in Europe, among them, a standardised set of paranoid nightmares about ex-Nazis and Communist forces that corrupt ordinary citizens and encourage them to consume American innocence and essence. Such nightmares also afford insight into fears about the limits of state protection; like witch beliefs everywhere, they bring to the fore contradictions in the world – a world eminently suited to anthropological treatment.

QUESTION: What role can Anthropology's micro studies play in a broader understanding of post-Fordist economies?

J. C.: I often do an exercise with students when we talk about postcolonial relations between the West and the non-Western world. I ask them to take off their jackets and lay their pens and pencils out on the table. Where are all these things manufactured? They soon discover that practically nothing is made in the United States, and that their most intimate possessions have an international history. This helps them to understand that we live in the global village – or at least, in a universe constructed by a global division of labour. Thus the working classes of America are to be found in South Korea, the Phillippines, Puerto Rico. It is easy in a late capitalist context to confine oneself to what seems a disconnected fragment, and take that for the world. As I said earlier, it is easy, in the West, to believe that we have moved from being a society based in production to one made through consumption, because the distance between their sites is so great. Yet we can trace the career of a commodity and ask where its raw materials come from, where the value-added labour is done, where it is perfected, where it is marketed, where it is consumed and reconsumed. The total process is very complex; no one can see it in the round, on the shop-floor of the Fordist factory. That is why our division of intellectual labour must trace out such global connections without reducing them to a mechanical, unitary analysis. Each of us works on a piece of the process, but we also have to keep our minds and our models open to the interconnections.

Take *Roger and Me* – a film about the closing of a GM plant in Michigan which reveals something of the fantastic interconnections between very local worlds and global forces. In it, a maverick film maker tries to find his way to the head of GM. He fails, but in the process he uncovers the impact of the removal of the factory – the major local employer in the town of Flint – to Mexico. (Such things will only be more frequent with the ratification of the North Atlantic Free Trade Agreement.) One point of the film – part drama, part ethnography – is to show how the "culture" of the community is affected by this economic shift, itself a classic instance of David Harvey's notion of the flexibility of late-capitalist corporations. Increasing financial hardship affected people's sensibilities about themselves and the world; it reshaped local class relations and the topography of the town. Ingenious victims set about trying to create an alternate economy, among other things, attempting to turn the derelict town into a tourist resort. This is a text-book illustration of the transition to a post-Fordist economy in what was the heartland of Fordism. We see here the marking out of a new frontier, one that encloses a kind of "Third World" within America itself. Making visible such conjunctures seems crucial to me, and the ethnographic eye can make it plain. It is possible, in other words, to get at very large articulations in very concrete contexts.

QUESTION: How can anthropologists engage in field studies when people in local communities no longer wish to have us near them? How can the discourse of anthropology persuade people that it has a useful purpose?

J. C.: I think that ultimately a discipline has to earn respect through the relevance and interest of its work. Some of the cherished methods of anthropology cannot be used in certain circumstances, and that should make us think hard about their nature. The problems that some researchers might be having here at present are very telling; they are part of the very process we are trying to comprehend and act upon. We are caught up in a total system of relations and forces, relations at once political, intellectual and symbolic. The mere fact that participant observation is impossible in certain places now is extremely significant. Our very presence as anthropologists in some communities is now a hindrance. We have to ask where else we can work, what else we can do? We also have to think carefully about the question of relevance. What is relevance? In the present situation this is a difficult call, because it is all too easy to take rather simple, theoretical criteria and discount all intellectual pursuits that seem irrelevant to them. Yet, especially in a time of brute necessity, one has to keep intellectual curiosity and independent reflection alive, and what seems beside the point now might become important later on. On the other hand, we can grossly overvalue our significance as scholars. A lot of what social science agonises over in America presupposes that what we are doing is consequential: that we are writing history and representing Others – and people read and believe us. I wish we were more significant! We have to take our cue from the place where we find ourselves. Sometimes scholars can serve by *not* "going in" and doing anything; there are times when one should not commit social science. Sometimes our job is to be primary educators, teaching about the social construction of reality, history, race, gender and the like. Sometimes we reveal a good deal about a society by drawing attention to the kinds of discourses that are (and are not) possible across social and cultural divides. We have to make a virtue of necessity. I also think there are lots of things we learn by looking, for example, at media, at texts, at public activity, at the breakdown of certain kinds of communication and the opening up of other sorts of possibilities. New phenomena constantly present themselves for all to read and decode: new public spheres in which television now does what certain rituals did before; new signs which present themselves in multiple modalities, from bodies to billboards. In this sense there is no field "out there"; it is the ground on which we all stand. But I cannot presume to know what the politics of research and writing is here, now.

QUESTION: Is the preoccupation with Satanism not a return to the primitive?

J. C.: I get very worried when people talk about witchcraft in America – both in academic and non-academic contexts. They always seem to have Salem in mind; periods of mass hysteria, when innocents are at risk, rationality is in abeyance and otherwise civilised people descend into primitive passion. The witch in this discourse is always a sign of the pre-modern. Anthropology has contributed to this too: The functionalist tradition, after all, portrayed witchcraft as a safety valve that kept "primitive" societies intact and unchanging. But the kind of witchcraft at which I am looking is as American as apple pie and as modern as the electronic media. If we cut ourselves loose from the baggage we bring to the notion of witchcraft or satanism, it becomes clear that they are aspects of, products of, a *contradictory* modernity. Witches do not always ride on broomsticks. But they do give malevolent human motive to otherwise reified forces and tell us a lot about the failure of our discourses of practical reason, rational economics, even established religion, to engage the moral issues that vex people in their daily lives. Those caught up in the pursuit of child abusers, in a celebrated case in small-town America recently, came from what have been called "fundamentalist" backgrounds; the town was also the site of a nationally renowned New Age "channeller" or medium. These things are occurring at a moment when the hold of mainstream modernist institutions and categories is slipping. In high church services, ecstatic rites and the laying on of hands is now quite common. It has become very chic, since Nancy Reagan introduced crystal gazers to the White House, for middle-class people to consult "readers" or diviners, to attend tarot sessions, and so on. Yoruba *babalaos* and Afro-Caribbean *Santaria* healers now have large followings, not only among African-Americans, but among white Americans as well. Alternative medicine is thriving as never before. There is a fascinating play of orthodox and unorthodox forms. These things do not necessarily eclipse conventional processes and discourses; there has even been some argument that in some ways they strengthen them. But they are conducive to a kind of pluralism of intellectual and imaginative possibilities, an open flirtation with forms and identities that would have been pejorative or embarrassing in earlier times. There is a wonderful playfulness about the way in which some American feminist groups have picked up on the rhetoric of witchcraft and created witch covens that seek to recover the suppressed powers of cunning women in the past, and so on. Radical dance groups emerge in the centre of New York with names like the Urban Bush Women and perform things they call – with a high level of irony – primitive rituals. Such manifestations appear in formerly unthinkable places. Somebody I met the other day was beside herself about the prevalence of satanic cults in Fish Hoek! The interesting issue about these anxieties is not whether they have "real" grounds, but how they create a space for the moral imagination. Witch beliefs in America, or in Africa, personify highly rarified processes and ungrounded experiences. They are an effort to embody, to bring down to earth, abstract forces that seem to dictate the rhythm of peoples' lives; to attribute to human agents the experience of loss, of inequality, of threat; to give fear hands and feet. This is a very old idea, but I think it is still salient – especially in a world driven by commodifying forces that dehumanise history, culture and society.

QUESTION: Does your work concentrate on subjects which are sometimes unspoken or unspeakable?

J. C. Like most of us, I have become very aware of the political sensitivities surrounding what we study. In this respect, I think back on my work on resistance in the African Independent and Zionist churches. My approach has been controversial, which I anticipated. But at the time I did not consider whether certain kinds of practices ought be best left alone – in particular, practices that seek, in various ways, to escape authority. Maybe they ought not to be opened up to scrutiny? I have become increasingly troubled by this problem. Do we have the right to expose certain kinds of things by writing about them?

Having said this, I acknowledge that it is the realm of the unspoken, the less-than-evident, the mundane and the embodied that most excites my interest; how it is that whole schemes of power and meaning can "come without saying", as Bourdieu (167) puts it, "because they go without saying". Notwithstanding our faith in discursive awareness and explicit truth, it is not primarily through them that we get to the complex motors that drive social forces – or to the multi-levelled meanings that reside in bodies, objects, and our orientations towards them. Perhaps this is why I find the essays of Ndebele so suggestive. He seems to be making precisely this point: that we need a more complex view of power, of the imagination, of everyday popular discourses and their role in the making of history. He argues that all of society is the domain of the political, despite the more limited image of heroic, "spectacular" action that many of us – especially in hard-edged authoritarian societies – retain. He goes on to outline the sorts of issues that cultural critics should be concerned with: rural consciousness, the creative world of sport, fashion, the popular media, and so on. These are precisely the kind of things that my instincts would lead me to in pursuit of a more nuanced sense of the making of the South African present. They make visible the politics of the everyday, the domain in which most of us are formed and re-formed.

One of the things that strikes me in coming back to Cape Town is the extent to which the terrain has been transformed. It speaks of a contest for the control of space. Who determines where the bodies move and cluster, how bodies themselves use space and place to signify ownership, defiance or submission? One gains a strong visual sense of the rise of the informal economy; casual commerce is bursting out everywhere and mocking the formal structures of a colonial past. There is an explosion of transactions – of material and cultural exchanges – across formerly closed frontiers. One cannot but become aware of the struggle to command the public sphere – its sounds, its look, its materiality. People confront each other in ways that are playful, threatening, dangerous, interesting. Apartheid's engineers understood the theatrics of space; theirs was very much a politics of controlling place and movement within it. Squatting, in this situation, was hardly an arbitrary form of resistance. Now the hard lines of the apartheid map are rapidly being smudged: Someone was telling me recently that along the freeway that borders Khayelitsha, there are cattle on the highway. There is a politics in these sorts of things – in the current sense of the tentativeness of certain spaces.

Contestations have also erupted around the visible and the audible, over what gets transmitted by the media to the world beyond. One thing I find distinctive, after being away, is the way in which violence is depicted here. It struck me especially forcibly after having lived through a Gulf War sanitised by CNN. Americans never saw a blasted body, they viewed the action from a distance, as if in a video game. We *heard* about "soft targets", but seldom saw them. Depictions of domestic violence, especially among those who inhabit internal colonies like the black inner city, are sometimes more graphic; yet there is always care to keep the news fit for family viewing. Commentators have noted how shocking is the impact, in America, of images of damaged foetuses wielded by anti-abortion activists. They shock because they flout the unspoken ethics and aesthetics of representing violence in the United States media.

Here, by contrast, the visual impact of newspaper and television depictions of, say, the Umtata massacre suggests to me that there is something different going on. Representation is graphic, blatant, shameless. To my long-absent eye, the gaze is disturbingly callous in its depiction of the dead, the damaged and the distressed. Is this an honesty bred of having to face brutal truths, a kind of honesty we are denied abroad by cosmetic camera work and a censorship of bland "good taste"? Or does it imply a brutalisation born of years of a politics of spectacle and of a violent disregard for the bodies and dignity of the dispossessed?

QUESTION: How are we to understand the issue of multi-culturalism and its impact on European academic discourse? How do we characterise the "culture" and "identity" of people who pray in Arabic, converse in English and swear in Afrikaans? How do people like Rushdie and Spivak fit into a dialogue that is often characterised as being between the West and non-West?

J. C.: These are the difficult questions. First of all, I could not agree more about the multilateral nature of so much of the intellectual discourse taking place right now. To call someone like Edward Said a "Third World" scholar is ludicrous. Apart from all else, the phrase "Third World" is itself a simplification. But beyond that, Said is a Palestinian, educated in Paris, who is at home in the academies of Europe, teaches at Columbia, and is involved with the politics of the Middle East in complicated ways. He is typical of a whole category of displaced elites – or, as he calls them, exiles: People who are at second or third remove from anything one might call "home"; who speak the language of Western scholarship but have a foot outside it through displacements of race, ethnicity, culture, religion, and so on. In a Brechtian sense, they experience an alienation effect – they feel the discrepancy. To me it is this kind of tension that generates the most interesting work in the arts and the academy. One has to be careful, though, not to essentialise a dialectical process here. When we talk of, say, current "African writing" we evoke a complex dialectical history; an interplay, that is, among colonial education, European texts and genres, the postcolonial predicament - all in a long-term dialogue with local African cultural forms. In this process, for instance, the novel is seized, creatively reworked and thrust back at the West. At the same time, we do not all swim in the same melting pot. Multiculturalism is a complex and misleading term. Everybody in America – from right, left and centre – seems to espouse the virtues of "multiculturalism". But they often imply different things by it; as long as the term remains inadequately examined, it may justify old forms of cultural imperialism in new guise.

For example, courses are taught in Comparative Literature where students read Achebe one week and Rushdie next week, and Coetzee the week after; and their works are laid side by side as if they were are all comparable products of the same brave new world. It's-a-small-world-after-all, in the comforting, Walt Disney sense; and we can easily take it in from our centred vantage point, where cultures are all alike in their differences and their products lie comfortably together like commodities in the supermarket. This kind of multiculturalism ignores the politics and the histories that differentiate peoples and make for inequalities of wealth, power and representation. Ours might be a global world, but we occupy diverse positions within it. Nor are those differences simply reducible to a cultural common denominator; they are often etched in warfare and blood, in colonial disjunctures and in irreconcilable inequities and values. If we simplify these relations and disjunctures, we allow the text to fly loose from its context, and in consuming it we merely consume a commodity on our own terms, in ways that reinforce our entrenched ethnocentrism. The fact that, in some classrooms, students read Buchi Emecheta, Nadine Gordimer and Jane Austen, without really locating the authors or the circumstances surrounding the production of their novels, reinforces an insidious idea: that there are great men and women everywhere and all cultures can ultimately yield the great bourgeois European novel – some more readily than others. Achebe can be read simply as another text; doing so may enhance one's literary repertoire. But to call this a multicultural exercise is to diminish the term. Multiculturalism ought to be disruptive and politically contentious. It ought to lift "difference" above the level of doggerel and allow it to decentre taken-for-granted assumptions and core values.

QUESTION: Is there a sense that the West has collapsed under a failure of moral will?

J. C.: To generalise at such a level is ludicrous, yet one cannot help but feel that, at least in Europe, "modern" institutions such as the "state" are under threat. The social democracies of Western Europe seem to be rapidly unburdening themselves of their collective responsibilities. They are privatising education, health care, and appear increasingly incapable of supporting such state institutions as asylums and prisons – institutions that, in Foucauldian terms, were hallmarks of the modern state. Of course this tends to be presented as an innovative, liberalising move, a move of "deinstitutionalisation". In Britain, for instance, government divests itself of responsibility for the disturbed and the dangerous, returning them to the "community". The Western capitalist state is not in a position any more to finance its own institutions. Capitalism is in severe crisis - ironically, just at the point where the cold war is "won", socialism is "dead", and we are supposed to enjoy a "new world order". This is one of the more fascinating aspects of the current moment. In America, the end of the cold war is marked by a rising sense of internal chaos: Violence soars, we struggle to fund education, and kids have to be frisked for weapons at the school door. In parts of Chicago we have undeclared war in the streets, and the illegal economy – that of drug capitalism – outstrips all else. And this is the triumph of the West!

The "crisis of modernism" is not lost on students. It certainly affects our work in American universities at the moment. Professors might continue to teach undergraduates about "rational choice" economics and still espouse the triumph of the liberal market. But counter examples are readily to hand, often in the street outside the classroom. This explains, in part, the appeal of alternative philosophies and politics, like ecologism. It also accounts for the appeal of postmodern nihilism; the postmodern, as Hebdige notes (195), lacks the hopes and dreams that made the modern bearable. In such a climate, I feel, a critical politics ought increasingly to begin in the classroom with undergraduates, with young people who are *not* going on to graduate social science – but may one day be actively engaged in such neo-colonial fields as development, or may go to work for corporations, NGOs, the World Bank, and so on. Pedagogic politics should involve such students in discussions about the global order; it should have them read writers who are differently positioned in that order, and who tell unsettling stories about colonialism, modernity and the current universal division of labour – that is the sort of pedagogic politics I aim for.

The West is obviously not bankrupt in any straightforward sense. It still foists a good deal on the non-Western world – intentionally and unintentionally, for good and ill. But there is definitely *angst* in its heart. It is an *angst* that comes of the dawning recognition that we have entered a world without clear centres: one that no longer promises unlimited progress, one in which the secure dualisms of modernism – west and east, right and left, white and black, male and female – have been destabilised. It is not a world that our models predicted. And it will not be responsive to band-aid solutions – like bland notions of multiculturalism or identity politics – that ignore the global politics of our age.

QUESTION: Are we at a point when we can start representing real issues again instead of continuing to represent "representations"?

J. C.: This is a crucial problem. In the American academy we are facing a new kind of essentialism, a pluralist Tower of Babel in which only you can speak for yourself – and for yourself only. If one teaches courses on anything that touches on identity – on gender, race, the body, and so on – one faces distrust and animosity among students whose strongly moralised identities conflict with, and delegitimise, each other. Differences are not reducible to any common basis. They permit no sense of social and historical *relationship*, no building of commonalities or coalitions. The African-American students suspect the white students and see no basis for dialogue; as the T-shirt proclaims: "It's a black thing, you wouldn't understand!" Their mistrust is reciprocated. But so it is, also, between male and female, gay and straight, Latino and Gringo, and on and on. It is an infinite regress, a *reductio ad absurdum* of ever proliferating identities based on essentialist notions of personhood, culture and representation. People feel passionately about these identities in a world where the differences they proclaim have become all too real. We social scientists may urge that difference not be taken at face value – that we try to understand the historical and contemporary forces that has produced and often profit from it; but we have to recognise the depth of these feelings to which it gives rise if we wish to engage politically or pedagogically.

It seems absolutely crucial to me that we *do* try to engage this discourse, because its consequences are grave. In the United States, it feeds into an ahistoric folk culture in which people understand the world to be made through individual action, unconstrained by society and history. Social class is not a phenomenon that finds a place easily in American views of "reality", though its effects would seem palpable to many of us raised with European or colonially-produced sensibilites. Class is entailed in the kinds of difference that underlie United States identity politics in complex ways, but the language of pluralism masks the political and economic production of inequality. For me, the problem with identity politics is that it tends to depict each group as distinct, rather than as positioned relative to others, within fields of power and resources. A relational vision of the world recognises difference - but sees it as a product of certain historical conditions, just as it sees identities as positioned. An other's view of you is different from your view of yourself. As an observer, I will never know the intimacies of your subjectivity; yet there are things I can know about you that you cannot – and vice versa. This knowledge is never absolute, archimedean. Nor should it claim to be a "representation" in the sense of speaking *for* "an" other (as if there ever is such a reified being!). To argue over the legitimacy of representation in these circumstances seems to miss the point. In any case, the idea of a social science is impossible unless there is some sense of dialogue between subject and object, the known and unknown.

QUESTION: You seemed to be critical of postmodern approaches. But is deconstruction not a way of getting at what you are advocating – of questioning dominant institutions in our society – not taking them at face value.

J. C.: The term "deconstruction" is often used, rather loosely, to imply critical examination: a making strange of the taken-for-granted or the naturalised. The gesture of "making strange" is at the root of modern critical theory: Marx advocated it, and applied it supremely in his analysis of that "trivial thing", the commodity – which turned out to be very different from what it appeared! Mistrust for the self-evident, the pursuit of the hidden logic beneath surface realities, is the core method of critical modernism. If this is deconstruction, I am all for it. But deconstruction in the more radical, Derridean sense is an altogether more nihilistic exercise. It denies the possibility of a stable critique of any form of logocentrism, claiming that all critique falls prey to the tyranny of that very logic. Taken in its own terms, this mode of deconstruction also denies the possibility both of social science and of politics. In my own view, it is possible to criticise dominant narratives by working through their own discrepancies. If one reproduces some of a system's tyrannies in critique, one can expose others. There are no total revolutions, no pure acts of resistance. Marx was ultimately a victim of his culture, but he did a good deal to reveal its mysterious logic.

In this positive sense, deconstructing the surface appearances of things, including the claims of ruling ideologies, is for me the essential anthropological task. Many of our colleagues and students in America are now interrogating their own world in this way – working on the "culture" of development, formal economics, medical ethics, ultrasonography, the abortion debate, supermarkets, and so on. The rhetoric of economics is where we find "voodoo" in our society; corporate moguls are our head hunters. But here we soon run into the limits of our traditional methods; which goes back to the earlier question about the limits of "fieldwork" among people who do not want us in their communities. One cannot simply "do ethnography" in corporate board rooms. It is impossible to walk into the "village" of Wall Street and observe, survey, interview, map interactions and carry away local knowledge! Efforts to "study up" soon make plain the degree to which anthropology has classically relied on colonial or neo-colonial conditions to do its business!

Long ago, in England, I applied for a position in medical anthropology funded by the Department of Health and Social Security. They had advertised for someone to study the doctor-patient relationship in general practice; as I had been studying Tswana doctors (both biomedical and indigenous), I figured that I was qualified for the job. When I presented my credentials to the panel of sociologists and physicians in London, they fell about laughing. They thought it was the funniest thing in the world that I felt qualified to study practitioners in England because I had studied healers in Africa. But they gave me the job anyway, and I found that I *was* particularly well-equipped to study the symbolic politics of doctor-patient interactions, the fetishism of the drug trade, the magic of prescriptions in Latin, and so on. I even wrote a paper on placebos which was based on ideas about African divination and the power of certain objects in therapeutic exchange – all of which made perfect sense to me. This is another instance of the effort to estrange the ordinary by refusing to take established institutions on their own terms. Anthropologists have long done this elsewhere, and there are some classic instances of how it can be undertaken at home with striking effect: Horace Miner's wry piece on "Body Rituals of the Nacerima" (American) for instance! Similar things are being done more and more.

QUESTION: If you were somebody doing research in South Africa now, and not necessarily as an anthropologist, what would you study?

J. C.: I can only speak again from my own situated perspective. I have long worked in Tswana communities in the Northern Cape. When I came from Britain in the heyday of structural functionalism, I had been trained to study "traditional religion". I spent a lot of time trying to understand what that was among people who had been missionised and colonised for generations, and had never inhabited anything like a "closed" society. I became concerned with the way in which the Tswana world had been made into a periphery of the modern South African state; but one thing I did not grapple with adequately myself (J. Comaroff 1974) was the making of apartheid in South Africa – and, with it, the formation of the so-called homelands as sociopolitical entities. When John and I recently went back to Bophuthatswana, we realised that it had become an even more sinister, small-scale replica of government in Pretoria than we had anticipated early on. We were struck by its entrenched, officious bureaucratic class, its authoritarian statute book, the violence of its armed police, and the obvious lack of freedom of movement of its populace. I would be very interested to study the making and unmaking of these enclaves of condensed apartheid; it is possible, from the periphery, to get at aspects of a complex system that are invisible at its centre.

John and I have long been in communication with Mafikeng and Mmabatho, and have been aware of the involvement of ordinary people in various forms of resistance and struggle – and of their attitude toward those who have benefited through collaboration. We went back last year and found that – inexplicably – large numbers of people with whom we had worked, people of our own generation, were no longer alive. They had died in diverse ways: in car accidents, in accidents on the mines, from disease, or just by disappearance. Where I come from – sociologically, that is – there really is no such thing as an accident. Such incidents and incidences have a social logic. What happened to that generation, personally and politically? Why were they so unnaturally vulnerable? Why were their lives so cheap? And what does this have to do with the history and structural predicament of the "homelands" under apartheid? In the early '90s, an entire social and economic structure was in place in Bophuthatswana that had not been there 20 years before - a space-age capital with postmodern buildings and a MegaCity Mall. What kinds of collaborations of power and capital built such places? The fascinating fetishes of late apartheid! The whole ediface: the Bophuthatswana "International" Airline, with its stops at such places as Hammanskraal and Taung; the Sun City, Lost City – part Las Vegas and part Disney World in an impoverished labour reserve, itself undergoing a stifled civil war! And so on and on. Perhaps here we would run into the limits of our methods. But not, I hope, before we have the opportunity to study how apartheid itself will come apart.

Part Two

CASE STUDIES

Demonstrations of the Study of Culture in Africa:

Poison, the Lydenburg Heads and

the representation of slavery

The Brown Serpent of the Rocks:
Bushman arrow toxins in the Dutch and British imagination, 1735 – 1850

David Bunn

In the afternoon, we were honoured with the company of the boor's vrouw and her sister, to witness the method of preserving birds: they were both . . . paying great attention to the process until they ascertained the composition which I applied to the skins, and which had a pungent odour, was gift or poison; when they immediately sprang from their seats, and covering their mouths with their aprons, hurried from the tent. The dread of gift is universal throughout the country, originating, no doubt in the horrid effects produced by the poisoned arrows of the Bushmen, with which most of the farmers in these districts are familiar.
Steedman, *Wanderings and Adventures*, 1835

On their way to the Cape of Good Hope, Carl Thunberg, surgeon-extraordinary of the ship *Schoonzigt*, together with twenty members of the crew, became violently ill, having consumed quantities of pancakes accidentally tainted with white lead. Unlike conventional narratives of the period, so often preoccupied with island visits, flocks of gannets, flying fish, and mysterious phosphorescence at night, Thunberg's is a pharmacological drama. His account of the two months at sea becomes a harrowing tale of the struggle against poison, a battle in which a series of hopeful, bizarre, remarkable and terrifying treatments is deployed in the attempt to make bodies well again after they have been attacked by a substance that is at once malevolent and misunderstood.

This is a story of the drama around poison in colonial contexts, with particular reference to the Cape in the period immediately following the Batavian interregnum.[1] While my argument makes use of some principles of discourse analysis – examining, for instance, the dispersion of statements with a common object across a variety of fields – my primary interest is in poison as an element of material culture. Thus what may seem at first like an arcane subject, the colonial dread of indigenous poison technologies, is also an opportunity for commenting more generally on certain problems of historical method: the influence of Geertzian textualism; the relationship between local microhistorical formations and the global transmission of knowledge; and the question of colonial science and indigenous resistance, as debated by historians working on the analysis of colonial discourse. To limit what is, perforce, an infinitely expanding argument, I shall concentrate on the history of one artifact, the poisoned arrow, and European representations of it between Thunberg in 1775 and Orpen's *Reminiscences* of 1846.

"Gift"

During his two month shipboard ordeal, Thunberg describes a panorama of medical treatments, including, amongst others, "emollients externally applied", emollient draughts, simple clysters (enemas, that is), tobacco clysters, gargles, doses of laudenum, emetics, "cooling" medicines, laxatives, bleeding, "antiphlogistic regimens", febrifuges and suppositories. Overcoming our surprise that anyone could survive these cures, we may find in this record evidence of a body remarkably different from our own. Essentially, this is a pre-modern body, a somatic order still dependent on medieval notions of the humours and an inner economy of symbolic fluids:

> On the 6th I was in a complete, but gentle, salivation, and my mouth was ulcerated, especially at the sides, a circumstance which was accompanied with a disagreeable stench. My teeth were covered with a yellowish slime. My urine was reddish. In order to carry the peccant matter downwards, I took a gentle laxative. (13)

Symptomatology, here, entails reference to the symbolic mapping of the body according to liquids that travel up and down, the visible colour of substances, and to disturbances of heat and cold. Hence the major purpose of an "electuary", according to Thunberg, is not its laxative effect, but a "cooling" of the hot belly. Similarly, once the white lead enters the system, it appears to be preserved and circulated, he believes, by that same inner economy: Mouth ulcers "seemed to contain white lead", but then he claims that "the leaden matter moved from my head in to my stomach" and outward into the knees, where particles are literally deposited. Two months later, his body only partially restored after its terrifying ordeal, the botanist recalls that this episode "taught me to be more particular and careful with respect to my diet in the course of my travels afterwards" (16).

Poison is an intriguing substance. Its interest lies not only in its exotic appeal, but also in the fact that it is both a tropological figure and an object of direct contestation in the exchange between Enlightenment travellers, a population of indigenous users, and emergent medical science and colonial law. Its danger, therefore, is not only intrinsic, in the fear of its mortal effects, but also potential, in what can be done with it once its secrets have been revealed.

We do not yet know much about the history of the body at the Cape in the period Thunberg describes. Nonetheless, for Europeans and slaves enough evidence surely exists in hospital registers, burial registers, and the like, to prevent a history of somatic inscription from "floating off into the stratosphere of discourse analysis", as Roy Porter once warned.[2] Fifty years before Thunberg, long before an understanding of epidemiology and vaccination, when only the most rudimentary understanding of infectious disease transmission held sway, the Company sick were clustered snugly together in wholly inappropriate sociable units, unsequestered from the public. In 1725, the Council of Policy found it necessary to institute visiting hours for the hospital, on the grounds that "het gemeene volk . . . continueel daar in enuijt loopen".[3] The prospect of communicable diseases muddled together, wards open to the public and pigs foraging between the beds (Searle 46), suggests a relationship between the body and public culture very different to what we encounter in the next century. Indeed as Yvonne Brink has argued in her reading of early Cape architecture, Dutch social identity depended not only on the visible display of rank, but also the circulation of identity. Social circulation and rounds of visiting between houses became, by the eighteenth century, "an essential strategy for the consolidation of the [free burgher] discourse of dwelling" as it sought to undermine VOC domination of the symbolic field (17).

Shortly after his arrival in the Cape, Thunberg made an exploratory survey of the botanical riches of the surrounding regions. From the outset of these tentative expeditions, we are made aware of the dependency of burghers and scientists alike on Khoisan herbal and pharmacological knowledge. For Dutch colonial medical practitioners, extrapolating the still medieval pharmacopoeia of Europe to South Africa was a hit-and-miss affair at best:

> Surgeons, apothecaries, and others, when they cannot find in this country the usual and genuine medicinal plants, look for others that resemble them, either in their flowers, leaves, smell, or habit, and then give them the same name. (Thunberg 43–4)

As many commentators have observed, free burghers in the colonial hinterland were almost entirely dependent on home-nursing practices, with an arsenal of local cures kept in the "Huis Apotheek" being occasionally supplemented by patent medicines received from travellers (Searle 55). Not surprisingly, the fear of untreatable injury such as snakebite was profound. Much faith was put in cures such as turtle blood, which, Thunberg tells us, "the inhabitants dry in the form of small scales and carry out about with them when they travel in this country, which swarms with this most noxious vermin" (43). Eighteenth-century travelogues abound with references to the poison ordeals of Dutch colonists; the treatments listed offer interesting insights in to the medical discourse of the time. So, for instance, Thunberg speaks of a colonist who, after being bitten by a cobra, applies a tourniquet, scarifies and washes the wound, then drinks new milk "copiously, and that to the quantity of several pails full in a night". "After this", he goes on to say, "the serpent-stone was applied to the wound" (43), and so the afflicted man recovers.

We shall have more to say about the serpent stone later; it is sufficient now simply to note that most burghers appear to have set great store by this talisman, rumoured to be of Oriental origin. Of course the country fear of snakes is nothing unusual, but this does not explain the almost medieval preoccupation with poisoning that seems still to have circulated in eighteenth-century Cape Town. According to a sceptical Thunberg, most people of distinction carried a rhinoceros horn goblet, which, it was asserted, if taken "from a young rhinoceros calf that had not yet copulated", would "discover a poisonous drought that was put into [it], by making the liquor ferment till it ran quite out of the goblet" (131–2). What is significant, therefore, is that the idea of poison inhabits public awareness, not only because of the real fear of snakebite, or quack medical treatment, but also because the Cape stirs a lingering folk memory of Machiavellian court politics, as though the arras and chilly battlements of Elsinore were suddenly transported south.

Poison, in the Dutch colonial period, is thus both a threat from without, from out there, and from within, inhabiting the distinction between social classes that allowed only the rich to purchase poison cups "at a rate of 50 rix-dollars a goblet". In a milieu where sumptuary laws tried to prevent the circulation of social identities beneath a certain rank, while burghers, slaves and Khoisan jostled elbow to elbow in the same spaces, poison threatens close at hand as well as from the margins of the colony.

If the question of the antidote so preoccupies the burghers of Cape Town, how does this discourse accommodate the fact of poison being deployed as an indigenous technology? Venomous arrows were an object of curiosity for the earliest European travellers to southern Africa.[4] However, as one of the pre-eminent botanists of his day, Thunberg is a different class of witness. He has a habit of meticulous observation which he applies in his descriptions of poisoned arrow technology, remarking on fine details of construction such as the fact that the projectiles consist of "a thin triangular piece of iron, fastened with a string to a bone of a finger's length, to the end of which is again fastened a reed" (292). The arrow poison itself, he says, is obtained from the venom sacs of snakes, and it is then dried and mixed "with the juice of a poisonous tree" (293).

For its time, this is an unusually accurate observation about regional variations in Bushman arrow technology.[5] Nonetheless, insisting its way into the rhetoric of this empirical observation is the nervous suspicion that for each known toxin there is, somewhere, both a hidden antidote and a class of immune individuals, and it is there that fear inhabits the narrative once again.

In the midst of a discussion of vegetable toxins, including descriptions of the ubiquitous *Boophane disticha*, the *gifbol* dreaded by Dutch farmers, Thunberg pauses to make the following observation: "The Hottentots and Boschiesmen are said to fortify themselves against poisoned darts and the bite of venomous animals, by suffering themselves to be gradually bitten by serpents . . . till they become accustomed to it; but these trials sometimes cost them their lives." (293). Snake venom, toxic plants, arrows, together seem to make up a lexicon of resistance to the would-be European settler, as though the body of the colonial world were turning against an intruding element. Because of the fear of local toxins, and the perception that local inhabitants may be able to make themselves immune to them, poison starts to resemble a symbolic medium in which indigenous inhabitants are at home. Ultimately, this fear is manifested tropologically in the figure of the "poison drinkers", those who can apparently transform the symbolic body, invert its chemistry, through a combination of dangerous experiment and detailed local knowledge, until it is able to withstand substances which deliver death immediately to the unwary colonist.

In Sparrman, rumours of the poison drinkers crowd in upon the scientific traveller when he tries to prevent Khoisan servants from drinking his preserving alcohol (178–9). This occasions an additional alarming thought: "How the uncultivated Hottentots should arrive to the knowledge, that the poison of serpents maybe swallowed without danger, it is not easy to conjecture."(179). At this epistemic moment the body is still clearly a symbolic system, and thus the suggestion that savages work upon their own corporeal resistance, producing immunity as an effect of dangerous experiment, is something of an insult to rational science. To cap it all, this is a symbolic order Thunberg believes to be constituted around binary opposition: "The urine of a Hottentot thus prepared", he says, "is esteemed an excellent antidote or counterpoison." (293). The prospect of fearful white travellers seeking out Khoikhoi to urinate upon them is too tantalising an idea for even the most postmodern theory of resistance not to entertain!

Let us return now to the case of the poisoned arrow, for nowhere else does the fear of poison combine more forcibly with the fear of indigenous epistemology. It is as well to remember that European contact with these weapons is at least as old as the Columbian voyages (Bisset 2-6, Clark 127), and seventeenth- and eighteenth-century travellers to South Africa often have what Edward Said calls a "textual attitude" towards such objects (92–3), frequently associating them with other forms of bodily violation like cannibalism. Some visitors, like Sparrman, brought with them a bank of proto-ethnographic knowledge accumulated from contacts in the mercantile colonial world or on voyages of discovery. As a staging post for returning East Indiamen, and convalescing British military personnel, the Cape participated in the transmission of encyclopaedic knowledge about indigenous technologies back to metropolitan archives. Sparrman, arriving at the Cape after joining Cook's *Resolution* for the first eastward circumnavigation, had fresh in his mind recent dangerous experiences in the New Hebrides "with a diminutive race of people, with a language peculiar to themselves, and poisoned weapons" (118). "More than once", he goes on to explain, "we were exposed to the poisoned weapons of these natives, from the slightest wound arising from which, we had every reason to dread as painful and terrible a death, accompanied with madness as happened to some of Captain Carteret's crew, when they were wounded on the coast of New Guinea."(119). Unlike other arrow preparations, the poisons of New Guinea, Melanesia and Polynesia are mainly microbial in origin, and arrows are often simply polluted by placing them in rotting flesh (Bisset 11). It is telling, though, that for Sparrman, the prospect of "madness", the dramatic collapse of ego defences, is quite as horrifying as death itself.

Thus far, I have been tracing the history of poison at the Cape, or, more accurately, I have been discussing the epistemology of poison, since the figure of poison marks a contestation of the grounds of knowledge more than a simple fear of mortality. What is especially interesting, is the way in which charting references to toxic substances enables at the same time an approximate history of competing somatic metaphors and of what Turner calls the "social skin": the incorporation of ideas of corporeal boundedness into a symbolic matrix. Also intriguing is the discovery that examination of references to poisons reveals the complex interdependency of colonial and indigenous understanding: Dutch colonial homeopathic practices derive both from experience of Khoisan medicinal knowledge, and from the circulation of reports about antidotes throughout the colonial world. News of poisoned arrows and news of local medicine travel the same global route in the seventeenth and eighteenth centuries, along the "commodity pathways" of the mercantile empire. But that entails, at the same time, that the figure of poison has a different valency at different places, and this suggests that there are profound problems with "discursive" analysis of colonial texts that treat them as bounded rhetorical units without readers or publishers.

Reading cultures as texts, following Geertz's ethnographic textualism, or deploying Foucauldian analyses of the relationship between discursive power and epistemic formations, may be one way of coming to terms with the manner in which dominant cultures enforce their meanings. At the same time though, we must be alert to Giyatri Spivak's critique:

> It is well known that Foucault located epistemic violence, a complete overhaul of the episteme, in the redefinition of sanity at the end of the European eighteenth century. But what if that particular redefinition was only a part of the narrative of history in Europe as in the colonies? (281)

For Spivak, Foucault's textual analysis of power, whilst eschewing any notion of the autonomous subject, at the same time locates itself within the practice and purview of European intellectuals. Discursive analysis that privileges micrology, she continues, omits the fact that "the new mechanism of power in the seventeenth and eighteenth centuries (the extraction of surplus value without extra-economic coercion is its Marxist description) is secured by means of territorial imperialism" (290). Reading the figure of poison, which insists itself in tropological displacements through any number of texts, is thus not simply a "textual" matter. Travelogues themselves circulate within certain privileged domains, and they accumulate knowledge that passes between different points in a mercantile colonial order in a manner reflective of different political hierachies and different relationships between administrators and local elites.

Administering poison

One modest proposition which underpins this argument is that the fear of poison depends on increasing contact between groups in an asymmetrically ordered social domaine. Internationally, as colonial encounters become more protracted, so news of spectacular foreign poisons seeps into travelogues, administrative reports, and journalism. Ironically, therefore, in the case of colonial toxins, a sort of Hegelian reversal becomes visible: as colonial wars proliferate across the globe, and indigenous communities are exterminated or pressed into wage labour, so there is a compensatory psychological mechanism that tends to exaggerate the strength of poisons, their morbid nature and the arcane knowledge needed to manipulate them. Furthermore, throughout the world, poison enters the discursive system as an effect of the presence of the slave in the master's house. In South Africa, as Sue Newton-King has demonstrated, Dutch freeburgher identity depends in large measure on a distinction between slave owner and Khoisan servant that is in some senses fictitious, because in fact both groups share a very similar experience of the land, food and livestock.[6] Given colonial dependency on indigenous forms of botanical knowledge, it is not surprising that most slave owners live in fear of the day their servants' botanical understanding is employed in sly homicidal practices.

Throughout the centuries of British colonial administration, poisoned arrows were collected for cabinets of curiosities, to be shown and classified. Furthermore, from a very early point in Britain's overseas history, we find metropolitan gentry reacting with shock at the news of savage expertise with poisons. For Richard Mead (1702), it is not so much the virulence of African or Indian poisons that is at issue, as the insidious ability of natives to manipulate them. There are persistent rumours, he says, that they "are so expert in killing, that they can do it in a longer or shorter time as they please" (125). For the as-yet rudimentary science of symptomatology, in a Newtonian universe, the prospect of death at a point temporally removed from the precipitating event, is cause for considerable alarm. Characteristically, in many of these popular treatises, news of poison is usually combined with speculation about antidotes, for medical officers throughout the colonial world, it seems, were already passing information about imaginary local antidotes back to the metropole. An "Ingenious Surgeon, who lived in Guinea", for instance, informs Mead that "the Antidote by which the Negroes would sometimes Cure those who were poisoned, was the Leaf of an Herb *which purged both upwards and downwards*" (125 original emphasis). Even more significant perhaps, is the evidence of interaction between slaveowning communities around the world, sharing knowledge about toxins, and their cures, gleaned from servants. In the last quarter of the eighteenth century, for instance, we see the publication of Prestwich's *Dissertation on Mineral, Animal, & Vegetable Poisons; Containing a Description of Poisons in General, their Manner of Action, Effects on the Human Body, and Respective Antidotes.* After extensive discussion of curare, the spectacular toxin of the period, the editor includes a reprint from the *Carolina Gazette*, 9 May 1750, containing the poignant record of "The Negro Caesar's Cure for Poison", "for discovering of which, the general assembly hath thought fit to purchase his freedom, and grant him an allowance of 100 1. per annum during his life" (216). Given the novelty of an emergent European print culture, it is interesting to see how the planters of Carolina are already helping to still the fears on plantations everywhere.

Not all influential scientists of the period were prepared to accept that native poisoners could manipulate at will the period of suffering before death. In another widely read eighteenth-century handbook (Dr Allan 1730), we find the following outburst: "That Opinion is Vulgar and False, that says, that the Indians, and from thence the Italians, have such an Art of Poisoning, that they can kill all Persons certianly [*sic*], to a certain Year, or determined Time, whether Weeks, Months or Days for Nature equally opposes herself with her whole Strength to all Poison, and overpowers or frustrates the deadly Venom."(234 original emphasis). This is a remarkable piece of period propaganda. Faced with the news about this deadly native prowess, Allen undermines the claim by enlisting Nature as a benevolent female principle, working on the side of the British.

Let us now turn to the reports of two British travellers in whom is combined military training, colonial service in various far-flung corners of the globe, an Enlightenment scientific apparatus, and the desire to catalogue Cape manners and customs for the purpose of future colonial administration. Both these travellers, William Paterson and John Barrow, have been the subject of close scrutiny by the literary theorist Mary Louise Pratt, and this will be an occasion as well for commentary on the value of her interpretive method.

Most British travellers to South Africa, it seems, would have shared William Paterson's belief that "the subject of Poisons is one of the most interesting branches of natural history" (161). Many reports from this period abound with references to toxic substances, and, following Thunberg, most writers are aware of the commoner arrow poison ingredients such as *Boophone disticha* and various Euphorbia species.[7] But Paterson, apart from writing the first detailed European descriptions of some of these plants, is also very particular about a still relatively obscure element in arrow poison manufacture: "Their method of making this pernicious mixture", he says, "is by first taking the juice extracted from the Euphorbia, and a kind of caterpillar peculiar to another plant, which has much the appearance of a species of Rhus."(62). This early account of the derivation of Diamphotoxin from chrysomelid beetle larvae is unusually detailed, as is his description of arrow technology, which, like Thunberg's, includes reference to the use of detachable link shafts and small barbs bound on with sinew.[8]

The fine empirical detail in Paterson can be ascribed, in part, to his military experience plus the rudimentary training in Linnaean classification methods he received at the Chelsea Physick Garden (Forbes 17). Underpinning the entire narrative, in fact, is the binary logic of the binomial classification system. The text abounds with such divisions, most insistently in the distinction between "Hottentot" and "Bushman", but also in the division between separate spheres of animal and vegetable poisons. At the same time, the clinical gaze of travellers such as Paterson and Sparrman means that the human presence of the Khoikhoi is effaced from the narratives. As Pratt remarks, "while Kolb wrote the Khoikhoi primarily as cultural beings, these two texts of the 1780s produce them above all as bodies and append-ages" (52).

Pratt's is one of the most sophisticated and influential discursive readings of a colonial South African text. For our purposes, though, and for the purposes of the "new" African history, there are serious limitations to tropological analysis. Subal-tern presences are, it is true, controlled and managed by the generic conventions of Paterson's manners-and-customs portrait. Nevertheless, to look at the *Narrative of Four Journeys* as a discursive event characterised mainly by certain forms of tropological insistence – the reiteration of the idea of poison, for instance – is to miss the point of Paterson's book as itself an aspect of material culture, circulating within a regime of value dependent both on metropolitan class associations and core-periphery systems of knowledge transmission.[9] Like most eighteenth-century public figures, Paterson is involved in a logic of imitating metropolitan class paradigms. In sponsoring the botanical expedition, his patron, the Countess of Strathmore, is clearly mimicking the fashionable collecting expedition by Francis Masson, the King's gardener (Forbes 33). That is one extradiscursive connection. On the other hand, the Cape is also a staging post for a military career that took him to India, back to the Cape, Australia, and finally to found a penal settlement in Tasmania. Thus while the *Narrative of Four Journeys* has an internal tropological order that may be examined, it is also interesting, I would suggest, for manifest contradictions that have to do with the place of the book in the triangular trade of colonial ideas between India, the Cape and London.

William Paterson's interest in colonial toxins, I shall show later, actually begins neither in Chelsea, nor at the Cape, but in the East Indies, and there are frequent references in his work to this earlier sphere of experience. South African poisons are, however, an object of intense fascination to him. In the Brenthurst manuscript of the *Narrative*, for instance, we find a note for 29 July 1778 describing the suffering of a Dutch woman wounded in the arm with a Bushman arrow: "There had been great pains taken in the curing of her", he observes, "tho' to no purpose, as there are different times of the year that mortifications break out."(90). Apart from the insights this passage offers into theories of airborne disease transmission, it is a relatively bland description. In the reworked and edited *Narrative*, though, the same episode is relegated to an appendix on poison, where the body of the Dutch woman provides empirical evidence of the power of Bushman toxins: "she received a wound from an arrow on her shoulder; and so rapid was the effect of the poison, that before she reached the Cape, it had not only produced a mortification in the fleshy part of the shoulder, but had extended itself to both her breasts, in which state she died. This and many other instances have been related to me by the country folk. I shall not attempt to vouch for the truth of them" (162–3). Now it is quite possible to see a gendered textual metaphorics at work here. Arrow poison, a signifier of potent indigenous knowledge, invades the breasts, which, for the male narrator, are symbolically associated with reproduction and maternal nurture. But what makes this sort of analysis unsatisfactory on its own, and the problem with importing into historical analysis a crude understanding of textuality and reading, is that it conflates tropological analysis with the entire intertextual process. Throughout the colonial world, in this period, milk and poison are diametrically opposed substances, the former almost always being mentioned as an antidote for the latter. This in turn reveals a gendered European division of labour between the world of action, on the one hand, and the domestic world of cures. Not surprisingly, given these distinctions, the curative capacity of breast milk is particularly esteemed. Lichtenstein, for example, sensibly recommends washing the eyes with milk if they are polluted with cobra venom, and repeats earlier Congo missionary reports that in such instances "the milk of a woman is the only thing that can prevent total blindness ensuing" (119).

Our discussion thus far has ranged broadly from conceptions of the body in Dutch and Khoisan communities, to the mechanisms of classification at work in Enlightenment travelogues. What needs to be stressed, however, is that poison, despite its mortal danger, is also an ontological problem for the colonial imagination. It represents that place where the gridlike, empirico-medical discourses of the Enlightenment encounter a pure signifier of indigenous knowledge, indigenous difference. Reference to poison, therefore, entails reference to an already-present, elaborate, indigenous pharmacopoeia which is clearly adapted to the environment into which white settlers intrude. It would be grotesque to suggest that the systematic murder of Bushman communities by Boer commandos and British officials alike was not primarily the result of competition over land, livestock and access to labour power, but at the same time the problem of *knowledge* represented by the sign of the Bushman arrow should not be overlooked. For the post-Linnaean British imagination, local poisons required two sorts of answer: analysis and the discovery of antidotes.

In colonial texts of this period, considerable effort is expended on denying the scientific status of indigenous arrow poison knowledge. Moreover, for some metropolitan observers, settler fears about these toxins appeared to be unjustified, stemming from pre-Enlightenment ignorance about the treatment of infected wounds:

> Since musquetry has been invented, it has happened from reduced health, by a tainted atmosphere, or insufficient food, or both, that every wound has proved gangrenous or ill conditioned. This, at one time, produced the same suspicion of arrows: nor is there any thing bold in suspecting that many accounts of poisoned springs have no better foundation. (Adams 2)

Having witnessed the deadly effects of poisoned-arrow wounds, Paterson is not as quick to deny the potency of the toxin. Despite his sarcastic remarks about Boer gullibility, he is obsessed with discovering an antidote "such as might be carried in the traveller's pocket" (167). At the same time, the hope for such a cure stems from a comparison of colonial situations: familiarity with malevolent native practices in one of Britain's colonies may help to solve problems in another. So, for instance, in the appendix on poisons, he bases his hope for an antidote to Cape poisons on his military experiences in the East Indies:

> The Brahmins tell us, that they can administer complete relief in the most desperate cases; but their mode of practice has hitherto been kept a secret from Europeans.

Colonel Fullerton, however, procured a small box of their pills from the Reverend Mr. Swartz, a missionary at Tanjore; and at the siege of Carrore we had an Opportunity of proving the effects of them. One of our seapoys [sic] was bitten, and so ill that we despaired of his life. The Colonel gave him one of the pills, which seemed to act as a very strong opiate for some time . . .; in two days, however, the man was perfectly recovered. (166)

Notwithstanding the predictable irony that it is usually native servants or the lower ranks, who are the subjects of dangerous experiment, it is clear that in the case of poisons and their supposed antidotes, a military community of knowledge stretches from colony to colony and then to scientific institutions at home.

The Orientalism in Paterson's fantasy about the Brahman pills is frequently repeated in Cape poison cures. Throughout the eighteenth century, standard treatment for snakebite or poisoned arrow wounds included scarification, the application of warm milk, oil or live chickens with bleeding wounds matched to the human wound to draw off the venom, cupping glasses, and, invariably, the use of a "serpent stone". Carl Thunberg, ever interested in the relationship between Dutch rank and access to medical treatment, observes that the snake stone "is imported from the Indies, especially Malabar, and costs several rix dollars". He goes on to describe its use as follows: "When it is applied to any part that has been bitten by a serpent, it sticks fast to the wound, and extracts the poison; as soon as it is saturated, it falls off itself. If it be then put into milk, it is supposed to be purified." Apart from the fact that this repeats the structural antithesis of poison and antidote, venom and milk, Thunberg here provides us with few of the original beliefs surrounding this symbolic object. For that, we must go back fifty years to Peter Kolb. Discounting the common belief that there are magical stones in the heads of certain serpents, Kolb goes on to describe how artificial serpent stones are in common use at the Cape:

They are brought from the East Indies, where they are prepared by the Brachmans, who are alone, it seems, possessed of the secret of the composition, and will not let it go out of their own body at any price. I am heartily sorry the secret is not in the Christian world, and that the Brachmans are inflexible in this particular. (42)

In this passage, in the reference to the traffic of curative "native" artifacts between colonial officials and local elites, there is an ironic foreshadowing of similar collaborations later in the century, with the British manipulation of caste differences and intermediate classes in the administration of India.

The traffic in poison cures amongst wealthy Dutch burghers at the Cape thus speaks volumes about the inscription of the East as a place of hieroglyphic inscrutability. But in fact such palliatives as the serpent stone are essentially homeopathic, and metaphoric, based on visible homologies: the stone displays its supposed power by giving off bubbles when submerged, it cleaves to the flesh, and it drinks the antidote milk. Surprisingly, this is a much later reliance on theories of similitude than Foucault allows in *The Order of Things*: "At the beginning of the seventeenth century", he says, "during the period that has been termed . . . the Baroque, thought ceases to move in the element of similitude."(51) Perhaps in the colonial world the belief in resemblance, the visible signature of things, persists much later for it is on that basis that settlers attempt to incorporate indigenous pharmacological knowledge. Yet in the case of the serpent stone, another secret lies coiled in the descriptive phrases used by Kolb and Thunberg: when it is said to drink in the poison, and in the remark "as soon as it is saturated, it falls off itself", the stone appears to have volition and to become engorged. As you will have guessed, therefore, the "slangsteen" is a simulacrum of that exotic surgical device in use in South Africa until the end of the century – the medical leech. Unlike the leech, though, it has added value because of its Eastern provenance. Colonial poisons, it seems, are best combatted with a touch of their own medicine.

Poison denied

As a man of the Enlightenment, and a representative of British government, John Barrow is crushingly dismissive of country beliefs in the serpent stone: "To the porosity of the bone may be ascribed its healing qualities, if it actually possesses any; for which reason, any other substance made up of capillary tubes, as common sponge, might perhaps be equally efficacious." (292). Over the past five years or so, with the proliferation of colonial discourse studies in literature and historical anthropology, Barrow's *Travels* has played a more and more important role. Outstanding amongst those who have examined his narrative and rhetorical logic is Mary Louise Pratt, who, drawing heavily on the work of John Barrell and Johannes Fabian, has demonstrated the textual "production" of Khoisan identity in the work. This, she says, is a process designed to "dismantle the [Khoisan] socioecological web . . . and install a Eurocolonial discursive order whose territorial and visual forms of authority are those of the modern state" (64). Hers is a magisterial analysis, but what is unclear in the work, however, is the relationship between rhetoric and historical contradiction. To put it another way: what is it in the nature of material conditions on the Northern frontier in the late eighteenth century that causes Barrow's empirical classificatory mechanism to break down around certain iterative images? Once again, I suggest, our answer lies in the historical enigma of poison.

As Lord McCartney's personal secretary, it was Barrow's responsibility to begin extending a sense of British administration to the lawless interior in the period immediately following the capture of the Cape. As such, his primary purpose was diplomacy and mapping, not narration. What is also significant is that he was the first British official to delineate the northern boundary of the frontier, and so the

Bushmen have a special significance for him: they are that people around whom the extended authority of the Cape and its legal categories breaks down, and Boer lawlessness prevails.[10] What I wish to argue, therefore, in contrast to Pratt, is that there is not *one* dramatic contradiction in the *Narrative*, the commando raid on the Bushmen, but a principle of elision, and that is open to historical examination.

Barrow's epistemological frame of reference is the great empirico-ethnographic classificatory grid described so well by Foucault: "In the eighteenth century", he says, "the continuity of nature is a requirement of all natural history, that is of any effort to establish an order in nature and to discover general categories within it." (147). But the principle of the table and the taxonomic continuum, unlike the structural grammars that it attempts to imitate, as Foucault points out, leaves no place for the aberrations and deviations necessary for evolution in the system:

> But this essential nomination – this transition from the visible structure to the taxonomic character – leads back to a costly requirement. In order to fulfill and enclose the figure that proceeds from the monotonous function of the verb to be to derivation and traversal of rhetorical space, spontaneous language had no need of anything but the play of imagination: that is, of immediate resemblances. For taxonomy to be possible, on the other hand, nature must be truly continuous, and in all its plenitude. (159)

In other words, natural history tries to emulate the condition of a well constructed language, but this is in contradiction to the inflexible and ungrammatical underlying principles of taxonomy. In any of the eighteenth-century encyclopaedic systems, therefore, the principle of deviation, surplus and excess always threatens.

Interestingly, the first sign of this excess, or, as I would prefer to call it, the principle of the supplement, appears in Barrow's description of rock art:

> On the smooth sides of the cavern were drawings of several animals that had been made from time to time by these savages. Many of them were caricatures; but others were too well executed not to arrest attention. The different antelopes that were there delineated had each their character so well discriminated, that the originals, from whence the representations had been taken, could, without any difficulty, be ascertained. Among the numerous animals that were drawn, was the figure of a zebra, remarkably well done; all the marks and characters of this animal . . . were seemingly correct. The force and spirit of drawings, given to them by bold touches judiciously applied, and by the effect of light and shadow, could not be expected from savages. (239)

This is not simply a condescending statement. First, in his programmatically anti-Boer narrative, Barrow is delighted to confound intelligence he has received from the "peasants", who had led him to believe rock paintings were "similar to those on the doors and walls of uninhabited buildings, the works of idle boys" (240).

Moreover, rock art exceeds the frame of reference Barrow inherits from earlier travellers: it is not quaint, simple, from the infancy of mankind, but successfully representational, a form of drawing that uses perspectival shading and chiaroscuro. In one sense, this is an extraordinary admission. In Barrow's generation, the presence of affect (the "force and spirit of drawings" as well as "bold touches judiciously applied") and skillful use of contrast in painting, suggests the presence of "Taste", the central category by which Whig subjects identified civilised being. "So far then as Taste belongs to the imagination", says Burke,

> its principle is the same in all men; there is no difference in the manner of their being affected, nor in the causes of the affection; but in the degree there is a difference, which arises from two causes principally; either from a greater degree of natural sensibility, or from a closer and longer attention to the object. (21)

Modelling, representational accuracy and mood in the drawing provide ample evidence, for Barrow, of the sensibility of the individual artist. These qualities, in turn, provided the chief metaphorics for access to class mobility and citizenship in the late eighteenth century.[11]

Rock art is mentioned on several occasions in the *Travels*, but frequently it is also associated with the figure of poison. After meditating on several hieroglyphic marks above the animal drawings ("crosses, circles, and lines, . . . placed in a long rank as if intended to express some meaning" (240)), the administrator's attention is drawn to a bituminous substance coating the walls of the cave. His Dutch companions draw him back in sudden alarm, explaining that this material is deadly, one of the chief ingredients in Bushmen arrow poisons: "they all agreed in the baneful qualities of this black matter, from having experienced the fatal effects of it on several of their companions, who had suffered lingering deaths from wounds received with arrows poisoned with the klip gift" (240–1). Thus the dichotomy between poison and painting becomes a telling signifier in Barrow's work. Rock art provides evidence of Bushmen sensibility, of their potential amenability to reason and administration; but it is overshadowed by its obverse, poison, the source of direct conflict and mortality on the frontier. Painting, in the language of Whig individualism, is the work of Taste, of the fully individuated subject; poison, conversely, is an expression of the collective indigenous subject, the "horde".

Unlike the pre-Enlightenment Dutch epistemology analysed earlier, Barrow's encyclopaedic method cannot accommodate play in the system. Deploying the method of natural history, for him, means finding not only taxonomic connections, but also the logic of association between genera and classes. He explains this principle as follows: "Nature has seldom given a bane but she has accompanied it with an antidote; or, in other words, she has ordained that one half of the creation should destroy and devour the other, that the constant operations of reproduction might be going on." (256–7). This principle of the continuum plays itself out in the narrative in frequent reference to paired units, which in turn establish connections between classes: Plagues of locusts, for example, call up, as if out of nowhere, a superabundance of hungry finches who swarm down to devour them (257). But given the tightly controlled nature of this grid, the appearance of apparently new species challenges the integrity of the whole system. The gnu, for instance, troubles the entire Linnaean method, which is based on visible similarities. "Perhaps", he suggests, "the introduction of intermediate genera might without impropriety be adopted, to include such animals as are found to partake of more than one genus; which would also point out the fine links that unite the grand chain of creation."(260).

After Derrida's critique of structuralism, it is far easier, to understand how the principle of supplementarity, of differánce, is at work in any system.[12] In the *Travels*, ostensibly stable binary oppositions often break down, generating contradictions that have to be contained. One of the most important distinctions in the work, between Boer sloth, stupidity and cruelty towards slaves, versus British administrative efficiency and science, depends on the staging of an idea of Dutch excess. So, for instance, absurd marriage laws at the Cape mean that couples have to travel long distances together, and Barrow explains "nine times out of ten the consummation of the marriage precedes the ceremony" (252). The problem would be solved, according to Barrow, by the reconfiguration of Dutch Law along British lines. Similarly, in a passage that has been extensively analysed by Gilman and others, the excessive sexuality of Khoikhoi women is marked by their "protruded nymphae", a feature that is impossible to catalogue. But this remarkable and potentially unsettling element is stabilised once it occurs to Barrow that this is Nature's way of protecting women, and that the "Hottentot apron" has at least "the advantage of serving as a protection against violence from the other sex" (279).[13]

John Barrow is interested in the Bushman not only because of their exotic nature, or because they exemplify a problem of administration. They also hold the key to one of his personal obsessions--the quest to discover a unicorn. Dragging his reluctant Dutch guides with him, he flies from one rock shelter to another, searching for representations of one-horned beasts. Tales of unicorn drawings, always rumoured to be a "little to the northward" (that euphemism characteristic of so many resistant native informants) confound him, until finally he comes upon a drawing that does actually seem to capture the essence of the mythical beast (see Figure 1 on page 74).

Unfortunately, to Barrow's intense disappointment and the hilarity of "the peasantry, who could form no such idea of the consequence I attached to the drawing", he says, the bottom half has been painted over with another figure, rendering it useless as empirical evidence. Later in the narrative, this leads him to question the empirical method itself, since nature, he admits, "is too varied to be shackled with a syllogism" (317).

SOUTHERN AFRICA.   313

that was certainly intended as the reprefentation of a beaft with
a fingle horn projecting from the forehead.   Of that part of it
which diftinctly appeared, the following is a *fac fimile.*

The body and legs had been erafed to give place to the figure
of an elephant that ftood directly before it.

Nothing could be more mortifying than fuch an accident;
but the peafantry, who could form no idea of the confequence
I attached to the drawing of fuch an animal, feemed to enjoy
my chagrin.   On being told, however, that a thoufand, or
even five thoufand, rixdollars would be given to any one who
would produce an original, they ftood gaping with open
mouths, and were ready to enlift for an expedition behind the
Bambos-berg, where fome of them were quite certain the animal was to be found.   Imperfect as the figure was, it was
fufficient to convince me that the Bosjefmans are in the practice of including, among their reprefentations of animals, that
of an unicorn ; and it alfo offered a ftrong argument for the
s s   exiftence

Figure 1: Page 313 of Barrow's *An Account of Travels into the Interior of Southern Africa* (1801)

Despite the fact that the symbolic ambiguity of rock art appears to triumph over empirical observation, on a frontier perpetually armed against Bushman stock theft the problem of the poisoned arrow remains. Thus begins the most famous moment of the *Travels*, an eye-witness account of a commando raid on a small Bushman party. As Pratt suggests, this is the most traumatic moment in the text, when "Barrow's discursive order breaks down along with his humanitarian moral one" (67). But directly prior to this event, much is revealed about the contradictory nature of British administrative opinions about agency and the "free" subject of law. Perhaps anticipating the trouble that lies ahead, Barrow wishes to interrogate Bushman informants about local Dutch atrocities, especially rumours of slaughter by commandos and the kidnapping into virtual slavery of Khoisan women and children. In each case, however, one of two things happens: either the British conception of a free, conscious subject of law clashes with what appears to be a "collective" subject ("we had wished to speak with the captain or chief of the horde, but they assured us there was no such person") (275); or, contrarily, individuals precipitated, as it were, out of the group, exhibit such fear and are so distressed that they cannot function as subjects of legal discourse at all.

This oscillation between the idea of the "free" wild Bushman (part of the anti-slavery rhetoric that characterised later government interventions on behalf of the Grahamstown merchant elites) and the dangerous horde, characterises British rhetoric for the next three decades. For Thomas Pringle, in the "Song of the Wild Bushman", "free" Bushmen are a dying breed, limited to a few individuals in the mountains who still pursue the old ways. In the poem, when the Bushman speaks he tells that "The crested adder honoureth me,/And yields at my command/His poison-bag, like the honey bee". The same poem ends with a statement of defiance in which the warrior refuses to leave the mountain fastnesses to "crouch beneath the Christian's hand":

> To be a hound, and watch the flocks,
> For the cruel White Man's gain –
> No! the brown Serpent of the Rocks
> His den doth yet retain;
> And none who there his sting provokes,
> Shall find its poison vain!

This is, we must agree, a sympathetic account of San resistance, characteristic of Pringle's abolitionist drive. However, given what we have seen in Barrow, it constructs an impossible scenario. In the rhetoric of the period, for very specific reasons that have to do with the conditions of labour, servitude and peonage in the Eastern Cape, the idea of the Bushman as an independent, free subject of amelioration and British law, the subject who paints the images in Barrow's cave, confronts the opposing image of the marauding collective horde. Thus the two signifiers "poison" and "painting" represent the dispersion of a particular contradiction: that under the second occupation, despite ostensible attempts to Anglicise Dutch Law and ameliorate the condition of servants, Khoisan labourers remained in conditions of abject servitude.[14] So Pringle's lone mountain figure is really an Enlightenment fantasy (the cave with rock art on his own farm had long been abandoned), when in actuality the problem of the poisoned arrow was far closer to home. As Sue Newton-King has demonstrated, late eighteenth-century attitudes towards Khoisan labour were heavily influenced by the attempt to exterminate the Bushman. Even a casual trawl through the Cape Archives will demonstrate that trials around poisoned arrow usage frequently refer back not to encounters between mountain bushmen and pursuing commandos, but quarrels over labour on farms. Thus in the Cradock Circuit Court case of Andries Stockenstrom contra "Vrolyk, a Boschjesman Prisoner", one Gerrit Cornelis Olivier is described as having arrows shot at him by a group who have been given permission to take up abode on his farm, only to discover that he wishes to press them into work (CJ 816). The accused are sentenced to be severely scourged, branded and to work in irons on Robben Island for the next fifteen years.

Thus poison, in John Barrow, is initially subject to the same schematisation as in other travelogues, but the administrative logic of the narrative produces an irreconcilable contradiction between the Bushman subject as a free, conscious subject of law and the idea of collective resistance. This same dichotomy, between a nostalgically construed "free" Bushman subject and the thieving horde hardens into a stony racism in Grahamstown. Throughout Robert Godlonton, invectives against the Bushman are strewn with references to their collective, unindividuated nature (178).

The poisoned arrow as fetish

Earlier in this account, I suggested that the debate over toxic substances at the Cape provided access to a history of the symbolic body. I wish to take this one step further now, and suggest that "poison" often stands for the principle of antagonistic local difference around which a link between colonial biomedical practice and administration is constituted. It seems to me crucial to insist that debates over arrow poison concern aspects of material culture and symbolic practice as well as questions of ethnography and weapons manufacture. For early toxicologists, the problem of colonial poisons was solved by their pharmacological analysis and the discovery of antidotes; that is to say, the solution to the problem of poisons follows once knowledge passes back into the metropolitan archive. On the colonial periphery, however, poison occasions a protracted debate over the meaning of the body, healing and the nature of subjectivity. What frequently confuses missionaries and magistrates alike, is that poisoned arrow usage appears to have a *cultural* function in relation to a symbolically construed collective body.

Contemporary African cultural studies has been enormously enriched by the interaction between fields such as medical history and cultural anthropology. In particular, the work of the Comaroffs, Megan Vaughan and Elizabeth Elbourne on missionaries as complex ideological advance agents of mercantile capitalism has shown, for instance, how the political "conversation" between evangelicalism and African hierarchies focused on competing ideas of the symbolic body. "It was mission medicine", Megan Vaughan explains, "which competed with African healers on the same terrain, since missionary biomedical practice was explicitly about transforming existing meanings surrounding the body and disease and creating new ones in their place."(19). This is a crucial point to bear in mind in our discussion of method in cultural studies, for too often, following Foucault, Bourdieu, Jordanova, Laqueur, and a host of others, the understanding of the body as having a history, as being literally remade in different epochs, resolves itself down into the rather mundane practice of looking for somatic imagery. What starts as a radical theoretical break, allowing insights into a variety of new historical fields, too often descends into a conservative and formalist understanding of literary hermeneutics that few literary theorists would accept. Reading bodies, or societies, as "texts" has its uses, but that does mean that they are not involved in material, non-discursive practices.

If the body is disciplined and remade in terms of changing relations of production, and if it is true that missionaries and Khoisan, for instance, contest the symbolic meaning of the body differently from the way colonial doctors do, then one may anticipate that for missionaries poison is a rather special signifier. In most cases of Bushman and missionary contact, the symbolic logic of venom and antidote suggested by poisoned arrow usage occasions as much comment as does the threat of mortal wounds.

For some missionaries, the entire matrix of detail associated with poisoned arrow preparation is a serious threat, for it appears to be both a species of idolatry and representative of a complex, elaborated material culture. John Campbell's guide through Bushman country in 1822 could speak their language "as well as any native", but he nevertheless insisted that "they did not believe in a god or the great father of men, but in the devil" (29). The same informant, however, is so eager to please his companion, that he ascribes his quick recovery from a poisoned arrow wound to the fact that the blow of the deadly dart was cushioned by "a pamphlet of twenty or thirty pages". Perhaps this saving tract is the South African equivalent of the deputy's silver badge or the detective's cigarette case.

By far the most interesting and bizarre missionary reaction to arrow poison can be found in Arbousset and Daumas. In a chapter entitled "Idolatry", part of a general appendix on Bushmen customs, the French missionaries discuss the concept of deity prevalent in the group they interview. Buoyed by the hope that the "Baroa" seem to have a rudimentary understanding of the immortality of the soul, they are later sickened to discover that "they worship an insect of the caterpillar tribe, the caddisworm" (255). Such horrible discoveries confirm the very worst suspicions about African religions in developing missionary discourses. As Lewis-Williams suggests, it is likely that Arbousset chanced here on an oracular practice of the Maluti San, in which creatures such as the mantis, chameleon, or, in this case, the bagworm (*Psychidae*) are consulted on the success of the hunt.[15] What follows in the description, though, is an extraordinary, distorted record both of strategies of ideological containment and the intricate symbolic relationship between poisoned arrow use and material culture.

Though commentators have specifically identified this as a description of oracular practices, the story told by Arbousset's informant is clearly also about the symbolic nature of poisoned arrow hunting. On the principle that one worm is very much like another, it may also be that this description refers to the actual use of poison grubs. *Chrysomelid* beetle larvae, and, in particular, *Diamphidia* pupae and their *Lebistina* parasites, are what researchers usually have in mind when they speak about Bushman poisons. Despite the fact that most Bushman communities – as in fact arrow poison manufacturers around the world – employ polyvalent mixtures, combining latexes and other vegetable and animal substances, it is the poison grub that exemplified for ethnographers the complex relationship between hunter gatherers and their environment. In the case of *Diamphidia nigro-ornata* and *Diamphidia simplex*, probably the best studied primary ingredients, respectively, of *!Kung* and *G/wi* arrow poisons, knowledge of the substance combines with a detailed understanding of the beetle, its life cycle and its *Commiphera* host shrub.[16] What I am suggesting, therefore, is that Arbousset's description of the "caddisworm" takes one aspect of the complex ritual preparation before the hunt and reduces it to a form of fetishism.[17]

Clearly, for Arbousset, the creature the informant refers to as "N'go" is a close approximation of the original serpent enemy of man, sign of a degenerate form of worship directed away from "traditional" African ancestor worship. The source of the confusion lies in this part of the informant's translation:

> One of them of whom I asked if he did not pray to his deceased father like the other inhabitants of the land, said No; adding that this father had taught him otherwise, and had solemnly said before dying, "my son, when thou goest to the chase, seek with great care for the N'go, and from him ask food for thyself and for thy children". (255)

Arbousset misunderstands this as a directive to abandon ancestor worship, an injunction that has serious consequences for the advancement of missionary evangelicalism, since the law of the Father and of male agnatic politics, articulated well with missionary explanations of Christian belief (Comaroff 138). Nonetheless, reading through the various levels of misunderstanding, this remains a detailed account of symbolic preparation for poisoned arrow hunting. As Lewis-Williams points out, the hidden reference to hunting is confirmed when the informant likens the movement of the caterpillar to the sawing off of meat after the kill, and in the "prayer" to the oracular creature, "Lord, bring a male gnu under my darts" (Arbousset 256).

Missionary activity in South Africa is characterised both by a brutal disregard for indigenous cultural practices and by a complex, tentative exchange in which mission culture itself becomes parasitic on local forms of belief and symbolic production (Elbourne 18). Arbousset's glimpse of the symbolic intricacy of the Maluti San material culture, evidenced in reference to poison arrow hunting, causes him to recoil in disgust. "Every one", he exclaims, "may . . . see how material and gross is the prayer of an idolatrous people, which begins by questioning first the love of his god, and calls then for flesh and only flesh." (256). In one sense, he is right; this is, indeed, evidence of a "material" prayer. But that is because Bushman and Khoi societies of the period have a detailed symbolic matrix through which the practice of everyday life passes, and which allows for the interpenetration of material and non-material orders. Missionary culture could not accept this at face value. In cases such as the one we have been examining there was often an attempt to drain the symbolic stature from an event, reducing it to something dull and fetishised. Thus the object of rituals such as hunting is reduced to a mundane reiteration of biological need.

Poison in South Africa is a powerfully contradictory signifier which is taken up in a variety of articulating systems including missionary discourse and colonial medicine; in the process, there were unacknowledged battles over the control of symbolic production, with compromises often being reached on both sides.[18] But what is also important, and what makes it unsatisfactory to consider only the "textual" nature of the missionary enterprise, is the link between knowledge on the colonial periphery and the development of disciplines back home. Missionary activity in South Africa, as elsewhere in the world, provides a major impetus for the development of the British anthropological sciences; similarly, the ethnographic collections of metropolitan museums throughout Europe and America are bristling with poisoned arrow paraphernalia originally garnered by Nonconformists, Catholics and Anglicans abroad. Recent historians of anthropology have demonstrated the early reliance of the discipline on ideas of primitive fetishism, advanced especially in early nineteenth-century studies such as Knight (1818), and discussions of totemism and phallicism in Meiner (1805-7) and Tyler, (Simpson 57–8,

Clifford 219). Perhaps, though, the ability of early anthropology to generalise theories of the fetish to all colonial cultures is in part a product of museum collecting itself in the last century. "Fetishism", in this reading, is thus not something intrinsic to African religions, though one may choose for ideological or missionary reasons to describe them as such. Instead, that process of ascription is aided by the international transfer of objects with a specific symbolic valence in non-metropolitan cultures. Once detached from their context, objects like blowpipes, darts and curare pots are resituated in a new information order that addresses both the metropolitan public and the idea of a distant colonial extension of British national identity. By mid-century, according to Carol Breckenridge, the display of colonial objects in permanent and semi-permanent contexts, like world fairs and museums, contributed to a new "Victorian ecumene", which "oriented the cultural flows that lay at the heart of an emporium in which the nation-state was not an entity *sue generis*" (196–7). Museum artifacts, to put it another way, rearrange the cultural productions of the colonial world in a manner that both celebrates and helps bring into being the European definition of the nation-state. Bushman poisoned arrows collected by Sparrman, Barrow, and others, form part of a new international order of representation based on core-periphery distinctions.

Ironically, psychological theories of the fetish have been returned to the study of colonial discourse, and some attention to this is needed if we are to confront the problems associated with "reading" cultures as texts. Most famously, the term fetishism has been deployed by Homi Bhabha in his dense, confusing commentaries on the psychological aspects of colonial discourse. For most Africanists, Bhabha's work is dismissed as inappropriate, idealist psychobabble, and he is not even mentioned in Raphael Samuel's recent survey of "textualist" influences on historical studies. That is a pity. Whatever the drawbacks to Bhabha's elliptical, difficult texts, they make a very important point about reading colonialism: if the central narrative and ideological mechanism of the colonial text is, as most people believe, the "Manichean" deployment of stereotypes, then very little is to be gained by simply categorising these binary oppositions. This, it seems to me, is one of the main problems in the "textual" drift of historical analysis today. The stereotype, we need to remember, is a profoundly ambivalent form, having to do both with "projection and introjection, metaphoric and metonymic strategies, displacement, over-determination, guilt, aggressivity" (34). References to poisoned arrow preparation in terms of the stereotype of the fetish, in other words, are not in themselves simple; rather, they attempt to stabilise an order of information disturbed by the discovery of competing epistemologies. Not to see the stereotype as contradictory is to ignore its historical functioning.

Since the reinscription of the poisoned arrow as fetish is an effect, not of the material culture in which the artifact has currency, but of the new colonial archive,

that process is visible in the records of any great metropolitan museum. Coincidentally, the Pitt Rivers Museum in Oxford offers particular insights into these cultural
flows, because its catalogues and displays retain their original nineteenth-century
form, in many cases preserving records not only of the original provenance of
articles but also the whimsical remarks of their original donors. For students of
material culture, it is a goldmine. Colonel Lane Fox (later Pitt Rivers) designed a
unique classificatory system for the museum which attempts to dramatise the
development of human material culture (see Figure 2 below). He firmly believed
that "the various products of human industry are capable of classification into
genera, species, and varieties, in the same manner as the products of the vegetable

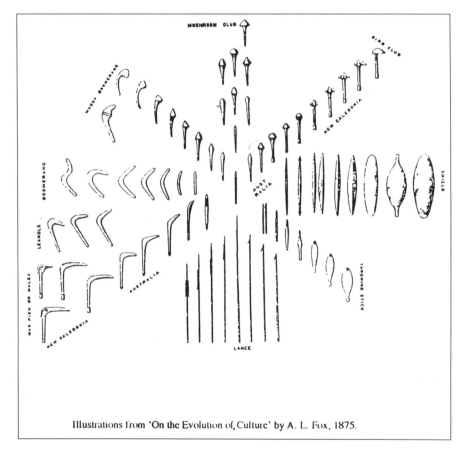

Illustrations from 'On the Evolution of Culture' by A. L. Fox, 1875.

Figure 2: Lane Fox's method of classification (Blackwood 4)

and animal kingdoms" (Blackwood 3). Using the museum's regional and subject card index (itself based on a central accessions register), it is possible to get a remarkable overview of the movement of artifacts from periphery to core in the colonial period.

There are literally hundreds of articles relating to arrow poison manufacture in the Pitt Rivers, originating from all the main arrow poison regions of the world: China, Borneo, South Asia, West, Central and Southern Africa, and, of course, South America. The oldest objects date from the seventeenth-century Tradescant collection, later combined with the Ashmolean and transferred to the Pitt Rivers in the late nineteenth century. (Not surprisingly, these early items are poisoned reed arrows from one of Britain's original areas of colonial engagement, the East Indies.) Another feature of the older part of the collection is that there are numerous artifacts from South America and from South-East Asia, a reflection of the fact that British interest in poisons in the late seventeenth and early eighteenth centuries centered almost exclusively on curare, with increasing attention thereafter being paid to *Upas Antiar*, the deadly arrow latex of the Malay Peninsula. In fact it is no exaggeration to say that there was a scientific traffic in arrow poisons in this period. After the spectacular experiments of Charles-Marie de la Condamine, who brought a stock of curare back from his ten years sojourn in Ecuador and French Guiana, scientists around Europe scrabbled to get hold of experimental samples of the poison. Most of their antics are recorded in the *Philosophical Transactions* of the Royal Society. In 1747, for instance, Brocklesby reported that the heart of a cat appeared to beat two hours after its apparent death; in 1751 M. Herrisant repeated de la Condamine's tests in London; and then, most spectacularly, after the success of Bancroft (1769), Abbé Felix Fontana conducted extensive if brutal experiments on arrow poisons he obtained in a complex deal with London physician William Heberden, a member of the Royal Society that was, by this stage, acting as a sort of broker for scientists working on the mystery of "the South American poison".[19] Unbeknownst to Fontana, the results of these tests proved that the only "antidote" for curare is artificial respiration. In the next decade, scientists began to make clinical use of its powerful anaesthetic effects.[20]

Typically, artifacts transported to the Pitt Rivers are sent by military personnel (Item A.M. 895: 5 "South American poisoned arrows collected by Lieutenant Maw R. N., 1828"); colonial officials (Item A.M. 890: "small globular urari pot, J.Barnett, British Consul, Mexico"); scientific travellers (Burchell, R. F. Burton, Captain Cook); or other colonial museums (Item B.I. 23: "wooden spatula with arrow poison on it, bought through L. Wray, Curator, Perak Museum, 1891"). When Bushman arrows arrive at the museum – and the museum holds an extensive selection, including the Burchell collection – it is in the context of this global network of classification and transmission. Traces of the violence inherent in the dislocation of these objects from their original context of use and symbolic value can be seen in the accessions records: several Gold Coast poisoned arrows are described by a District Commissioner as "Confiscated from the Konkomba Tribe". Still others are placed within the syntax of nineteenth-century ethnographic practice: darts from Malaya poisoned with Strychnos and Upas juice are described as being "marked by Sekai omen". "This is always done", the donor continues, "both among Sekai and Semang". (What Fabian has called the "ethnographic present" here recontextualises the objects under a new analytical gaze.) Finally, there are those cards which speculate wildly on the provenance of the arrows. Item V. 21, from the Zouaragu District of the Northern Territories of the Gold Coast, is described as "3 quivers full of arrows poisoned with crocodile gall and by insertion in decomposing human bodies". "No antidote is known to humans", the donor's note continues, "though the natives are said to possess one."

What I have been tracing in the first stage of this collective project really comes to an end in Victorian museum culture, where the work of both missionary and collector enables the display of the poisoned arrow as a fetish object rather than as the unstable signifier of earlier explorer texts. In part, as I have suggested, the work of displacement and fetishisation is completed because of the syntax imposed by a museum like the Pitt Rivers: In Figure 2 (page 81), for instance, the centripetal radiating lines reorganise world material cultures in terms of a new proto-evolutionary model.

As the extermination of the Bushmen reached then passed its genocidal zenith, a new regime of poison took over in South Africa with the commercial introduction of white arsenic and strychnine. The process is quite clear in Orpen's *Reminiscences*. Orpen ended up as Landdrost of Winburg and played a key role in the suppression of Bushman "squatters" near the town. Increasingly, in this period, the conflict was around sheep farming, and as William Beinart has suggested, there was a close association in the minds of farmers between jackal predation and stock theft by humans (19). New poison regimes were beginning to be established in the region, a process advanced by the Landdrost himself:

> I think we were the first who introduced strychnine into that part of the country. We had brought a little from England and it was very expensive. White arsenic had been tried and was called "Rotte kruid"..., and *nux vomica*, the seed of the Strychnos was already in some use . . . But nothing was nearly so effective as strychnine. (30–1)

With the widespread manipulation of the environment for sheep farming, and the prospect of growing numbers of jackals already refusing poisoned baits, the eradication of Bushman squatters seems to have been viewed by Boer farmers as an extension of pest control methods. Yet it is in this narrative, late in the grim war against the Bushman, that some of the most graphic descriptions of the effects of arrow poison on humans are given. Calling up a commando from Winburg, Orpen arrives at the Bushmankraal very early, on the advice of one Adrian Stander who claims that "in the early morning the strings of their bows were damp and useless". Riding in alone and unarmed, Orpen announces himself as Landdrost, and then occurs a series of spectacular misunderstandings. Pulling back some karosses, he finds a quivering mass of people hiding beneath, one of whom stabs at him. A member of the party shoots the Bushman, and a full-scale battle breaks out. The passage is full of what Ian Watt, with reference to Conrad's Congo experiences, has called "delayed decoding" effects, where the mind cannot quite process the flood of detail: the shower of poisoned arrows about them is described as "just like flying bees", and very quickly several of the whites are wounded. Stander is struck by an arrow which breaks off, leaving the poisoned head in place. Orpen treats the man with brutal urgency: "[I] carved out a bit of skin and flesh more than one inch square, with my wrist grasped in my left hand to steady it, scraped the bone, sucked the blood and spat it out." (276). He survives. Not so lucky is the young Hendrik Wessels, wounded in the upper arm: "He had pulled it out, but the barbed point had remained in the wound. There was only a round hole to be seen. . . . He told me his arm was already numb to the shoulder from the poison." (277). After sucking ineffectually at the wound, the Landdrost orders the boy carried to a neighbouring farm, for the application of a cupping glass. But it is too late: "Hendrik fell dead before they reached the top of the rise, within twenty minutes of his being wounded." (277).

From mid-century onwards, increasingly, Bushman arrows become objects of exotic nostalgia. This attitude is already visible in James Chapman's mid-century expedition to the Kalahari, which is full of scorn for local medical practices, but noteworthy also because it is the first, as far as I can tell, to photograph poison beetles and their host trees. There is, moreover, a complete description of the life cycle of *Diamphidia simplex*.[21] Further, Chapman claims to have fooled his Bushman informants into revealing the name of their antidote for arrow poison when they are distracted "talking about my consulting the stars, and . . . astounded by my camera". On the whole, though, it is a model for future ethnographic expeditions in the region. Only once does poison enter Chapman's narrative as an unstable element, and that is when a member of the party is roused early in the morning by a Bushman carrying a dish of water: "He hesitated, thinking it might contain poison, but an older Bushman, who spoke Sechuana well, explained it was a custom to serve water next morning to a man who had killed an animal." (144). This is a sad echo of something we have only touched upon until now: that as a signifier, poison is an unstable element in colonial discourse not only because it is hieroglyphic, and deadly, or because through it is revealed a wealth of dangerous pharmacological knowledge. Rather, in many travelogues, repeatedly in Bleek and Lloyd's transcriptions, and here in the Chapman text, Bushman poison moves beyond its horizon of use into a world of interrelated symbolic domains.

Arrow poison, wherever it is found in !Kung, G/wi, Heikom and other San communities, has never been solely a use value. That is why, of course, its meaning can never be exhausted in the ethnographic description of hunting methods or mass spectrographic analysis of its constituents. Janette Deacon's fine analysis of Bushman arrows in museums around South Africa remarks the fact that many have decoration on the reed shafts (6-8), for, apart from their value as trade items, arrows are individually marked so that hunters are able to recognise their own projectiles, in order that the ritual order of meat distribution can be determined. Thus the meaning of the arrow far exceeds its context of use in hunting. Yet the fact that Bushman communities chose not to use bows with a stronger pull weight, or larger cutting arrows, continues to puzzle some archaeologists. "From a global point of view", says Hans Dieter Noli, "those Bushman communities of Southern Africa who preferred the combination of weak bows and poisoned arrows were all but isolated in their decisions to do so."(25). The point, though, as Noli all but admits, is that prolongation of the hunt with relatively slow-acting poisons and close-range weapons, makes possible the extension of the event into a complex, ritual semiotic, governed by particular gender asymmetries and avoidance rites. Bleek and Lloyd's account of "first eland kills", together with Lewis-Williams's reading of such events, illuminate a range of symbolic practices that tie the hunter to the dying animal in a detailed metaphoric process that enters the practices of the community as a whole during the performance of the event.[22] This symbolic matrix extends thinly through time and space, associating itself with the agency of the poison. The hunter, according to Diä!kwain, one of Bleek's informants, is tied both to the dying animal and the action of the toxin; the least infringement of a number of avoidance rules causes the poison to "cool" and the animal is released into health (Lewis-Williams 58). Arrow poison, as far as we can know it, thus has a penumbra of value that at times incorporates the entire material culture of the group deploying it. Placed in museums throughout the world, artifacts associated with arrow poison manufacture move in another dream world far from their performative context – one of the colonial spectacle, and then the commodity.

The Poison Pen

Jane Taylor

Of histories – Dr Barry –
the Royal Society's schemes for language reform –
Gulliver and Lagado – Linnaeus – the first platypus examined –
God's plenitude – the English and the Dutch at the Cape –
Sir Francis Galton's daring travels – poison, finger-prints, detectives

It should come as little surprise that, in the Whig histories which dominated South African English historiography until the 1970s, the second British occupation at the Cape is synonymous with the advance of reason, civility, harmony and mercy. Dorothea Fairbridge, that lady of Edwardian letters, in her history of South Africa, refers to "The Second Coming of the British". The event is characterised, perhaps unwittingly, as a new dispensation, a millennial triumph.[1] For Laidler and Gelfand (1971), the end of Batavian control at the Cape marks the point of entry into modern health administration. Gelfand, in his "Preface" to the book, which functions in some ways as an obituary to his colleague, Laidler, points to a line of inheritance which marks their project for liberal enlightenment humanism. Laidler's second wife, we are told, is the granddaughter of Dr John Atherstone, an 1820 settler who was to become District Surgeon for Albany, and the grandniece of Thomas Pringle, the advocate of a free press in the Cape. A tenuous but vital line of inheritance is thus established between early British settlement and late twentieth-century liberal historiography. In order to foreground, simultaneously, British liberal individualism and enlightenment, Gelfand and Laidler refer to the years of sweeping transformation at the Cape as "The Barry Period", using the celebrated medical practitioner as a synechdochic figure for the new regime. Here they have instituted a shift in their own procedures, which, in the early sections, periodises medical history in terms of various moments, such as "The Eighteenth Century" or "Progress in Turbulent Times". We are told, in the opening lines of this section, that

> Dr. James Barry was one of the most outstanding medical practitioners ever to have practiced in South Africa. It must be contended that he was also one of the foremost social reformers in South Africa. (132)

The stabilising authority of this statement, which seeks to construct an unambiguous narrative of emergent modernity, must, of course, repress the contradictions necessary for such a story. This act of repression is, as it were, allegorised in these lines about Barry, for they absolutely occlude any reference to Barry's ambiguous sexual identity. In fact, the lengthy opening paragraph uses the masculine pronoun, and treats Barry as a male subject. It is well known that after Barry's death there was testimony given that the corpse was in fact that of a woman. It is not that this question is without interest for Laidler and Gelfand: In the service of biological investigation, they spend some time examining the record in order to consider whether Barry was "a male, female, or hermaphrodite" (132).[2] The possibility that Barry may have been homosexual is avoided, alluded to only obliquely in a later section on Lord Charles Somerset's heavy-handed censorship policies. Laidler and Gelfand speak in evasive terms about a scandalous bill which was posted, "concerning Lord Charles Somerset and Dr. Barry, a diabolical accusation as filthy as it was unnecessary". (161) Barry thus constitutes a problem: In the terms deployed, Barry is enlightenment medicine; however, he/she also dramatises enlightenment discourse's inability to deal with contradiction, with excess, with ambiguity.

The enlightenment project sought to fix the relationship between terms, within a matrix of non- contradictory positions. To this end, language had to be pared of its metaphorics, and used only denotatively. Such tendencies can be seen early on in Thomas Sprat, the official historian of the Royal Society, who advocates a separation of rhetoric from grammar, for rhetoric is the enemy of science:

> Who can behold, without indignation, how many mists and uncertainties, these specious *Tropes* and *Figures* have brought on our Knowledg [*sic*]? How many rewards, which are due to more profitable, and difficult *Arts*, have been snatch'd away by the easie vanity of *fine speaking*? . . . And, in a few words, I dare say; that of all the Studies of men, nothing may be sooner obtain'd, than this vicious abundance of *Phrase*, this trick of *Metaphors*, this volubility of *Tongue*, which makes so great a noise in the World. (113 emphasis in original)

Sprat calls for a return to "the primitive purity, and shortness, when men deliver'd so many *things*, almost in an equal number of *words*". This obsession with rigorously referential paradigms is parodied in Swift's *Gulliver's Travels*. Gulliver describes a linguistic experiment being undertaken at the Academy of Lagado:

> the other [Project], was a Scheme for entirely abolishing all Words whatsoever: and this was urged as a great Advantage in Point of Health as well as Brevity . . . An Expedient was therefore offered, that since Words are only Names for *Things*, it would be more convenient for all Men to carry about with them, such *Things* as were necessary to express the particular Business they are to discourse on. (158)

It seems not wholly incidental that this model of language, with its pretensions to more adequately explaining the world for science, is promoted in the era of burgeoning mercantile endeavour, under which ethos *value* was to become assimilated to *exchange value*. The exchange equivalent of a commodity, one might say, stands in the same relation to that commodity, as the word to the thing it names. McKeon, in his study of the emergence of the novel as a dominant literary form, points to the links between the Royal Society's expressed scientific objectives, mercantile interests and literary style, citing the Society's instructions to voyagers, on how to keep daily journals, accounting what has been witnessed (101). It is thus not simply in order to track English discursive history that I cite Sprat here; rather, it is to foreground the relationship between Enlightenment linguistic philosophy, global mercantilism, colonialism and nascent nationalism. Sprat gives the project of the Society a national character, and celebrates "the general constitution of the minds of the *English* as one which naturally inclines toward plain style" (113 emphasis in the original). The split between grammar and rhetoric is implicitly recast as a split between England and the continent, and plays upon the conceit of scientific apprehension:

> These Qualities are so conspicuous, and proper to our Soil; that we often hear them objected to us, by some of our neighbour Satyrists, in more disgraceful expressions. For they are wont to revile the *English*, with a want of familiarity, with a melancholy dumpishness; with slowness, silence, and with the unrefin'd sulleness of their behaviour. But these are the reproaches of partiality, or ignorance . . . So that even the position of our climate, the air, the influence of the heaven, the composition of the English blood; as well as the embraces of the Ocean, seem to joyn with the labours of the *Royal Society*, to render our Country, a Land of *Experimental knowledge*. (114 emphasis in the original)[3]

There is for Sprat something inherently *English* about empirical enquiry, which depends upon a referential model of language, in which an unambiguous parity is constituted between a word and the thing to which it refers.

This conception of order becomes synonymous with enlightenment science as epitomised in the work of Linnaeus, the "second Adam" von Haller called him, because he sought to give a name to each of the species (Schiebinger 383). Certain species that would not easily yield to the propriety of taxonomy, such as the platypus, presented formidable challenge, but were ultimately stabilised through the effacing of discrepancies. Thus the platypus was classified as a mammal because it lactated, a signifying feature for Linnaeus, despite the fact that Everard Home, the English anatomist who dissected a pair in 1802, could find no uterus, no nipples and no obvious mammary glands in the female (Schiebinger 391).

When the British settled at the Cape, they brought with them the problematics of Enlightenment logic, although unevenly distributed across the genders and classes of the British settlers themselves. This positivism must have engaged uneasily with the languages and practices of Calvinism, which carries, at its heart, a theological coherence based upon asymmetries and surplus. There are no balanced scales under this law; there is always both an excess of sin and an excess of mercy. Forgiveness is no longer the handmaiden of justice; rather, it is qualitatively described in terms of its quantity: it is always more than was deserved. The language of charity is one of superfluities, "pressed down, and shaken together, and running over" (Luke 6:38). This conception engages with medieval ideas of God's plenitude. If it is more perfect to be than not to be, which the very existence of God asserts, then the universe must be teeming. There can be no neat discontinuous, non-contradictory identities; rather, all is flux, and flow and fullness. Similarly, human sinfulness is beyond the reach of rationalising description, and thus cannot be redressed through a system of equivalences. Furthermore, the discourse of Calvinism is rich in metaphorics, for various orders of meaning are at once both present and transparent, for it speaks of one sequence in terms of another, through the structures of allegory and typology. Interpretation must constantly be played across a field of simultaneous possibilities.

Given such distinguishing differences between Dutch and British discursive possibilities, it is interesting to consider certain specific constructions around poison, as well as the range of attempts to classify, use and legislate toxic substances. The unease instituted by the incapacity to know and control the production of meaning and knowledge in the colonies gets figured in the work of the Victorian writer, Conan Doyle, as *the problem of poison*. The powerful organic toxins used in the colonies are associated with alternative systems of intelligence, unreadable representations, political logics which flout rationality, and medical and cosmological practices that defy the English imagination. The instability introduced, via competing epistemologies, is contained through the proliferation of western technologies of investigation. For this reason I shall be considering the Victorian man of science, Sir Francis Galton, as a special case. He was in fact nominated as a Fellow of the Royal Society after his extensive travels in the south-western regions of Africa; and I shall discuss how this relates to his other major contribution to the domain of western enquiry, that is, his role in establishing finger-printing techniques in metropolitan centres of surveillance. At the same time, I will inevitably be making certain assertions about the articulation of local systems of knowledge within a global logic which is predicated on English imperial expansionism in the nineteenth century.

I

"Let us have some fresh blood", he said, digging a long bodkin into his
finger, and drawing off the resulting drop of blood in a chemical
pipette . . . "I have to be careful", he continued, turning to me with a
smile, "for I dabble with poisons a good deal". He held out his hand as
he spoke, and I noticed that it was mottled over with similar pieces of
plaster, and discoloured with strong acids.[4] (Vol. I 150-151)

If the spectacular literary success of Sherlock Holmes is anything to go by, the Victorian imagination must have been deeply engaged with the problem of poison: how to detect it, classify it, how to control it; even, at times, how to yield to its seductions, for the detective who is its master is also its slave, as Watson occasionally reminds us.

> Sherlock Holmes took his bottle from the corner of the mantelpiece, and his hypodermic syringe from its neat morocco case. With his long, white, nervous fingers he adjusted the delicate needle, and rolled back his left shirt-cuff. For some little time his eyes rested thoughtfully upon the sinewy forearm and wrist, all dotted and scarred with innumerable puncture-marks. Finally, he thrust the sharp point home, pressed down the tiny piston, and sank back into the velvet-lined arm chair with a long sigh of satisfaction. (Vol. I 610)

At one level, a fear of poison is an inevitable and explicable result of human subjectivity: It threatens to secretly invade us, to insinuate its way into our system, and to unseat our little monarchy from within, with no sign of warning until it is too late. It is a persistent reminder that our non-material self is held hostage to our biological being, and must thus have had particular meaning for a generation coming to terms with its own loss of faith. The contradictions implicit here are evident in the split between Sherlock Holmes's materialist cynicism and the mystical hankerings of his author, Conan Doyle, who in his later life became a somewhat ridiculous advocate of spirit-mediumship. Following this logic, the fear of poison is a reasonable fear, one based upon deep anxieties about our own boundaries as human subjects. However, it does not take a great deal of scrutiny for one to realise that there is a category of poison which is deployed over and over within the Holmes canon, and that is, generally, poison from the colonies, and more particularly, arrow poisons.

In the novella *A Study in Scarlet*, which introduced Sherlock Holmes to the reading public, the plot turns on the revenge of Jefferson Hope who, while a janitor at a university laboratory, happened to overhear a lecture on South American arrow poison, an alkaloid which is "so powerful that the least grain meant instant death" (Vol. I 227). The tormented Mr Hope works the malevolent substance up into tablet form, which he subsequently feeds to his victims. It is, I think, fair to assume that the alkaloid described by Hope is in fact curare, also known as *wourali*, which had been familiarised to European science by de la Condamine in the mid-eighteenth century. Now, it had been well-established by the middle of the nineteenth century, through extensive experiments carried out by Claude Bernard and others, that curare was a neuro-muscular poison which was ineffective if taken orally, and had to enter the bloodstream in order to do its work (although Brocklesby, Fontana and others had reported that large doses taken orally could kill birds[5]). There is, it would seem, in the dissemination of tales about arrow poisons, an affective surplus which cannot be neutralised by scientific findings: In symbolic terms, what is of significance is the entry of the noxious substance into the body-system; of less significance, is the path of entry. Further, Doyle has taken the arrow poison as raw matter, and has removed it from the system in which it was found in order to rework it, in this instance into the profoundly European form of the tablet. Doyle himself, as a qualified medical practitioner, has transformed the toxin into a form within his own symbolic lexicon.[6]

By the time that Doyle published his second Sherlock Holmes saga, *The Sign of Four*, there has been a significant alteration in this procedure. Poison is once again at work, once again a "powerful vegetable alkaloid". This time, however, the means of transmission is integral to the meaning of the stuff. Holmes directs Watson's scrutiny:

> "On getting into the room I at once looked for means by which the poison had entered the system. As you saw, I discovered a thorn which had been driven or shot with no great force into the scalp . . . Now examine this thorn."
> I took it up gingerly and held it in the light of the lantern. It was long, sharp, and black, with a glazed look near the point as though some gummy substance had dried upon it. The blunt end had been trimmed and rounded with a knife.
> "Is that an English thorn?" he asked.
> "No, it certainly is not." (Vol. I 639)

There has been a significant change between *A Study in Scarlet* and *The Sign of Four*. In the second story, it is not just the poison which has ended up in England; it is, effectively, an entire system: poison, darts, even the poisoner himself, an

Andaman Islander. Poison is no longer treated as a raw material which can be reworked at the metropole into a commodified form, although the act of incorporating the arrow poison into the story is, via a discursive appropriation, itself a commodification. In *The Sign of Four*, the very presence of the poison precipitates a confrontation between cultures, and it seems that by this stage Doyle has undertaken some further research into the field, for he describes the "glazed" blackened appearance of the projectile in terms directly drawn from earlier documentary accounts. The foreignness of the paraphernalia is foregrounded in Holmes's query, "Is that an English thorn?" to which Watson must reply, "No, it certainly is not." Here the poison is seen to penetrate the skin, and it is thus appropriate that it is in *The Sign of Four* that Doyle exposes us for the first time to Holmes's cocaine addiction. We are treated to a sensuous description of the moment, with the agitated detective sliding the needle under his skin in an elaborate ritual of self-annihilation, relinquishing himself up to the velvet arm-chair. The eroticism and exoticism of the scene mark Sherlock Holmes as a creature born of the repressed Victorian obsession with its colonial territories, and his body, as it surrenders itself to the charms of cocaine, is a metaphor of the permeable frontier which separates coloniser from colonised.

The thematics of colonial infiltration abound in Sherlock Holmes, in a metaphorics closely related to the trope of poison. In "The Adventure of the Dying Detective" Watson finds Holmes stricken with "a coolie disease from Sumatra – a thing that the Dutch know more about than we, though they have made little of it up to date" (Vol. I 440). Here old colonial rivalries play themselves out within medical terms, and the early supremacy of the Dutch in colonial enterprise is turned to ridicule, for despite their protracted contact with foreign diseases, they have made no gains in medico-scientific understanding. Poison and disease thus form elements within a global system of competing powers and knowledges. The coolie disease is identified by Holmes as "the black formosa corruption", and he then accounts for his diagnostic insight:

> There are many problems of disease, many strange pathological possibilities, in the East, Watson . . . I have learned so much during some recent researches which have a medico-criminal aspect. It was in the course of them that I contracted this complaint. (Vol. I 441)

Several of the strategies associated with Orientalist discursive practice are here overtly deployed: The East is inscribed as a single, enigmatic, vast system and is identified with the corruption of the flesh and, implicitly, the soul. Holmes, whose intellectual obsessions keep him from immersing himself in the stuff of common mortality, is set up as a stay against such seductions and contaminations.[7] He, of course, does not actually have the disease of which he bears the obvious marks:

These are simply theatrical effects he is deploying in order to ensnare the diabolical Culverton Smith, a British colonial from Sumatra, who has used microbiological technologies to poison his nephew with "the black Formosa corruption".[8]

In "The Adventure of the Sussex Vampire" the metaphorics of difference are also marked for gender, as the Victorian bourgeois household is assaulted from within. Holmes is called in to deal with the case of an Englishman who

> married some years ago a Peruvian lady, the daughter of a Peruvian merchant, whom he had met in connection with the importation of nitrates. The lady was very beautiful, but the fact of her foreign birth and of her alien religion always caused a separation of interests and feelings between husband and wife. (Vol. II 464)

The protagonist of this tale is both the agent and the subject of infiltrations, for he is clearly in the business of cross-continental trade, and he has taken a Catholic Peruvian woman to bear his children. This is, however, his second marriage and there is thus already a child in the family. When his second wife gives birth, he discovers, to his horror, that she appears to abuse the older boy; the distress induced by this knowledge, however, is nothing compared to his shock at discovering that she seems to be practicing vampirism, for she is revealed, one day, to be sucking blood from her own infant's neck. At one level, this lurid tale can be explained as a paradigmatic expression of British male phobias about feminine sexuality, which are particularly articulated in terms of female bodily fluids; at the same time, it plays into the metaphorics of anxiety about the threat to British cultural identity inherent in protracted colonial contact. For my purposes here, however, what is of interest is the resolution of the story; we discover that in fact the firstborn son is so consumed with jealousy that he has attempted various assaults on his changeling half-brother. The mother's supposed vampirism is a misreading of her attempt to suck poison from the neck of the child, after an attack by his older sibling. Holmes is quick to read the signs, for he discovers, upon the oak-lined wall, "a fine collection of South American utensils and weapons" (Vol. II 468). He renders his interpretation to his client:

> "A South American household. My instinct felt the presence of those weapons upon the wall *before my eyes ever saw them*. It might have been other poison, but that was what occurred to me. When I saw that little empty quiver beside the small bird-bow, *it was just what I expected to see*. If the child were pricked with one of those arrows dipped in curare or some other devilish drug, it would mean death if the venom were not sucked out." (Vol. II 473, emphasis my own)

Holmes reveals himself here to be an avid and experienced museum-goer: The bow and arrows are hung upon the wall, in typical display, where objects avail themselves to consumption by the eye; the bow and arrow, what's more, are already known to the detective. He calls them up, as it were, because they provide the necessary answer to the enigma. He blames the bow and arrow, before he even sees them, for they are "just what I expected to see". The objects have been dislocated from the logic within which they were produced, and have been overwhelmed by the dual imperatives of phobic paranoia and curatorial punctiliousness. There is a system of apprehension being pointed to here, one in which colonial discourse, museum techniques, patriarchy and detective procedures all participate, in a circulation of the languages of domination.

The relevance, for South African studies, of Doyle's strategies here becomes evident when we turn to a passage from his little-known, and rather complacent, *Our African Winter*. After a varied literary and political career, Doyle visited South Africa in 1929. This was not his first trip: He had spent some time in the country in the role of doctor during the South African War. This time, his objective was to proselytise for spiritualism. His rather quaint message from the Victorian parlour looks somewhat anachronistic at the brink of '30s South Africa and is filled with fanciful meditations. On a visit to the South African Museum, he encounters representations of indigenous culture and technologies, and this shifts him into speculative comparative mode:

> But the really interesting point is that these paintings are so like the paintings done by primeval man in the caves of Spain that when they are placed alongside each other they are practically the same, save that the old craftsmen were the more artistic. There cannot be any doubt that the same race did both, though the whole length of Africa lies between. In addition to this the Bushmen's women have an extraordinary deformity of their hind-quarters which is also found in the drawings and sculptures in Spain. The clear deduction is that the whole of Africa was inhabited by the little yellow men, and then that the big black negroid people, coming from some flank, gradually pushed them down until now there are only a handful of the poor creatures lurking in the Kalahari Desert. (38)

This passage is a horrible blend of English and colonial South African fantasies, registered through such familiar tropes as the steatopygia in Bushmen women, the recent arrival of "black negroid people" on the stage of South African territorial dispute and the archaism of Khoisan society. In all likelihood, Doyle would have seen not only the examples of rock art, but would also have scrutinised the display of Khoisan lifecasts made for the museum, under the instruction of the director Dr Louis Peringuey, between 1907 and 1924. Doyle's comments read like a gloss on the main label to the exhibition of the casts taken in Prieska in 1911:

> CAPE BUSHMEN: The Bushmen of the Cape appear to have been the purest-blooded representatives of the Bushman stock, much purer than those of the Kalahari and other more northerly districts. They are now practically extinct. They were light in colour and of small or medium height; the prominent posterior development (steatopygy) of the women was a characteristic feature of the race.

> To anthropologists the Bushmen are one of the most interesting races in the world.
> There are strong grounds for suspecting that they are of the same stock as the remote
> Upper Paleolithic period. This cannot yet be definitely asserted but recent discoveries
> in North and East Africa have tended to strengthen the probability considerably.[9]

In this museum inscription, we find the same logics as are evident in Doyle: The
Bushmen are related to the lost peoples of the Upper Neolithic period, a claim which
will be substantiated once further evidence of a trans-African network is verified
by finds in the north and east of the continent. Doyle's commentary, then, is more
than the sum of its parts, for it is not just an example of tropological description. It
also suggests the way in which colonial knowledge is circulated. It is quite evident
that Doyle knew how to read the ethnographic display before he arrived at Cape
Town; however, having wandered into the Museum, what he knows to be true is
confirmed by what he meets there, and it now has accrued to it the solid affirmation
of empirical observation, and Doyle can return to England with a first-hand account
of Khoisan history. Doyle deliberately eschews anything like an emergent scientific
discourse, in favour of familiar terminology: he refers to "the Bushman stock" (the
formulation found in the museum label) noting that he prefers to "avoid the scientific
jargon". Is he avoiding the phrase "the same stock as the remote Upper Neolithic
period"? It seems likely, since ethnic identity is distilled into the biologistic
designation, "stock" in both instances. The colonial museum is thus a site for the
reproduction and confirmation of metropolitan cognitive violence.

Doyle subsequently engages in a discussion of various "primitive" weapons,
demonstrating the Bushmen's apparently unlikely technological superiority in the
region:

> The great negroid races did not use the bow, and I saw today a cave picture where
> the little brown men were cheekily driving off the cattle of the negroes, and covering
> the operation by a line of bowmen, who were holding off the blacks who pursued
> with shield and assegai. The bow may prove very important in tracing the origins of
> the human race. There seems to have been a great watershed on one side of which
> every one knew the bow, while on the other side it was unknown. (39)

Doyle's reading here displays a naive reflectionism, that assumes that a figure
representing the Bushmen defeat of the Bantu-speaking warriors is a literal depiction of an historical saga. He seems to have forgotten his own narrative of the
displacement of the Bushmen by stronger forces; further, he gives no suggestion
that the painting may have symbolic significance, or that desire can figure itself as
wish-fulfillment in an art which is not pure mimesis. Further, Doyle's limited
ethnographic knowledge leads him to assume that the bow and arrow are unique in
southern Africa to the Bushmen; Noli, in a recent dissertation, describes the use of
large powerbows by Bantu-speaking peoples prior to their contact with the Bush-

men. For Noli, the powerbow is "technically more advanced" and "more effective", by which he clearly means that it is a more efficient killing instrument (207). The religious and epistemological system within which the poison arrow functions, is overlooked in such a single-minded description. In fact, the preference of European, and particularly English, observers for a large bow and cutting arrow has a long and distinguished history. Shakespeare's *Henry V* uses the longbow's glorious victory at Agincourt as a metonymic celebration of the stalwart yeoman soldier, and as a metaphor for English national identity. In the nineteenth century, Burton (1961) spurns the cowardly poisoned arrow, favouring the virtu of the soldierly weapon of valour:

> The East Africans ignore the use of red-hot arrows; and the poisoned shaft, an unmanly weapon, unused by the English and French soldiers even in their deadliest wars, is confined to the Wanyika of Mombasah, the Wazaramo, the Wak'hutu, the Western Wasagara, and the people of Uruwwa. (305)

The broad arrow of traditional English weaponry becomes synonymous with British sovereign power, and a trace of this signifying logic is to be found in the arrows which mark convict clothing and signal the wearer as a subject of administrative control.

In a strikingly trivial and poor volume of poetry, entitled *Songs of Action*, Doyle writes out a maudlin vision of the English heroic type, ranging from the pre-Raphaelite courtier to the happy wanderer. The first of the poems, tellingly, is entitled "The Song of the Bow", and is a celebration of English values, through the metaphor of archery:

> What of the bow?
> The bow was made in England:
> Of true wood, of yew-wood,
>
> The wood of English bows;
> So men who are free
> Love the old yew-tree
> And the land where the yew-tree grows.

Inevitably, the self-complacency expresses itself in terms of global enterprises, for the poem continues:

> What of the mark?
> Ah, seek it not in England,
> A bold mark, our old mark
> Is waiting over-sea.
> When the strings harp in chorus
> And the lion flag is o'er us,
> It is there that our mark will be.

In his discussion of the Bushman bow and arrow, Conan Doyle makes no mention of the use of arrow poison. This is a noteworthy aporia, because Sherlock Holmes, who was singularly obsessed with such poisons, would never have neglected the opportunity to inquire into the chemical and botanical properties of Bushman poisons. As Watson had noted, in his little table of Holmes's erratic domains of learning: knowledge of "Botany. – Variable. Well up in belladonna, opium, and poisons generally. Knows nothing of practical gardening . . . Knowledge of Chemistry. – Profound" (Vol. I 156). It seems unlikely that Doyle was unaware of the use of poisons for hunting in the sub-region. The potency of southern African toxins was legendary by the end of the eighteenth century: as Paterson comments, "there are few countries in the world which abound more with deleterious vegetables than the country adjacent to the Cape of Good Hope" (169).

Although Doyle does not make use of contemporary discourses around arrow poisons in South Africa for his crime fiction, there is one Sherlock Holmes saga which points to the special relationship which Doyle had with South Africa, "The Adventure of the Blanched Soldier". We have seen how in "The Adventure of the Dying Detective" *disease* is used literally as a *poison*, which elision constitutes the two terms as one large semiotic field, in which either can be used to signify in similar ways. Disease, for Doyle, is generally marked as foreign, in much the same way that poison is; further, both infiltrate the unknowing victim and undermine the system from within. Thus, in "The Adventure of the Blanched Soldier", the body to be read is one that bears the traces of disease, although the structure of the story sets up the enigma as if poison were once again in the bloodstream. Written in 1903, the tale turns around the South African War. Mr Godfrey Emsworth, a British soldier, has gone missing after having been shot in the shoulder with "an elephant gun in the action near Diamond Hill outside Pretoria" (708). As the narrative proceeds, we find that Emsworth is in hiding in England, carrying the marks of leprosy, having unwittingly taken refuge in a South African leprosy hospital after being injured. There is high literary precedent for the conflation of leprosy and poison: in Hamlet, the ghost of the prince's father describes the poison poured into his ear as a "leperous distilment" (Act I v line 64). Doyle's narrative choices here can thus be seen to engage with convention; however, they must also be a consequence of his close experience of medical circumstances during the South African War. Early in 1900, Doyle was asked to supervise a medical unit travelling to the colony, and by April was at Bloemfontein. His *The Great Boer War* ("With Maps") documents Doyle's experiences, observations and speculations; the work has only two protagonists, the Boer and the Briton. Published in 1900, it is a blend of jingoism and respect for the rough energy of the *boer*, with the medical practioner's observed scrutiny of physical suffering and rampant disease. The pestilence which was decimating the British troops was enteric fever, and Doyle locates it as a feature of place: "[it] is always endemic in the country, and especially in Bloemfontein", although he does concede that the outbreak amongst the soldiers was due to poor field practice and inadequate attention to clean water supplies (371). His commentary on the war is so close to the moment that it is effectively a military brief advocating the urgent modernisation of the British army:

> The army proper should, according to this scheme, be drawn from a higher class than is done at present, for modern warfare demands more intelligence and individuality than is to be found in the peasant or unskilled labour classes. (530)

Doyle's conclusions, in the final chapter of *The Great Boer War*, "Some Military Lessons of the War", take a rather singular turn, as British imperial interests get rewritten, in part, as an extension of national defence: one of the "most certain lessons of the war, as regards ourselves, is once for all to reduce the bugbear of an invasion of Great Britain to an absurdity". However, it would seem that Doyle cannot discriminate between the British home territories and Britain's strategic possessions abroad, for he moves unproblematically from the "country of hedge-rows" to discuss "the wars of the future, where a soldier has to be conveyed to the centre of Africa, the interior of China, or the frontier of Afghanistan" (514–5), and the "defence" of Britain is synonymous with imperial aggression.

Doyle is preoccupied with the notion that technological supremacy is the means to domination. In his *The Great Boer War* he rails against outmoded British weaponry, with the injunction that the "magazine rifle" is the only instrument of modern warfare. "Lances, swords, and revolvers have only one place – the museum." (519).

In July 1901, Doyle left South Africa to return to Britain, where he set about his campaign for justifying the British role in the war. He raised a subscription fund to finance the free European distribution of a pamphlet which, we are told, "had a steadying effect on European opinion", for Doyle was of course not just another war correspondent: his reputation and public stature were considerable, because of the stature of Sherlock Holmes as a man of penetrating insight. In 1902 Sir Arthur Conan Doyle received a knighthood, not for his contribution to the world of letters, but for his service to the nation (Pearson 143).

II

"Did it not occur to you that a bleeding wound may be sucked for some other purpose than to draw the blood from it? Was there not a Queen in English history who sucked such a wound to draw poison from it?"

(Vol. II 473)

The quest for poisons and antidotes becomes an internal principle of self-justification in many of the later explorer narratives, which struggle to legitimate themselves in terms of some greater principle. This project, the investigation of toxic substances and their effects, is an overdetermined coincidence of morbid rapture, prurience, epistemological competition and enlightenment beneficence. The discourses around poisons are thus frequently an intriguing combination of self-abnegation and self-indulgence. The pursuit of an antidote takes, as it were, two paths, one which attempts to harness modern techniques and enlightenment procedures, the other which remains committed to the cosmology of Renaissance thought, with its structures of sympathetic magic, and similitude, in which the relationship between poison and antidote would be a manifest one. Traditional cures would be based upon rumour and hearsay, the evidence derived from custom and anecdote; modern cures would make claims from documented experiment. The difference thus also, significantly, marks a divide between an oral and a written practice. Many of the explorers are caught between the two epistemes: Someone like Farini, writing in the last decades of the nineteenth century is, on the one hand, a literate man producing arm-chair excitement for a community of urban literate (male) readers, whose relationship with frontier experience is extremely tenuous. However, his informants are active participants in the transmission of local knowledge about botany, animal toxins, symptomology and homeopathy. Farini becomes a hostage of his foreignness, his brand of literacy, within a signifying system that he cannot read. Having briefly separated from his party in the Kalahari, he loses his way, and after some hours in the blazing sun he goes into shock, and becomes desperate for food or water. Finding nothing else to hand, he digs up some roots [*inchies*: bulbs?] which he cooks and eats. The sustenance gives him temporary relief, however it is not long before he discovers that his tongue and mouth are as if aflame, and he is overcome with a choking sensation. His legs collapse beneath him, as he realises that the plant material is poisonous. However, the oblivion which has begun to overwhelm him, is replaced by agonising spasms:

I was seized with terrible griping pains in the stomach, and a feeling of nausea arose, and as it increased the numbness and burning sensation diminished. Death was not going to be calm and easy. Instead of a narcotic, it was an irritant poison I had taken, and instead of quietly passing away as in a dream, I was to have a struggle with the grim reaper. (139)

There is no easeful death for Farini, and the scripted, literary decline into unconsciousness is replaced by violent anguish. The episode, for all its flirtation with finality, concludes with Farini being discovered, at the brink, by members of his party. Somewhat later in the narrative, Farini is out walking with one of his guides, when the latter is bitten by a snake. The Bushman ministers to himself:

Coolly taking out some dried poison-sacs he reduced them to powder, pricked his foot near the puncture with his knife, and rubbed the virus powder in . . . extracting the fangs, [he] drank a drop of the poison from the virus-sac, and soon fell into a stupor which lasted some hours. At first the swelling increased rapidly, but after a time it began to subside, and next morning he inoculated himself again. That night the swelling had disappeared, and in four days he was as well as ever. (367)

This account reveals a curious mix of ethnographic interest, superstition and modern medical science. The traditional practice, of treating snake-bite with dehydrated venom, is here characterised as "inoculation", conflating toxicology and virology, in a pseudo-scientific amalgam of indigenous practice and Western medicine. The efficacy of inoculation against smallpox was first demonstrated by Jenner at the end of the eighteenth century; by the late 1800s, it had become synonymous with Western medical management of infectious disease, and it is striking to see it being used here to characterise Khoisan traditional practice. The metaphoric use of the term here is singularly ironic, given the devastating effects of smallpox on indigenous populations throughout the early modern period.

Stanley (1890) reveals similar attempts to control African poisons through the exploitation of advanced technologies and learning; however, he has less tolerance for local systems of use and knowledge. His interest in local plants, for instance, is largely governed by a desire to see them garnered for Western exploitation, and he has little conception that they may have uses imperceptible to the colonial imagination. The great harvest will take place once "one sensible European has succeeded in teaching them what the countless vines, creepers, and tendrils of their forest can produce" (111); in other words, Stanley has scant concern that these plants may already be identified and understood within a competing logic. His response to the threat of poison is not ambiguous, like Farini's: rather, it is based upon a model of penetration and control which serves as an allegory of imperial enterprise:

If this pale poison be of this material, one must confess that, in the forest, they possess endless supplies of other insects still worse, such as the long black ants which infest the trumpet tree, a bite from one of which can only be compared to cautery from a red hot iron. But whatever it be, we have great faith in a strong hypodermic injection of carbonate of ammonium, and it may be that stronger doses of morphia than any that I ventured upon might succeed in conquering the fatal tetanic spasms which followed every puncture and preceded death. (108)

Stanley has no interest in engaging with indigenous knowledge or signifying systems: His is a paramilitary project to get in and out as efficiently as possible and, where necessary, to neutralise any local effects which may threaten the integrity of his purpose.

The urgency of the project to find appropriate antidotes, is compounded by the burden of a colonial administration which has to safeguard its emissaries against subjugated peoples. There are abundant cases cited, in which indigenous slaves and servants are had up for murder or attempted murder, with poison cited as the means deployed. By the late 1870s, such episodes have clearly become tropological, for the pseudo-document, "The Diary of an Idle Hottentot", written by the fictive "Adonis Jager", facetiously invokes what is obviously popular current mythology. The "idle Hottentot" of the title recounts the events of his day:

> When we were at breakfast Frans Boerland, an old chum of mine, arrived. He was on his road home from the town. I noticed that he had two bottles of brandy in his saddle bag and made him thoroughly welcome accordingly. He told me all the news about my friends and relatives in town. One of my uncles, who is a leper, was gradually getting worse; a brother of mine had got married. I asked, "Who to?" Frans said, "I should remember that Bushman girl who some time ago was charged with attempting to poison her master's family – that was my sister-in-law!" (161)

This exemplum of colonial stereotyping, written in 1877, can take for granted a range of shared attitudes and assumptions, and exploits what must have been a wide-spread dread of the vulnerability of a household which brought together coloniser and colonised in relations of considerable intimate hostility. In October 1872, the *Standard and Mail* proclaims in a sensational headline, "ATROCIOUS ATTEMPT TO POISON A MISTRESS", and decries the "unenviable situation which masters and mistresses hold when they have the misfortune to raise the ire of native servants".[10] The sorry saga recounts the story of a young Fingo woman who is kept from marrying a worker from a neighbouring farm, and who allegedly obtained poison from her lover, in order to kill her employer. The same newspaper, in April 1873, reports how a "Bushman girl, who was scolded by her mistress, and who, in revenge, tried to poison her" was subsequently sentenced to six years imprisonment. This episode is particularly intriguing, for the girl involved is linked, in the popular imagination, with a series of similar poisonings:

> How often have I asked, and heard it asked, why was that girl who caused so much

anguish at Middleburg and Graaf-Reinet allowed to go free? There have been two
attempts at poisoning since the death of Dr. Coward's family and the death of Mr.
Reeve.[11]

Without romanticising acts of violence, such documents suggest the way in which
poison becomes associated with the contestation of power and knowledge around
settler homes. The Cape Archives abound in the circuit court records of similar cases
in the second half of the nineteenth century. Jannetje Swaartboy, Kaatje Magerman
and Griet Abrahamse are sentenced to three, two and one years of hard labour
respectively, for administering milk laced with strychnine to Martha Sophia, wife
of Isaac Lodevicus van Heerden.[12] Aquillus Adolpho is found guilty of attempting
to poison one Andries Jacobus Burger, "agriculturalist", with six grains of strychnine, and is sentenced to twelve years of hard labour.[13] A third case resonates so
with surplus meanings, that it is worth recounting in some detail: Othello, a domestic
cook, in the service of the Cape Town merchant, William Berg, on 30 May 1857,
in preparing a meal for the merchant's wife and children, mixed with the rice "one
drachm, of a certain deadly poison, called Strychnine". A portion of the rice,

> was then and there taken and swallowed by Augusta Berg, the wife of the said
> William Berg, and Julia Berg, one of the children of the said William Berg, who
> thereupon became by means of the said poison, very sick and disordered in body,
> and so remained for a long space of time; and thus, the said Othello, did commit the
> crime of causing poison to be taken, with intent to murder, or otherwise, with intent
> to do some grievous bodily harm.[14]

Othello was found guilty of attempted murder, and sentenced to seven years of hard
labour. The specific mention of the preparation of the family meal, taken with the
fact that it is one of the children who is so severely stricken by the poison, emphasise
what may be characterised as *domains of intimacy* between master and servant
classes in the Cape, despite constant demonstrations of profound distrust, and
spheres of absolute separation.

In this case, as in many, if not most, of the similar cases cited in the archives,
commercial strychnine is the substance used, not some organic compound such as
might be associated with local toxins. This demonstrates, amongst other things, the
limited administrative control over toxic substances during the period. In fact, in
the mid-nineteenth century, there was cause to bewail the poor administration of
dangerous substances even in Britain:

> In this country any chemist or druggist can furnish the means of self- destruction or
> murder for a few pence, and in too many instances have done so with the utmost
> indifference. The sale of a poison is regarded as a mere act of commercial intercourse;
> *tant pis* for the unfortunate victim of error or passion; he has the benefit of a coroner's
> inquest; the vendor of the poison receives a reprimand, and things resume their

natural course – that is, arsenic and oxalic acid are retailed without compunction, and men are hurried from time to time into eternity.[15]

It was not until 1851, with the Arsenic Act in Britain, that legal measures were introduced to control the movement of such poisons. It seems fairly evident from contemporary documents that the drive to manage pharmaceuticals is integral to the professionalising of medical discourses generally. In 1848, the President of the British Pharmaceutical Society addressed the society in the following terms:

> When, gentlemen, I think how important a position is held by the Chemist, of how useful a member of society he is designed to be, I turn with sorrow to look upon those with whom the name is in many parts of the country associated. At present, as the law stands, any man, however ignorant – an individual unable even to sign his own name – half of whose shop is stored with butter, bacon, cheese, or tape, shall from the other half have the power of dispensing, to any person applying, preparations of mercury, arsenic, opium etc. etc. (Bartrip 60)

Similar moves, to professionalise medico-pharmaceutical practice, were to follow in the colonies. In 1855 a meeting was held in Grahamstown, at the house of Dr William Edmund, with the objective of starting a medical society in South Africa. The first president was Dr Alexander Melvin, Deputy Inspector General of Hospitals and Inspector of Colonial Hospitals. Andrew Geddes Bain, famous as the engineer of many of the most spectacular and unlikely mountain passes in South Africa, was invited to be a member, in recognition of his contributions to scientific learning, a gesture which today looks uncannily like a metaphor for the relationship between medical investigation and territorial conquest. At the society's meetings, papers deemed to be of general interest were presented. Dr Atherstone read a paper on "The Medicinal Qualities of Cannabis Indica", and a sub-committee was appointed to draw up a list of subjects which would make suitable papers, amongst which were "The Bites of Venomous animals found in South Africa, Symptoms, Progress and Treatment" and "The Bushmen Poison" (Laidler and Gelfand 332–3). It was not until 1885 that the South African Pharmaceutical Association was formed at King William's Town, and in 1891 a Bill was introduced to establish The Colonial Pharmacy Board, which decreed that a Poisons Book be kept by each pharmacist in order to record all sales; a general dealer who wished to sell poisons had to obtain a licence, as did a medical practitioner who wished to compound prescriptions (Laidler and Gelfand 352).

Inevitably, medical, taxonomic and popular discourses around poisons intersect with forensic practice. Any substance suspected to be the noxious cause in a murder inquiry, was generally sent for chemical analysis by a medical specialist: in the case of the "ATROCIOUS ATTEMPT TO POISON A MISTRESS", a sample from the bottle of liquid in the young woman's possession was sent to Dr Atherstone for examination.

The procedures and techniques for investigation must have been somewhat rudimentary at the Cape, for Forbes has argued that even at the metropole, British forensic medicine "lagged centuries behind this science on the Continent" (296) and points to the expert testimony given in the murder trial of Charles Angus as an indication of "the still primitive state of English forensic medicine in 1808" (306). Other technologies, however, were beginning to facilitate the surveillance and management of, shall we say, ungovernable subjects. One such tool is so pervasive and transparent a feature of forensics, that it is effectively identified with what is now conceived of as detective work, and that is the finger-print. Some decades before South Africa was to institutionalise finger-printing procedures, it entertained the man who was to become synonymous with this forensic device. Francis Galton, accredited with initiating modern finger-printing techniques, is perhaps better known in southern Africa as the author of *Narrative of an Explorer in Tropical South Africa, being an account of a visit to Damaraland in 1851*, first published in 1853. He was the grandson of Erasmus Darwin, and the constellation of ideas which engaged him throughout his career demonstrates his easy fluency in prevailing Victorian intellectual pursuits. Apart from his travel writings, he was also to publish extensively on the concept of heredity and intelligence, which works constitute a major contribution to eugenics debates. His method was informed by the empiricist's optimism at the potential of statistical and cartographical procedures. Such strategies obtrude at various points of his *Narrative*, and are at times used to humorous effect, but are often simultaneously a demonstration of the inherently violent inequities within the logic of the scientific gaze. Such an instance occurs early in the *Narrative*, when Galton seeks to draw a woman in the household of Mr Hahn, a contact at the start of the trip.

> The sub-interpreter was married to a charming person, not only a Hottentot in figure, but in that respect a Venus among Hottentots. I was perfectly aghast at her development, and made enquiries upon that delicate point as far as I dared among my missionary friends. The result is, that I believe Mrs. Petrus to be the lady who ranks second among all the Hottentots for the beautiful outline that her back affords, Jonker's wife ranking as first; the latter, however, was slightly *passee*, while Mrs Petrus was in full *embonpoint*. I profess to be a scientific man, and was exceedingly anxious to obtain accurate measurements of her shape; but there was a difficulty in doing this. I did not know a word of Hottentot, and could never therefore have explained to the lady what the object of my foot-rule could be; and I really dared not ask my worthy missionary host to interpret for me. I therefore felt in a dilemma as I gazed at her form, that gift of bounteous nature to this favoured race, which no mantua-maker, with all her crinoline and stuffing, can do otherwise than humbly imitate. The object of my admiration stood under a tree, and was turning herself about to all the points of the compass, as ladies who wish to be admired usually do. Of a sudden my eye fell upon my sextant; the bright thought struck me, and I took a series

of observations upon her figure in every direction, up and down, crossways, diago-
nally, and so forth. (53–4)

I do not wish to get drawn into the debate around European representations of
Khoisan female sexuality; I want simply to note Galton's metaphorics here, in which
he likens the desirability of the clothed Victorian female form with the natural form
of the Khoikhoi woman.[16] What is of particular interest, for the purposes of this
essay, is the deployment of cartographic and surveying strategies in order to capture
the distinguishing marks of individual human anatomical features. A similar coincidence of factors comes together in Galton's project for the deployment of
finger-prints as a signifier of individual identity.

III

With dramatic suddenness he struck a match, and by its light exposed a stain
of blood upon the whitewashed wall. As he held the match nearer I saw that
it was more than a stain. It was the well-marked print of a thumb.
"Look at that with your magnifying glass, Mr Holmes".
"Yes, I am doing so".
"You are aware that no two thumb-marks are alike?"
"I have heard something of the kind". (Vol. II 425)

Sir Francis Galton, F. R. S. (1822-1911), may be characterised as the quintessential
Victorian man of science. The *Encyclopedia Britannica* summarises his career in
the pithy catalogue "English explorer, anthropologist, and eugenicist" (97). To those
South Africans who do know him, it is generally in the identity of "English
explorer", based upon his attempt to find a Western route of access to Lake Ngami.
The account contains, like so many which precede and which follow it, discussion
of indigenous hunting techniques, with particular attention paid to archery. As is so
often the case, the episode invokes nationalist rhetorics, as Galton compares the
poor skills of the local archer, with those back home:

> I planned a shooting match; there were twenty competitors, and each shot six arrows,
> so that of these one hundred and twenty shots were made; but out of these one hundred
> and twenty only one hit the target fairly, and another brushed it. At very near
> distances, as from five to ten yards, the men shot perfectly. I have frequently given
> prizes to Damaras, Bushmen, and Ovampo, to shoot for, but I have only seen
> wretched archery practice, far worse than that of our societies in England. (124)

In this narrative, there is something of that patriotic appropriation of archery as somehow an Englishman's skill, in much the way that Burton uses it. Galton makes no attempt to decipher why it is that the archers are so skilled at close range, choosing not to see it as, say, an indication of the tracking and hunting skills which would bring the bowmen into such close contact with his prey. It also suggests that the bow is primarily a tool, and not a weapon. A logic similar to Galton's, as I have suggested, is implicit in Noli, who despite his regard for Khoisan archery, cannot mask his sense of the superiority of the power bow as an instrument (201-07).

Galton is well aware of the symbolic authority which accrues around the idea of Khoisan poison: He writes of having dressed several arrow wounds caused by Damara arrows which, he argues, are of relatively slight danger because the "poison becomes so hard and dry on the arrows that it will not dissolve". By contrast,

> [t]he Bushman poison is far stronger and more complicated, the manufacture of it is kept secret, but many ingredients are put into the composition. Beside vegetable poisons the Bushmen assured me that the poisonous black spider (a kind of Tarantula) is an important ingredient. It seems to be, for its size, the most venomous of creatures. (176)

Although Galton's objective, of reaching Lake Ngami from the West, was not attained, he was, as a result of the discoveries and documentation of this trip, elected as a fellow of the Royal Geographical Society in 1853, and three years subsequently, of the Royal Society. Thus his major works, on the subjects of heredity and identity, found a ready audience and a context of debate which had been constituted around his travels in southern Africa. It is as if the exploration is a rite of admission into an order of patriarchal knowledge, and he is given access to metropolitan discursive intervention. His *Hereditary Genius*, which argues for selective breeding in humans, and was so influential as to be cited several times in Darwin's *Descent of Man*, was written some seventeen years after his *Narrative of an Explorer*. Clearly, in the context of the later nineteenth century, Galton's work was instrumental in arguments around race and intelligence, and he is thus pivotal to the production of colonial discourses justifying racial legislation. However, it is not this work which engages me at present: rather, I am interested in considering his work on finger-printing techniques, for this remains one of the most successful and readily administered technologies for controlling human populations. Carlo Ginzburg, in an extremely cunning article, has discussed how with the emergence of modern social organisation, class conflict emerged and was increasingly marked as criminal activity (25). Older methods for identifying repeat offenders, such as the mutilation of the body or the brand, were no longer deemed acceptable. Signatures were not entirely stable signifiers, because of forgery; some new method of fixing identity seemed to be urgently required. A photographic archive was suggested, but the inherent problems such as aging and disguise, together with the more practical difficulties of the classification and accessibility of such an archive, rendered the project impracticable (Ginzburg 25).

In 1888, Galton proposed the use of finger-prints, of which he had learned from Sir William Herschel, who was at the time District Commissioner of Hooghly in Bengal. Herschel had observed the use of the finger-print as an identifying mark amongst the local populace of Hooghly, and decided to deploy its possibilities to help in the effective administration of Bengal. By 1880, Herschel was sufficiently confident to announce in *Nature* that, after seventeen years of experiment, finger-printing techniques were being successfully deployed in Hooghly. As Ginzburg notes, the"imperial administrators had taken over the Bengalis' conjectural knowledge, and turned it against them" (27). Thus the appropriation of finger-printing for the management of subordinated populations had already been initiated before Galton became involved in the process. What he institutes is a way of making such techniques generally available, by classifying prints into various types, and identifying certain differential features. This work he made available in his *Finger Prints* (1892), which is elaborated in the supplementary chapter, *Decipherment of Blurred Finger Prints* (1893). There is thus a system of exchange established, which circulates knowledge, colonial administrators and strategies of containment between Britain, India and southern Africa. Galton's intended purposes for his work on finger-printing are transparent. The first sentence of *Blurred Finger Prints* opens with the phrase: "The registration of finger prints of criminals, as a means of future identification." Galton's work must have been disseminated rapidly and widely, for by 1894 finger-printing had been used by Mark Twain to resolve the dilemma of criminal identity in *Pudd'nhead Wilson*, a work which was expressly influenced by Galton.[17] At much the same time that psychoanalytic inquiry was destabilising the Cartesian subject, by suggesting that the individual was crossed by ambiguities and contradictory drives and desires, the British imperial machine was committed to defining and naming individuals who would thus be unequivocally subject to colonial law. It is the interest of such administrative orders to deny the fluidity of identity, in order to constitute "personhood" as a stable ground upon which to enact British justice.

Galton's metaphorics, in describing the persistence of the individual print over time, are most intriguing:

> I have lately come into possession of the impressions of the fore and middle fingers of the right hand of eight different persons, made by ordinary officials, in the first instance in the year 1878 and secondly in 1892. They . . . afford new evidence of the persistence of the *minutiae*, that is of the forks, islands, and enclosures, found in the capillary ridges. (1)

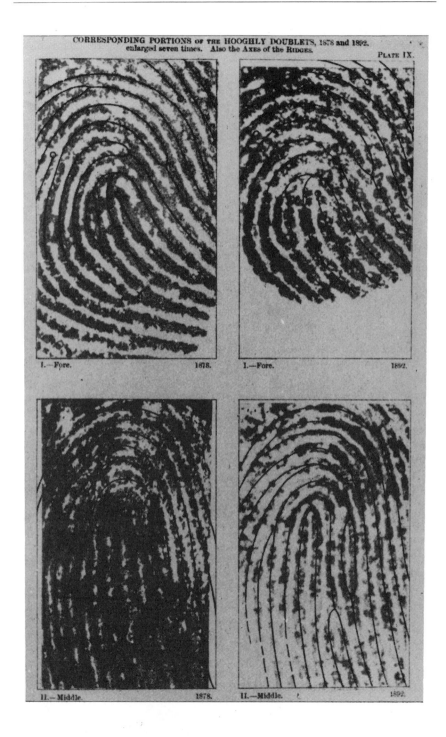

CORRESPONDING PORTIONS OF THE HOOGHLY DOUBLETS, 1878 and 1892,
enlarged seven times.   Also the AXES of the RIDGES.
PLATE IX.

I.—Fore.   1878.   I.—Fore.   1892.

II.—Middle.   1878.   II.—Middle.   1892.

The features of the print, are encoded in a language taken from cartography, and in fact even a cursory look at Galton's representations of finger-prints shows that they are contour maps (see Figure, page 108). Through the isolation and designation of certain features as *significant*, a maze of irregular scratches is transformed into a charted terrain, such that anyone faced with the same irregularities would be able to recognise the terrain: the procedure is repeated for the reading of maps and for the deciphering of finger-prints. Again, the logic of territorial acquisition provides a method for inquiry. Galton and Herschel use this method to determine whether the landscape of the finger-print can adequately be tracked over a period of time. The "Special Sub-Registrar of Hooghly", Babu Ram Gati Bannerjee, is instructed to visit, in 1892, a group of individuals whose prints had been taken in 1878. The sets of marks is then sent on to Galton, who observes:

> The documents are characteristically Oriental; they are on a common kind of apparently native-made paper, worm-eaten with many holes, and abundantly subscribed with attestations, names, ages, and dates, partly written in English and partly in native characters . . . The only thing which I cannot commend is the method of printing, which is by using dye or watercolour . . . The impressions obtained from these eight persons cannot compare in clearness with those regularly and rapidly taken at my laboratory by means of printer's ink, in the way fully described in Chapter III. of *Finger Prints*. The ink is spread uniformly and *very thinly* on a smooth slab by a printer's roller, the fingers are pressed on this and then on paper, and the results are uniformly of a high-level order of goodness. (1893: 4–5 emphasis in the original)

Galton's logic here is itself something of an identifying mark, for it shows all of the "forks, islands and enclosures" of his Victorian administrative imagination. There is the standard invocation of the "characteristically Oriental", which is associated here with poor paper and, seemingly, a rather anarchic chaos of text. These lines reveal Galton to be ridiculing the administrative pretensions of the "Special Sub-Registrar of Hooghly", a member of the subaltern classes now so familiar to us because of the work of Spivak.[18] It would appear that Galton is shadow-boxing with Bannerjee and that the contest is over differing technologies. Finally it is by fixing his own practice within the domain of modern print expertise that Galton affirms Western superiority.

As is suggested in the opening to *Blurred Finger Prints*, there was some initial resistance to the wholesale deployment of the new technology, or its admissibility as evidence. Once the surveillance applications of prints were recognised, however, the colonial offices were quick to exploit them. William James Clarke, who was

Illustration on page 108:
From: The appendix to Sir Francis Galton's *Decipherment of Blurred Finger Prints*.

appointed criminal investigation officer in Natal in 1895, was the first to set up a finger-printing department in the colony. When he initially set up his office in Pietermaritzburg, criminal statistics were based largely on circulated descriptions, drawings and photographs.[19] In 1902, Clarke was invited to accompany Colonel Albert Hime to the coronation of Edward VII, and Clarke took the opportunity while in England to visit Scotland Yard. We are told that "in the company of Pinto-Leite, he made a careful study of the finger-print system of identification" and on his return to Natal purchased the equipment, and began a series of visits to the prison staff around the colony, instructing them of the correct procedures. By 1903 he had assembled 3 500 specimens (Hattersly 161). Such was the perceived urgency of the task, that a finger-print office, as a distinct entity, was instituted a year before a similar office was established at Scotland Yard (SESA 627).

Thus the technology which had been adapted by Herschel to manage Bengali subjects, was developed and advanced through Galton's experiments, which in turn were directed principally, although not exclusively, at providing evidence of his claims about heredity and intelligence. He had hoped, in fact, to demonstrate that different races would be revealed to have distinctive features. This particular avenue of his work was, not surprisingly, picked up by apartheid scholars. A curiously archaic tract, *Portents of Violence?* (1983), from Unisa's Institute for Criminology, investigates "the causative role of heredity in the perpetration of crimes" (1). Of course, this interrogation of the criminal classes is inflected for race, in van der Westhuizen and Oosthuizen as it had been for Galton:

> It appears that different racial groups show both differences and coincidences with respect to the presence of whorls on their fingertips. However, we can make no reliable and valid generalizations to explain those coincidences and differences. (*Portents* 7)

The authors indicate that Galton, some ninety years earlier, had come to much the same conclusion, rendering their discussion rather futile. Galton's sample group is telling: it is made up of "250 Britishers, 250 Welshmen, 1 332 Jews and 250 Negroes" (7). The transparent taxonomy deployed here passes without comment by the Unisa academics. Jews, Negroes and Welshmen are all constituted as "not British".

The Unisa study then proceeds to pursue other categories of discrimination, listed under the headings of "Sexual Differences", "Schizophrenia", "Intellectual Ability", "Feeble Mindedness" and "Criminality and Degeneracy". The apparently disappointing determination at the conclusion of the study is that,

> Fingerprints are an indication of but one of numerous variables which constitute a criminal's personality; we should not underestimate the role of social, emotional and intellectual variables. At the utmost we can associate fingerprint patterns, as a biogenetic factor, with a predisposition towards crime. (15)

By leaping from Galton's study in the last decades of the nineteenth century to a Unisa publication in 1983, I do not wish to efface the differences between Victorian imperial science and criminology studies conducted in apartheid South Africa. However, it is worth noting that Oosthuizen and van der Westhuizen uncritically took much of their methodology and their ostensible project from Galton. In this way, modern forms of domination practiced by racial capitalism are parasitic upon earlier forms of imperial control.

IV

> *"The band! The speckled band!" whispered Holmes.*
> *I took a step forward. In an instant his strange headgear began to move,*
> *and there reared itself from among his hair the squat diamond-shaped*
> *head and puffed neck of a loathsome serpent.*
> *"It is a swamp adder!" cried Holmes – "the deadliest snake in India.*
> *He has died within ten seconds of being bitten. Violence does,*
> *in truth, recoil upon the violent, and the schemer falls*
> *into the pit which he digs for another". (Vol. I 261)*

Poison is "any substance which, taken into or formed in the body, destroys life or impairs health"; it is thus material. However, it is also "any malignant influence", which suggests that it can be as insubstantial as a rumour, as undetectable as a miasma.[20] It is to be feared from one's enemies, and one's intimates, as Hamlet's father knew too well:

> Sleeping within my orchard,
> My custom always in the afternoon,
> Upon my secure hour thy uncle stole
> With juice of cursed hebenon in a vial,
> And in the porches of my ears did pour
> The leperous distilment, whose effect
> Holds such an enmity wi'th' blood of man
> That swift as quicksilver it courses through
> The natural gates and alleys of the body,
> And with a sudden vigour it doth posset
> And curd, like eager droppings into milk,
> The thin and wholesome blood. (Act I v)

It is because of those "natural gates and alleys of the body" that we are always vulnerable to the fear of infiltration, such a fear as will not be stilled by a pharmacopeia of antidotes. Nonetheless, enlightenment logic set into motion a battalion of emissaries, to harvest, name, distil and neutralise, all of the toxic substances that could be found within the purview of British Imperialism. Such an inquiry generates its own monsters, for soon the known world began to proliferate in unknowable venoms, which was only exacerbated by the phobias generated through the protracted contact between the colonial classes and the colonised. The task of enlightenment exploration coincided with, and legitimated, the drive for territorial acquisition, the extraction of raw materials, the global relocation of the displaced English peasantry and "criminal classes", culminating in the forging of an English national identity. The contradictions inherent in such a project become visible in the production of texts which attempt, through narrative strategies, to resolve competing versions of the world; however, these texts themselves become bearers of such contradictions. Tales about the daring adventures to obtain the truth of the antidote to arrow poison become crossed with rivalries, unforeseen dangers, competing epistemologies.

Galton's advocacy of finger-printing techniques is an attempt to control the literal bodies of peoples who are a threat to class and national interests, and the surpluses of meaning generated by the clash of cultures consequent to English adventurism abroad. The sciences of pathology and criminology are, as it were, tested in the colonies, at the same time as they are used to control labour resources. It has been suggested that there is a distinction to be drawn between the old-style police forces in the Cape, and the new detective force that was introduced in the 1870s in order to eradicate illicit diamond dealing: new relations of production require a new order of investigation.[21]

In this sense, then, Galton is the ally of Sherlock Holmes; as Watson observes of Holmes's intellectual labours, "Surely no man would work so hard or attain such precise information unless he had some definite end in view." (Vol. I 154). Both Galton and Holmes are in the business of making England *safe*, by developing the technologies of surveillance and domination.

Postscript

Recently, I went through to the South African Library, in order to read the article by Herschel in *Nature* 1880, from which Galton allegedly first heard of the deployment of finger-printing as an administrative tool. The volume which is supposed to contain this article was somehow not retrieved for me. However, in browsing through the other volumes of Nature for 1880, I came upon two striking pieces of information. The first is that Galton was himself a regular contributor to the journal in 1880; in fact, there is an article by him entitled "Pocket Registrator for Anthropological Purposes", in which he describes an instrument which he has designed, which can be used, in one hand, as a kind of miniature surveyor's tool, in order to covertly take the physical measurements of any human being from a distance. The development described in the article in 1880 is surely a refinement of the technique used in 1851 when, on his travels around South-Western Africa, he had used surveying techniques in order to chart the physical form of a San woman he meets, and it is being advocated as a universal procedure. The second point of interest was an article by one Henry Faulds, from Tsukiji Hospital, Tokio, Japan, entitled "On the skin-furrows of the hand", in which Mr Faulds, having noticed the distinctive presence of finger-prints in Japanese ceramics, seizes upon the usefulness of these traces. He says,

> There can be no doubt as to the advantage of having, besides their photographs, a nature-copy of the for-ever-unchangeable finger-furrows of important criminals. (Sept. 1880 605)

Galton's *Finger Prints* is published in 1892, some twelve years later. It is obviously only after distilling a range of such preliminary findings, and having seen the practical uses tested by Herschel, that Galton advocates the finger-print as a scientific technology.

So the circuit of colonial information expands its horizon for us, to include Tsukiji Hospital in Japan; and the journal *Nature*, like the Royal Society, constitutes a forum for the circulation of such knowledges amongst a community of British male administrators, scientists and interested amateurs.

Response to Bunn and Taylor

Isabel Hofmeyr

I have been asked to comment on two papers in a session on interdisciplinarity. Because of the theme of the session, I am going to focus less on the content and detail of the papers and more on the model they put forward and what this may mean for the pursuit of African Studies.

However, before doing so, I would like to note that both papers are extremely elegant and accomplished. They show a rare combination of rigour and imagination, and as general models for cultural studies I find them extremely exciting. Where I come from, there is of course a long and distinguished tradition of social history. Increasingly, however, this body of scholarship shows enormous rigour but plummeting levels of imagination.

Returning to the models of interdisciplinarity put forward by the two papers, they both situate themselves at the boundary of local and imperial forms of knowledge. Or as Bunn phrases it, "the relationship between local microhistorical formations and the global transmission of knowledge". In Bunn's words, the issue involves "articulation of local systems of knowledge within a global logic which is predicated on English Imperial expansionism in the nineteenth century". African Studies must always straddle these two areas and indeed it would seem that increasingly the trend within area studies in the rest of the world is towards embedding local/area concerns in an international matrix.

The model suggested, therefore, is an excellent one. However, I do think that there are problems with how the two papers have put it into practice. The first point to note is that both papers are much stronger on the global, imperial end of things rather than on local knowledge, and I want to put forward two reasons for why this might be so.

The first concerns problems relating to Colonial Discourse Analysis, the areas in which both papers locate themselves. I should, of course, note that both papers offer exemplary and often shrewd applications of this model. They also make some deft theoretical manouevres in so doing, which are not insubstantial contributions to the debate. Yet, in my view, these limits are very real and relate in essence to the question of what can and cannot be read off from texts – more especially imperial texts. It must of course be noted that the papers provide us with ingenious and often breathtaking ways of reading, that the choice of the idea of poison is an inspired one and that they do attempt to access knowledge from sources other than the imperial text. However, neither paper centrally addresses the question of whether local knowledge can be divined from such texts. Furthermore, the papers tend to create the impression – which I know their authors do not hold – that there is *one* local knowledge.

The second issue relates to the often asymmetrical or idiosyncratic way in which African Studies has, or more properly has not, been appropriated in South Africa. The point has been made that in South Africa we do not do African Studies. We do South or at best Southern African Studies. There has been little systematic and sustained engagement with Africanist scholarship. This lack of engagement is particularly striking in these papers, particularly when one considers that one of the key and driving questions behind Africanist scholarship has been how to understand local knowledge. This question has been posed by various disciplines since the 1950s and there is a long and distinguished scholarship around it.

It seems to me that if interdisciplinary African Cultural Studies is to expand here, then work of the type we are discussing would need to baptise itself in, and enter a dialogue with, this type of scholarship. The question can also be phrased as one of academic priorities and it should be taken for granted that this scholarship is one area in which one would be expected to do an apprenticeship.

One final point I have relates to questions of the appropriation and reception of texts, an issue that has cropped up frequently. The papers have relatively little to say in this area and it is an issue seldom broached in local scholarship. The type of analysis used here does not appear to me to be one that will hasten this set of issues onto the research agenda since it reduces all questions – even broader political ones – to questions of reading. If we are to address questions of reception properly, then minimally we will have to relativise our understanding of the book and reading rather than exporting this practice out to all other areas of social life. Academics are generally doomed to believe that the only things to do with books is to read them . . . and on that entirely anti-intellectual note, I will stop.

From Lydenburg to Mafikeng:
Appropriations of images of the past

Martin Hall

I

The Centre for African Studies at the University of Cape Town came into being in 1976. By 1979 it had adopted a drawing of one of the Lydenburg Heads as its symbol.[1] This terracotta sculpture had been restored by the British Museum in London and returned to South Africa in early 1979. Nick van der Merwe, Director of the Centre, recalled the Head's return as having "all the elements of high drama". Van der Merwe had been taken to a black wooden box in the basement of the British Museum:

> "A guard unscrewed the lid and invited me to remove and inspect the contents. I was quite taken aback by the magnificent piece of ancient art which emerged, restored from the broken shards to its original condition by expert hands."[2]

After "VIP treatment" at Heathrow, the crate was strapped into a seat next to its custodian:

> "Some cabin staff believed that the object in the box was a real human head and couldn't be persuaded otherwise."[3]

It was common cause that "one of the greatest archaeological finds in the history of African archaeology"[4] should be the visual focus for the fledgling interdisciplinary centre.

Through the years that followed, the Lydenburg Heads accrued a literature – a set of academic papers seeking to fix an original meaning for the set of artefacts that are their subject. In this paper I will be concerned with such appropriations and disavowals of images of the past. How do objects such as the Lydenburg Heads acquire meaning? How can they be understood as part of the endeavour to "read" the past? How are such objects "reinterpreted" in the present, and how can a productive critique of such reinterpretations be developed?[5]

II

A good starting point for this enquiry is the small archive of academic publications that have sought to pin down the meaning of the Lydenburg Heads within a bracket of time (the sixth century A.D.),[6] and within a cultural box (the Early Iron Age).

Broken fragments of the terracotta sculptures were found in 1956 or 1957, although it was a further ten years before the heads were brought to Cape Town and reconstructed. The first formal description was published by Ray Inskeep and Tim Maggs in 1975 (Von Bezing and Inskeep, 1966; Inskeep and Maggs, 1975). Although the aesthetic qualities of the finds were acknowledged, the main focus of the analysis was the incised patterns of decoration framing the facial features rather than the individuality of the objects.[7] This emphasis allowed Inskeep and Maggs to show stylistic connections between the heads and ubiquitous earthenware pots and bowls from two archaeological sites on the Natal coast north of Durban.

Between 1974 and 1978, T. M. Evers excavated at the heads' site in the town of Lydenburg, finding more fragments of terracotta sculptures, collections of decorated everyday earthenwares and samples for radiocarbon dating. In his report on his research, Evers further developed the interpretation put forward by Inskeep and Maggs, arguing that the heads and the associated ceramics formed part of a single assemblage, part of "the first phase of the Lydenburg-Natal cluster of the Early Iron Age" (Evers 1982). This located the heads within a stylistic system, mapped across southern Africa, and with a chronology based on affinities of form and radiocarbon dates. In turn, such "traditions" have been taken as the material residue left by migrations southwards of farming communities. Most of the subsequent archaeological literature has been concerned with the number of streams of movement, their routes and their sequence, rather than with the relationship between ethnic identity and the decoration of ceramics.[8]

When the heads' archaeologists have turned from generalising their subjects into subcontinental migratory patterns, and have returned to the problem of the specific meaning of the sculptures, the language of analysis has become tentative and hazy. Inskeep and Maggs stressed that the purpose of the heads could "only be guessed at". They suggested that the smaller heads may have been attached to posts, while the larger heads could have been worn "in the style of a helmet-mask". But,

important and exciting as the heads are as examples of African Early Iron Age art, they remain disappointingly silent as ethnographic documents . . . perhaps the farthest we can go at present is to suggest that the heads as a group represent part of the paraphernalia relevant to some ritual or ceremonial context. (136)

Evers concluded that the heads had been put in "a pit which was specially dug to contain them", that "they are certainly symbolic objects" but that "their use is more problematic". Perhaps, he reasoned, they were initiation figures, kept in the pits when they were not in use. "This", he felt, was "probably about as far as it is safe to go under the present circumstances." (30). Tim Maggs and Patricia Davison, writing in the journal *African Arts*, turned to the language of aesthetics. They felt that, seen in profile, the curved line of the ridge running across the forehead of all seven heads "perfectly counterbalances the curve of the ear". Although the significance of these ridges has been lost with time, "at the aesthetic level . . . the sensitive placement of this design element testifies to a well-developed artistic awareness" (29).

What can be made of this rather slim file of archaeological papers? Firstly, and consistently with the main flow of archaeological writing, there has been a claim of distance and distinction between head (subject of analysis) and archaeologist (analyst). The language of the archive is the language of science: the passive tense and the impersonal third person plural. The feelings of the analyst are out of court and any "subjective" impression is hedged in with qualifiers.

Secondly, and as a result of these rules of objectivity, very little is actually said about the heads at all. Since there is no evidence for the "ritual or ceremonial context", and speculation must be tightly constrained, the heads remain silent about "life in the Early Iron Age". The only recourse is to generalised aesthetic statements. These have the virtue of claiming the heads as art, but with the obvious limitation that the aesthetic standard is ours, rather than that of the heads' makers.

Thirdly, the meaning that is appropriated is acquired by disassembling the heads until they are no more than an abstract code: a set of numbered decorative motifs that can be marshalled along with similarly coded decorative motifs culled from everyday pots and bowls, and rallied in support of competing "traditions" and "cultures".

The heads' archaeological journey from the eastern Transvaal, via the basement of the British Museum, ended in a particularly liminal setting in the South African Museum – ironically appropriate, given the elusiveness of their archaeological meaning. For many years, they were displayed behind glass, half-way up the staircase; between floors, with the solid ground of ethnography and archaeology below and the safely taxonomic worlds of fish and birds above; between institutions, with the paradoxical legal status of "permanent loan" from the University of Cape Town; the backgrounds in the display cases sky-blue, enhancing the message that these heads do not have bodies to connect them to firm ground. Decapitated.

III

The archaeology of the Lydenburg Heads is not unusual. One of the beguiling characteristics of most writing about "material culture" is the absence of culture. Archaeological reports are usually numerically rich, groaning with the weight of tables and appendices, counts of stone tools, pot sherds and other debris, and well illustrated with profiles, section drawings, plans and maps. But rarely is much said about the people who made all these things, leaving us the traces of their lives. Indeed, the heads can serve as a metaphor for the discipline that has claimed them; richly detailed, hard surfaces enclosing empty spaces; inscrutably silent, ignoring demands for answers.

The root cause of this problem seems to me to be a lack of theorisation of the object. As Daniel Miller has pointed out, most modern theoretical trends have been away from the object itself, concentrating instead on production rather than consumption, on representation rather than materiality. Indeed, the last major theoretical work on materiality seems to have been Marx's long, and long neglected, passage on fetishism in *Capital*.[9]

Archaeologists have gone with this trend, offering interpretations of the past which avoid discussing the inherent nature of "things" in themselves. Looking back at my own writing about South Africa's past, for instance, I find that I hardly mentioned the Lydenburg Heads at all: a photograph, a phrase referring to them as evidence for "individual actions and identities" "occasionally perceived" and a map. I made much more of the characteristics of the heads' site: fragments of building plaster, animal bones showing that livestock were herded and the stream-side position of the village, on fertile soils, revealing the agricultural preferences of these early farmers (*The Changing Past* 2, 41–2, 53). The artefacts themselves have been reduced to little more than marks on the map.

One school of thought which has tried to break into the meaning of things has been "contextual archaeology".[10] A central concern is the relationship between material objects and language. Can material things be subsumed within the category "language"? Are assemblages of things analogous to language, or does the material world have different qualities to language? Such questions are seminal for, if the material world is just another set of grammars or vocabularies, then it can be "read" in Saussurian terms as a set of relationships between signifiers and signifieds. But if the material world is different to language, the problem becomes more complex.

A close reading of some of Contextual Archaeology's own texts with this problem in mind unearths confusion. On the one hand there is an insistence on the methods of postmodernism's own "master narratives", Ricoeur, Geertz, Barthes, Derrida, Foucault.[11] But on the other hand there is an insistence of difference (*différance*?), that material culture is not the same as other texts.

Ian Hodder's *Reading the Past* illustrates the problem. "Objects in their 'text'", Hodder writes, "may not be totally mute if we can read the language." But a few lines later, "it is important to make a distinction between language and material culture" and, later still on the same page, "in many ways material culture is not a language at all – it is more clearly action and practice in the world" (*Reading the Past* 123). The confusion continues. "Context", for instance, "can be taken to mean 'with-text', and so the word introduces an analogy between the contextual meanings of material culture traits and the meanings of words in a written language." (*Reading the Past* 146). But the analogy soon crumbles away as Hodder goes on to argue that verbal meanings and the meanings of material culture are articulated differently. Verbal meanings can be contradicted, or made up spontaneously, as parts of a social ploy. In contrast, Hodder sees "material culture" as "fixing" meaning.[12]

Elsewhere in his book, Hodder continues to worry away at these problems. Written language is "precise", "comprehensive" and "complex" and is interpreted through the use of grammars and dictionaries. Material culture is "more ambiguous", "simpler", "durable, restricting flexibility" and does not have grammars and dictionaries. Hodder argues that "for these varied reasons, material culture texts are easier to decipher than those written documents for which we do not know the language" (*Reading the Past* 123). But the only reason that Hodder gives for material culture being easier to read than a verbal language is what Hodder terms "materialism" – the "structured system of functional inter-relationships" between objects. But this contradicts Contextual Archaeology's central proposition that "ideas, beliefs and meanings . . . interpose themselves between people and things", resulting in the "structured content of ideas and symbols" (*Reading the Past* 121).

Hodder continues with these problems in a later paper, pointing out that "it is of course one of the central paradoxes of archaeology that the objects dug up are concrete and real things, yet it is so difficult to ascribe any meaning to them". The postmodernist concept of the "text" offers a solution – the concept of "reading" – but also a danger, the prospect of many "readings", none of them "right" or "wrong" (*Post-Modernism, Post-Structuralism* 67). Some archaeologists have grasped the possibilities inherent in such perpetual relativity. Bjornar Olsen, for example, sees material objects as polysemeous, with a "floating chain" of signifieds underlying their signifiers. Olsen sees the "logocentric" tradition of interpretation, which seeks to recover the preconceived meaning of an object, as impossible and nostalgic. Instead, material culture should be seen as "open" and "plural". Objects (in Olsen's example, European megaliths) should be seen as "empty sites", "eternally open to signification":

> These multitudes of ties and quotations drawn from innumerable sources are gathered in one place only, the reader, who carries in herself all alone the megalithic "difference". (200)

Olsen believes that such plural meanings cannot be ranked in order of veracity because they are in some sense all "true"; Hodder, in contrast, still seeks to establish veracity by "fixing" meaning – by establishing context – for "it is the context which allows us to fix meanings. It is the context in which a signifier is used (written) which screens out the polysemy and limits the interpretation." (*Post-Modernism, Post-Structuralism* 69). But, in turn, this is circular, as Hodder himself recognises, for the definition of the attributes of an object depends on the definition of context, while the definition of context depends on the definition of attributes (*Reading the Past* 141).

The only specific solution that Hodder can offer is to look for correlations between the objects studied by archaeology and other attributes of the "exterior" material world; "most material culture does have meanings through being associated with practical uses in specific contexts" (*Post-Modernism, Post-Structuralism* 73). But this seems to me to be the same as mainstream, traditional archaeology, with its failure to theorise the object. As for the Lydenburg Heads, *Reading the Past* would take us no further than their association with pits, water and fertile soils.

A leading exponent of Contextual Archaeology is Christopher Tilley, who has claimed Hodder's writing as "a fundamental change in the way in which archaeologists actually see the world of material culture" (*Interpreting Material Culture* 185). Tilley asserts that the material world is part of language. In accordance with Saussurian principles, meaning is seen to be resident in a system of relationships between signs, and not in the signs themselves. Language, conceived in this way, is the paradigm for understanding all other aspects of social life. Therefore an assemblage of objects is a meaningful significative system.[13] To this Tilley adds the Derridian conception of *différance*. Meaning is displaced along a chain of signifiers, and therefore there can be no "absolute" meaning and closure always escapes the analyst. Consequently, the task of archaeology is always to write, and to be constantly self-reflexive in its writing.

This argument takes Tilley inexorably towards the slough of relativism, where every interpretation is as good (or as bad) as another. Like Hodder, Tilley wants to pull back from the brink of this pit, which he calls "nihilism". As with *Reading the Past*, this reversal results in ambiguities which become evident with a close reading of Tilley's own writing. One paragraph is sufficient to make the point. Tilley writes:

> Material culture is a framing and communicative medium involved in social practice. It can be used for transforming, storing or preserving social information. It also forms a symbolic medium for social practice, acting dialectically in relation to that practice. It can be regarded as a kind of text, a silent form of writing and discourse; quite literally, a channel of reified and objectified expression. (*Interpreting Material Culture* 189)

Firstly, the material world is presented as "a framing and communicative medium". A medium is an agency of communication, a vehicle of transmission – something that stands between the origin and destination of a message. But to do this, it must have an existence outside the message. And since the message is linguistic, this statement implies that things have an existence outside language.

Secondly, Tilley sees objects as "transforming, storing or preserving social information". This implies both passive and active roles. "Storing" and "preserving" are an extension of the idea that the object is a "medium", and reinforce the implication that it stands outside language. "Transforming", though, indicates not only that the object stands outside language, but also that it has the power to act on language and change it.

Thirdly, collections of things are "a symbolic medium for social practice, acting dialectically in relation to that practice". This further develops the implications of transformation. Tilley is implying that objects do indeed have a power of their own, because they can act dialectically with the human agency of social practice.

Fourthly, objects form "a kind of text, a silent form of writing and discourse". In other words, things are not unambiguously a "text", in the sense that has been established in the postmodern tradition of Derrida and Barthes (both of whose authority is used in this paper), they are rather a "kind" of text. This must mean more than the observation that the material world is an extension beyond verbal expression, since work such as Barthes' weaves a wide range of social practice into textuality; in Tilley's words,

> Barthes . . . is not concerned with general structures, but with particular cultural practices. All such practices are endowed with signification, and this is a fundamental feature running throughout the entire gamut of social life from a wrestling match to eating steak and chips to hairstyles – the list is endless. (*Interpreting Material Culture* 187)

But the list must have an end, because the material world is outside it, as "a silent form of writing and discourse" – silent, that is, in comparison with wrestling matches, steak and chips and hairstyles.

Fifthly, objects provide "a channel of reified and objectified expression". This completes a circle back to the beginning of the extracted paragraph – the idea that the material world is a medium, outside language, than can contain and preserve social discourse.

It seems to me that this close reading illustrates, more than anything else, confusion. How can a text or a discourse be "silent"? How can a pot or a hand-axe, in itself, take part in a dialectical play? A wrestling match would be outside the ambit of what most archaeologists would regard as their field of study, but the study of food and dress styles are certainly within the discipline's self-asserted range. Why are they, then, accepted as fully textual (as part of Barthes's work) while other aspects of the material world are only part of "a kind" of text?

Such confusion is aporetic – and the aporia is that the material world seems to be, at one and the same time, both bound by language and outside language. Tilley asserts the boundedness of language, the impossibility of going beyond the text, but writes of the material world as beyond the boundaries of words.[14] But at the same time, Tilley wants to insist that there is nothing outside the text.[15] Therefore the artefact without the text must be meaningless – an "empty vessel" waiting meaning given by writing. But then, in turn, it follows that any writing can confer meaning on the artefact, and that such texts can refer to nothing but themselves. Again, Tilley finds himself poised at the brink of "nihilism".

Tilley effects his retreat in the same manner as Hodder – by returning to an earlier archaeology. "The artifact", he asserts, "cannot be reduced to its visible surfaces. Meaning resides both in these surfaces directly open to observation and beyond them." (Michel Foucault 334). But how could we make such invisible properties visible? Tilley does not tell us, but the answer must lie in correlations between the artefact and an external "environment". And such correlations could only be found by setting up propositions – hypotheses – and by testing them against empirical observation. In other words, the "invisible surfaces" of the Lydenburg Heads would be approached through a law-like generalisation that objects used in ritual are often hidden away to preserve their ritual potency. This would be "tested", and substantiated, by the association of ceramic sherds with pits dug into the ground – precisely the methodology of the "New Archaeology" that Contextual Archaeology has sought to sweep away.

In December 1992, in one of these rites through which academic disciplines lay claim to the vestments of their identity, Tilley was positioned against Lewis Binford, a leading exponent of the old orthodoxy (ironically, still tagged "New Archaeology"), in a public debate to mark the thirtieth anniversary of the publication of Binford's own, once-seminal paper.[16] Tilley was seconded by John Barrett, while Binford was backed by Colin Renfrew, Disney Professor of Archaeology at Cambridge and newly ensconced on the Conservative benches in the House of Lords. There were more than 600 people in the lecture theatre, while three prominently sited video cameras (left profile, right profile and audience reaction) relayed the proceedings to those unlucky enough not to get a seat, and added tangibly to the sense of occasion. And yet the result was palpably disappointing – old phrases and challenges, old responses and witticisms. Fresh approaches to the meaning of the past seem as chimerical as ever.

IV

Thus the archaeological meaning of the heads – constructed within the boundaries of archaeology's own disciplinary discourse – remains elusive. But, since their reconstruction, the heads have also been part of another discourse – the politics of Art and Identity. The hyperbole of the journey from London to Cape Town was symptomatic of the appropriation of far more than narrowly academic meaning. This political discourse was to be illustrated some ten years later by a short, but sharp, debate in the Centre for African Studies' *Newsletter*.

In 1988 Brenda Cooper suggested in an African Studies Newsletter, that the Lydenburg Head was inappropriate as a symbol for UCT's Centre for African Studies:

> The representation of the Lydenburg Head Sculpture as the Logo for the Centre for African Studies is, to my view, repulsive, and even worse, reactionary. Please note that this is a personal view. It projects that ghastly, old distorted image of the "authentic" "pure" pre-industrial rural Africa. Is a ceramic sculpture dating back to about 500–600 AD an appropriate sign for a Centre situated in the modern, industrialised South Africa of today? Does it not reek of that, distorted, image of a timeless Africa in which people and wild animals merge in a static safari jungle-like setting (or that of the South African Natural History Museum)? It is an image that the "true" art of Africa predates the present and consists of interminable drums, assegaais and ancestor carvings and fetishes ... the Lydenburg Head, however unwittingly, reinforces the Apartheid myth of a separate, monolithic and pre-urban black South African culture. Can the Centre for African Studies afford to propagate this image?

Given his paternal relationship with the object in question, Nick van der Merwe's response in a subsequent Newsletter was not altogether surprising:

> Brenda Cooper's diatribe about the Lydenburg Head is offensive. It is her privilege to think the sculpture is ugly, though few would agree with her. It is another matter to claim that it symbolises a vision of the African past which emerges from apartheid thinking. The reality is that the sculpture in question is one of the oldest of its kind not only in South Africa, but in Africa . . . Brenda Cooper would have us believe that an appreciation of things ancient and historically significant grows out of a wish to put down Africa with tribalism and primitivity. This is a very tired old argument which has long since been settled, particularly in the rest of Africa . . .

A second response was from Pippa Skotnes, Lecturer at the Michaelis School of Fine Art:

> The Lydenburg Heads are unique and significant art objects. To the trained eye they are works of immense beauty . . . Formal analysis quite reasonably suggests the heads were all made by one individual. One individual whose vision encapsulated an "ideal", perhaps a "dream" and whose "priorities" (like those of any true artist) were

ones of reparation and reconciliation. How much more appropriate could such a logo be? (Skotnes 1988)

How can these appropriations of meaning be understood? One quick response is to insist on disciplinarity. This argument would be that the domain of archaeology – the archive of formal papers in the *South African Archaeological Bulletin* and elsewhere – has nothing to do with the domains of identity (the appropriate logo for the Centre) or of art (the aesthetics of form). But the texts that have been written around the heads have blurred such disciplinary distinctions from the start. Thus several of the formal academic descriptions move between archaeology and art, while relative value judgements of "uniqueness" and "antiquity", clearly political, are given more authority by their archaeological presentation. To claim that archaeology and art are completely distinct from one another, and have in turn nothing to do with the politics of identity, would be naive, disingenuous or clever (clever, since such naivety and disingenuousness often enhance the power of academic statements).

Appropriations such as the 1988 logo debate are, of course, part of the concern of Hodder, Tilley, Olsen and other "postmodern" archaeologists. Their issue would not be with whether or not the logo debate was "relevant" to the archaeology of the heads, but rather with whether (and how) the different texts that have now become glued to the clay sherds can be evaluated. But perhaps archaeology's postmodernists, working mostly from Europe and North America, have been swamped by the complexities of advanced capitalism, which seems to transform everything (including the production of archaeological knowledge) into commodities which have value only in relation to other commodities. Working within the astringency of South Africa's political brutalities, I find that I can evaluate the logo debate, and set out a justification for the correctness and incorrectness of different "texts". I believe that it can be shown, by adducing a substantial weight of historical evidence, that to appropriate a Lydenburg Head as a symbol for a Centre for African Studies was indeed to appropriate a particular view of Africa as timeless, naturalised and primitive. I can think of no evidence for an interpretation of the Lydenburg Heads, in the eyes of their makers, as symbols of "reparation and reconciliation". I find it revealing that both responses fall back on the authority of their disciplines; of archaeology, in dating artefacts and in knowing interpretations in the "rest of Africa"; and of art, in claiming the "trained eye". I understand the vehemence of both the attack on the centre's logo, and of its defence, as revealing the politics of disciplinary territory within the institution of the university.

A subsequent appropriation of the Lydenburg Heads is equally interpretable. When the new museum in the town of Lydenburg was opened, the choice of its symbol was obvious:

A spanking new museum complex housing a permanent exhibition calls for an
eye-catching logo to represent its corporate identity. For this purpose a TPA [Trans-
vaal Provincial Administration] graphic artist created a stylised version of one of the
Lydenburg Heads. A beautiful wood carving was mounted on a wall panel in the
foyer. The logo looks strikingly effective while establishing a strong identity for the
museum. (Smit 6)

The appropriated symbol dominates the reception area of the museum, while
perspex-cased replicas of the Lydenburg Heads are surrounded by information
boards. But, with an ingenuousness which is a gift to a paper such as mine, the
Lydenburg Museum's chronicler describes the setting:

In the lush grass of a gently sloping Lowveld hillside near the Lydenburg-Sabie road,
there stands a strikingly attractive complex which enchants and educates the visitor
while enriching his life – the new Lydenburg Museum . . . The structure features an
attractive thatched roof that blends harmoniously with the scenery of the Gustaf
Klingbiel Nature Reserve in which it is situated. The tall, strong grass of the Reserve
provided the thatch. (Smit 4)

The themes of the museum are "the rich archaeology of the area", the "fascinating
cultural history of the region" and "the colourful indigenous Pedi people". In
addition, the museum "offers the added bonus of visitors being able to view a variety
of game from its premises. The area is regarded as a bird lovers' paradise." The new
displays are part of a long historical process of exploration and discovery: "a
never-ending fascination and interest for early explorers, hunters, travellers, traders,
fortune-hunters, transport riders, adventurers and settlers . . ." (Smit 4).

It would, I think, be widely accepted (although not universally, of course) that
this appropriation of the Lydenburg Heads is part of a long-standing colonial
discourse which naturalises the indigenous population (the "colourful" Pedi, living
in the "tall, strong grass" whose cultural history is part of a nature-lover's paradise).
I have no difficulty in rejecting this as a "bad" text about the Lydenburg Heads.

In other words, in the face of the practical problem of the heads, the theoretical
dilemmas in evaluating texts that have so concerned Hodder, Tilley and other
archaeologists seem to vaporise. Of course, Pippa Skotnes and Nick van der Merwe
will disagree with my choice of sides in the centre's logo debate and, of course, I
will defend my position; such has been the dialectic of academic practice for time
immemorial. The point is that I, like them, can come to a position in the first place. But
then again, perhaps the post-processualists' problem is itself illusory. For even Bjornar
Olsen, the arch-relativist, needs the right to claim a position, declaring, with missionary
zeal, that "our task . . . is not to recover a lost origin, but to create intelligibility for our
own time" (202). How can such "intelligibility" be achieved without insisting on a
differentiation of readings?

V

To these two, substantially overlapping, sets of meaning acquired by the Lydenburg Heads (the archaeological archive and the politics of symbolic identity) can be added a third – the heads as subjects for artistic transformation; inspiration for the icons of Malcolm Payne's terracotta Mafikeng Heads, and in his copper-plate etching titled "The Market Place".

Like many archaeologists, Payne has been centrally concerned with the relationship between form and meaning. He argues that prevailing traditions of South African landscape representation are narrative and allegorical, and that they therefore serve only to continue a long-established discourse. In seeking an approach to representation that is "revelatory", Payne has turned to objects that disturb and interrupt such narratives, culminating in a collection of paintings and etchings, titled "Market Forces"; a re-figuring of the South African landscape that concentrates on the ecological, economic and political effects of gold, diamond, coal and iron-ore mining.[17]

There is a rich universe of objects available to serve as icons in this process of re-contextualisation. But there is also the danger of what Payne calls "promiscuous appropriation", the re-use of objects without due regard to their prior histories. He seeks to avoid this charge by situating his work historically, and by choosing objects carefully; smokestacks, anvils, coal dust, bandages and mine machinery are drawn from the narratives that Payne's re-coding disturbs through arrangements in radical new forms.

Malcolm Payne has seen the Lydenburg Heads as appropriate icons because for him they recall the place of mining in the Early Iron Age, and extend the historical context of the central theme of mining that runs through his work ("Form and the picturing of Mining"). Re-coding has taken the form of a series of ten terracotta sculptures – the "Mafikeng Heads" – made in 1987 and 1988. The Mafikeng Heads have rudimentary implements in place of facial features, suggesting the "accountability of technology for the dehumanisation of man"; a device that Payne also employed in the earlier "Stacked Relief" series. The raging gorillas, and distorted elephants and rhinoceroses, on the crowns of the Mafikeng Heads signify ecological chaos, excluding the possibility of reparation: "the fantasy of reconciliation" ("From Lydenburg to Witbank" 40).

The Lydenburg Head/Mafikeng Head icon is used again in Payne's copper plate etching titled "The Market Place" (1989). The reference to the set of terracotta sculptures is important to the composition, as Pippa Skotnes has pointed out:

> The image is composed of an oval shape surrounded by four disks, each depicting an aspect of four major mining industries, coal, steel, diamond and gold. The central ellipse contains injured figures taken from a Sanoid Bandage given to soldiers in the first world war. These figures are situated amongst boxes of agricultural produce, and by association are seen as thinly veiled commodities. The figures in the region

of the sky, referring to the sculptural products of the South African Iron Age lend the image a sense of historicity and suggest an appraisal of the long term cost of both human and ecological exploitation.[18]

In writing about his own work, Payne has stressed the importance of the materiality of the Lydenburg Heads, implying that, for him, they were indeed "outside" language, focal points that enabled "the continuing articulation of my subjective experience through a primary emphasis on the articulation of form" ("Form and the Picturing of Mining" 40–1). But, as he has also made clear, they were not casually chosen – they carried a meaning about the pre-colonial South African past. In consequence, the symbol of the Mafikeng Head is a new combination that appropriates both an early past and a more recent history.

Again, it would be inadequate to insist that what Malcolm Payne "does" is art, completely distinct from archaeology and a consciousness of the politics of identity. Clearly his work has an aesthetic, inviting valorisation within the cannons of artistic appreciation (even if the artist himself would reject such cannons). But his landscapes are also expressly political, while the Mafikeng Head appropriates meaning from the archaeological archive; or, rather, misappropriates meaning, as the Lydenburg Heads are neither associated with mining or have been interpreted as evidence for human or ecological exploitation.

VI

The Lydenburg Heads, then, do not "belong" exclusively to archaeology, art or the arena of symbolic identity. Rather, these overlapping domains of appropriation are bound together by the act of appropriation itself – by a common interest in the heads, and by their materiality in the mezzanine limbo of the South African Museum. This returns us to the problem of the relationship between objects and words; a question which inhabits the archaeological archive, the transcripts of the logo debate and Malcolm Payne's studio.[19]

In a particularly helpful paper presented originally to an archaeological conference, Jean Molino has applied the principles of semiotics to this question. Molino takes the material world to comprise sets of signs. The central point about signs is that they have material existence, both as production, because language cannot encode a meaning prior to the existence of the sign, and as reception, because it offers access to knowledge; ". . . having been produced, the sign exists materially as an object of the world among the other objects of the world: image, word, rite, work of art, or scientific theory". The sign is thus "irreducibly new", a combination of form (17). Its fundamental structure is not purely formal, since it is a consequence of the "symbolic function", which is an autonomous function, alongside nutritative and reproductive functions. In other words, the symbolic function must be seen as prior to language. "Any social practice is symbolic through and through, and there is no tool, no activity, no product that is truly empty of meaning."[20]

As the "symbolic function" exists prior to language, the material world – as a set of signs – is distinct from verbal communication. But at the same time the Saussaurian distinction between signifier and signified ensures that objects such as the Lydenburg Heads, divorced and isolated from the original context in which they were produced, can only be partial traces of the full system of signs that once existed. By distinguishing between the objective reality of these traces and the necessary indeterminacy of later analysis, Molino draws a distinction between objects as constituted in past symbol systems (in the "Early Iron Age"), and objects as transcribed in successive texts (archaeological papers, logo debate and Mafikeng Heads).

Thus to recognise the priority of the symbolic function is to recognise the reality (although always incomplete) of a past represented by its material residues; post-modernist archaeologists need not fear ritual self-destruction by means of de-construction. But this same priority of symbolic function ensures that artefacts from the past are always available for appropriation as "irreducibly new" signs, different from one another: the Centre for African Studies' logo, the Mafikeng Head, the Lydenburg Museum logo. And, when signs in a set refer to the same inspirational source, they inevitably refer to one another as well, setting up chains of cross references. Thus the centre's logo referred to the newly reconstructed Lydenburg Head to claim an association with the historical depth and civilisation of Africa, contesting the apartheid view of a shallow, barbaric past. But subsequently, the Lydenburg Museum has also claimed the reconstructed Lydenburg Head as an apartheid image of tribal Africa. Appropriations such as this have led the centre to disavow its earlier image by appropriating Payne's Mafikeng Head – itself, of course, an appropriation of the earlier archaeological image. Attempts to string the barbed wire of disciplinary boundaries across such complex webs of association can be little more than spoiling tactics.

Objects, then – if they are to be fully understood – need to be granted their materiality, their priority over language. In this spirit I offer a set of images that share a common origin in a hole in the ground in the eastern Transvaal, each with a phrase or two attached to make the connection with its verbal texts.

Marx expressed the complexity of the material world in his discussion of fetishism:

> A commodity appears, at first sight, a very trivial thing, and easily understood. Its analysis shows that it is, in reality, a very queer thing, abounding in metaphysical subtleties and theological niceties. (76)

There are no single Lydenburg Heads. Rather, there is a series of symbols; a series that starts a thousand or more years ago, lies underground for centuries, and then

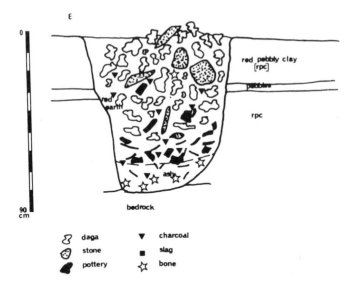

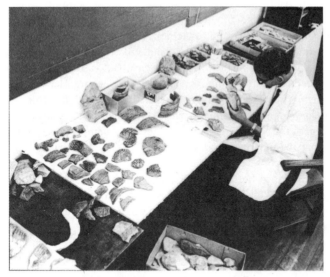

Top: Context: Profile of a pit at the Lydenburg site
Bottom: The heads assembled: Cedric Poggenpoel in the
              Archaeology Department Laboratory, circa 1970

Centre for African Studies
UNIVERSITY OF CAPE TOWN

Head as Letter-Head

fragments into parallel meanings; the "magnificent piece of ancient art" strapped into a Boeing seat, the logo of the new Centre for African Studies, a disassembled collection of decorative motifs, a mark of the timeless tribalism of Africa, a radical challenge to the history of South African landscape painting, a subversion of prior academic practise. Although part of language, the symbols in this series are also always more than language – not reducible to the words that describe them.

As signs, these many heads speak many discourses – the racist narratives of the past, essentialist ideas of Africa, concepts of universal aesthetics, challenges to apartheid history. Such "signified" discourses are in turn part of our current discourse, rendering the heads inherently political; powerfully reactionary, powerfully progressive, never neutral. Underlying this multiplicity of meanings is the power of materiality, the power of the object itself.

Equally complex is the identity of disciplines such as those which have claimed the heads – the nature of the internal relationships between practitioners and the dependency of discourse on the discourses of other disciplines.[21] Archaeology has subjected the heads to its recognised procedures, locating them in cultures and traditions. But in this same archive are frequent slippages into guesses and aesthetic judgement – beyond the rules for a "scientific" study of the past. Art has also claimed the heads and yet, in its own creative development of the icon, has depended on the archaeological archive for authority. The point, perhaps, is simple; creative disciplines are not those that fence themselves into exclusive compounds, but are rather those sets of practices which are always open to the possibilities of syncretism, that celebrate transgressions of their boundaries. Archaeology is enriched by the Mafikeng Heads, and art is all the better for the Lydenburg Heads.

What will be the next appropriation of meaning? Let us take a hint from "Banyoles Man", the sad stuffed San who has been the only point of interest in his small Catalonian museum since 1916 (Jaume *et al.* 1992). Robbed from an unknown grave in Botswana, this mounted body has become a symbol in the political battle between racial purists – demanding that if their stuffed trophy has to go, then Banyoles' African immigrants should go with it – and Barcelona's Inter-African Centre for the Promotion of Cultural Activities, which has condemned the continued display of the stuffed body as racist.

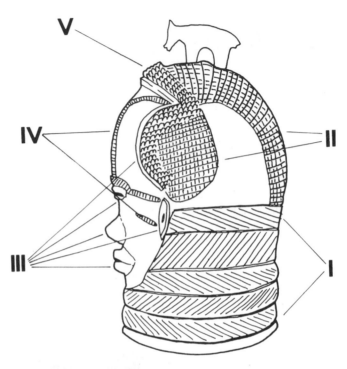

Above: Lydenburg Head as specimens (from Evers 1982)

Left: Head as postcard: South African Museum shop

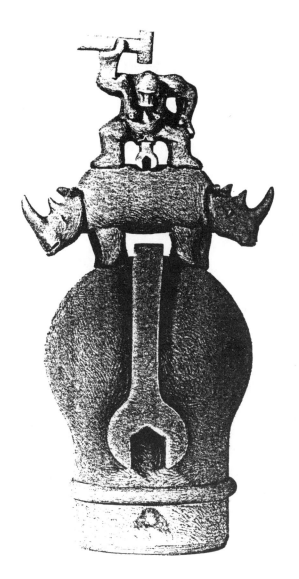

Head appropriated:
A Mafikeng Head (Malcolm Payne)

The terracotta sculptures from Lydenburg are corporeal rather than corporal, even though they seem often to have been animated almost into life. Nevertheless, along with other "ethnography" and a good many stuffed animals and reptiles, they reside in Cape Town's Natural History Museum. They are separated by long shady paths from the Cultural History Museum, where are stored the artefacts of white South Africa, and from the National Gallery, repository for our aesthetic standards. This map of the Company Gardens in Cape Town is a map of colonialism and apartheid, marking out the distinctions between Native and European, Primitive and Civilised, Own Affairs and General Affairs. If the rude awakening of "Banyoles Man" is anything to go by, the Lydenburg Heads will soon be back in the news.

Talking Heads
A response to Martin Hall

Patricia Davison

In keeping with the spirit of the conference, Martin Hall's paper discusses the fields of discourse surrounding the Lydenburg Heads and focuses attention on the issue of their cultural appropriation within the disciplines of archaeology and art, as well as the appropriation, in the late 1970s, of an image of the large restored head as logo for the newly established Centre for African Studies at the University of Cape Town. He also draws attention to a more recent appropriation of this image as corporate emblem for the Lydenburg Museum. Hall's paper is, of course, in itself an academic appropriation of prior appropriations.

A conceptual concern throughout the paper is to understand how objects acquire meaning, and the related issue of whether material culture is analogous to language or not. If not, how does communication through objects work? How do we read material things, in particular how can we understand the Lydenburg Heads?

He suggests, "There are no single Lydenburg Heads. Rather a series of symbols, a series that starts a thousand or more years ago, lies underground for centuries and then fragments into parallel meanings . . ." and in the following paragraph, "As signs, these many heads speak many discourses – the racist narratives of the past, essentialist ideas of Africa, concepts of universal aesthetics, challenges to apartheid ideology . . . underlying this is the power of the object itself".

I would like to raise two issues relating to these statements. Firstly, Hall seems to make no distinction between sign and symbol but rather uses the terms interchangeably. I find this problematic because in my understanding signs and symbols operate differently from each other, they signify in different ways. Within a shared system of communication a sign cannot afford to be ambiguous because it would simply not be effective. Within symbolic discourse, on the other hand, ambiguity is necessary in order to give the symbol the capacity to evoke many different meanings. A red traffic light is unambiguously a stop sign, whereas in other contexts the colour red communicates symbolically, signifying many complex associations. Symbols cannot be decoded as if they were linguistic signs – they work precisely because they do not have fixed meanings.

Secondly, the heads cannot literally "speak many discourses". They are implicated in discourse but discourse itself is part of social practice, and while material culture is surely actively involved in many fields of discourse, the power of the object is not inherent in its materiality *per se* but in the relationship between the object and the human subjects who invest it with meanings in particular contexts. I would suggest that here and elsewhere in the paper, the issue of human agency is not adequately taken into account. In short, the concern to theorise the object (see page 119) would be better expressed as a concern to theorise the object/subject relationship. One can then look at the history of an object and at the range of meanings that might be attached to it in relation to specific social contexts. This would be consistent with the notion of a biography of an object.

The Centre for African Studies logo debate seems to make sense in these terms. Hall correctly interprets the debate as revealing the politics of disciplinary territory within the institution of the university (page 125), the disavowal of the logo must surely be seen in a similar context. An image of the heads may yield many interpretations precisely because the original range of meanings of the heads and their contexts of use is little understood.

However, while the significance of the heads is open to many readings, the heads site has been dated to about 500 A.D. This constitutes an anchor that stabilises the range of meanings attributed to the heads to some extent, and gives the heads particular importance in the history of southern Africa. The paper underplays the role of this knowledge in challenging colonialist assumptions about the empty land prior to European settlement. The heads feature regularly in a growing body of revisionist history written for schools and the general public, including museum-goers. While I agree that in spatial terms the heads are in a liminal position in the South African Museum, in practice they provide a useful point of departure for correcting stubborn misconceptions about the time depth of African settlement in southern Africa (requests for photographs of the heads are most frequently for history books and encyclopaedias). Outside of a purely academic arena, and within the realities of contemporary South Africa, there is still a very real need to provide evidence of the early occupation of African communities in southern Africa. Hall's paper, I suggest, severs the heads from this discourse.

Face Value:
Old Heads in modern masks

This is a semblance of a paper by the author and visual presentation on aspects of the book and exhibition: Face Value: Old heads in modern masks. A visual, archaeological and historical reading of the Lydenburg Heads.

Malcolm Payne

The *Face Value* project was initiated with a series of sculptures I produced in Mafikeng, in erstwhile Bophuthatswana, in 1987, entitled the *Mafikeng Heads*. The project had no name at that time. It emerged as an attempt to make visual sense of the "post" in postcolonialism and the "euro" in eurocentricism – to create some sense of place for myself in the future – recognising, as Bhabha says, that "Our existence today is marked by a tenebrous sense of survival, living on the borderlines of the 'present', for which there seems to be no proper name other than the current and controversial shiftiness of the prefix 'post': postmodernism, postcolonialism, postfeminism . . ." (1).

South African cultural histories have in recent times become the focus of much critical debate. Indeed, the debate in itself may be considered a vital form of cultural expression. No exhibition, artist, artwork, political grouping, museum collection or museum-governing board is free from its complex scrutiny. The debate aims to re-structure representation, re-write history, to transgress stylistic and cultural boundaries; all in the search for dialogue that is meaningful. "History" is its focal centre. It is in this context that this project entered the fray, examined the production of meaning and, hopefully, has become a site of meaning in itself.

The most remarkable issues at play in the prolific global cultural debate today, are not dissimilar to ours. Traditional hierarchies have become unseated. We can no longer take our perception of images, the understanding of language or history for granted. Our cultural practices have been seen for what they are – complex ideological strategies that simultaneously veil and determine meaning. In the *fin de millennium*, as we cross the psychological divide into the twenty-first century, culture is being asked to speak in new voices. Some speak of multi-culturalism, some of "cultural nomadism"[1] – a kind of reposited internationalism, or new universalism or "new internationalism"[2] – to gain fresh insights and renewed creative impetus in defence against the pervading bankruptcy of postmodern fragmentation at the core of contemporary art. Faced with this crisis of creativity (which is really the recognition of the demise of Western sovereignty), Europe is desperately re-examining its modernist past, its second origin. By constructing a reading of the way in which this legacy was consumed, in particular by Africa, Europe is formulating a strategy of survival. Africa it appears, on the flip-side, is doing much the same. It is re-naming, re-positioning, re-claiming and re-modelling, a past created by the contingencies of geographical and cultural colonialism.

The first making of Africa materialised in a penumbraic half-light along the blurred edges of Europe's peripheral vision and was brought into focus as the exotic other. The obsessional avarice of colonial enterprise fed the retina with objects and materials of desire, which were to be quickly melted down, hallmarked by appropriation and set in anthropological and art historical discourse.[3]

Difference was constituted by the supposition that the entire body of world culture, from the first light of humanity, must be conventionally understood and appreciated in respect of the European visual experience formulated by the Renaissance more than half a millenium ago. Museum practice and expositions – spectacles contrived to conserve cultural division – of the late nineteenth and early twentieth century exposed exotic as well as erotic objects (curios) and people (curiosities) from other cultures. All of this was engulfed by a prefabricated imperialist paradigm placing Europe at the centre, mediating the peripheral shade.

One of the aims of the *Face Value* project has been to create a framework for the examination of these practices, and in particular as they are applied to the categorisation of the aesthetic, art/artefact, pluralist and appropriationist products of debate in South Africa. Seven terracotta hollow modelled heads found near the town of Lydenburg in the Transvaal in the 1950s, and estimated to be about 1 500 years old, are the stimulus for this project. They are in many senses empty[4] – they have no meaning and are opaque to interpretation. We do not know anything about their meaning, nor about the reality they inhabited. What we do know is that they are a part of those South African cultural histories that have been explored mostly by archaeologists, but also by historians and museologists. These sculptures, collectively called the *Lydenburg Heads* and presently residing in the South African Museum in Cape Town, act as beacons demarcating the visible field for these arguments.

The project is not about ethnographic declassification, the search for archaeological veracity or an attempt to celebrate the aesthetics of the *Lydenburg Heads*. If any frame is to be set in place, it would be in the context of co-existent voices harmonising in inter-disciplinary discourse amplified by the symbolising capacity of art. A notion of universality in art is firmly rejected. Such notions of authority are totalising and simply denote a form of domination of one set of values over another. This project steers clear of simple assumptions about transcending cultural boundaries. In fact, it may reinforce them in order to promote a sense of symmetry, ensuring identities are not consumed by a desperately expedient, panic-driven over-arching paradigm of faceless co-existence. The project may examine the past historically, but does so in clear recognition that this will always be ideological. The substance of this project is perhaps to constitute some psycho-cultural sense of this time in South Africa.

The intention to collaborate on one aspect of the overall project, a book, with practitioners from other related disciplines, was to smart-bomb the heads from different directions. My co-conspirators Martin Hall and Patricia Davison both have had, for some time, a working relationship with the *Lydenburg Heads* within their respective fields and therefore share, to some extent, common readings of the complex textuality generated by the heads.

My initial research for the extension of the project found form in numerous two-dimensional conceptualisations in various drawing media. Some were tentatively assigned to the etching plate towards the end of 1988 when two small plates were editioned which incorporated iconographic reference to the *Lydenburg* and *Mafikeng Heads*. It had always been my intention to supplement the possible range of expression prompted by this research, and in particular within some form of publication. The opportunity arose when in 1989 I co-founded the Axeage Private Press with Pippa Skotnes. The Press is responsible for publishing fine original hand-made books and prints. The books embody a union of the artistic, the scientific and the literary.

Besides my own contribution of visual interpretations, in the form of etchings, I provide a discussion of my approach to visual art engaging in this kind of plurality. I emphasise the parallel reality evoked when conjuring the means to experience the past in the present, catalysed or enabled by the form of the visual as found in works of art. The practice of inscribing relics with value, or consecrating memory in history formulated in faith, functions as a metaphorical bridge, forming an ideological cortex able to link various practices of enshrinement, whether in language, art, religion, the art gallery museum or iconoclast's tool-box.

Figure 1:
The *"context"* (size: various)

Figure 2: *Mafikeng Head* no. 10
(height: 605 mm)

Figure 4: *Face value*, title plate
(etching: 200 mm x 400 mm)

Figure 3: *Lydenburg Head* no. 7
(height: 210 mm)

As much as art and artefacts from the past are susceptible to becoming vague aesthetic abstractions or acquiring ambiguous classificatory status, so equally are products emanating from the contemporary art world. This was acknowledged by allowing the *Lydenburg Heads* to play an equal part by association, in context production, alongside my visual art in the exhibition of this project at the South African National Gallery between November 1993 and January 1994.

My request for the repositioning of the *Lydenburg Heads* in the South African National Gallery for the duration of the exhibition met initially with strong resistance. The practice of inscribing relics with meaning, I was told by the South African Museum, really meant – context by association – they owned the "context", the associated material (various bits and pieces of pot sherds, etc. from the site), in essence, garbage. A lending clause stipulated that the heads *would not* be lent without their "context" (Figure 1). A meeting attended by chief museum staff in the South African Museum board-room was called to thrash out our differences. The *Lydenburg Heads* did not attend, however their "context" did. It was dramatically wheeled in on a trolley (was the trolley also part of the context?). After much deliberation my point was taken. The heads were severed from their "context", and allowed out to visit another.

The completed project was finally presented as installation. The exhibition contained all seven *Lydenburg Heads* (Figure 3), seven of the ten Mafikeng Heads (Figure 2), fourteen etchings from the book (Figure 4), the book, seven large container-like constructions, seven supermarket trolleys and a large black dot painted directly onto the gallery wall.

An important sub-text in the form of a question emerged within the ambit of this production. Where do the *Lydenburg Heads* belong? It may be argued that their current siting in the South African Museum, keeping company with fossilised remains of extinct animals, stuffed birds, fragments of meteorites, veriest sculptures, body casts of Bushmen and whale bones, is entirely unacceptable. It may be equally argued that this question is a simple reiteration of the conventional debate which attempts to locate "material culture" in institutions of art, singling out and privileging the architectonic canon of the art museum as a site of valorisation, over the context of the ethnographic or other museums. My position asserts that the hierarchical grading of objects or material culture should be provisionally suspended. In either case, the concept of a value-free territory is problematised. As the essayists noted, the *Lydenburg Heads* occupy a liminal space – below the threshold of consciousness. Perhaps the value of this project, like any meditation on displacement, is that it demands risk taking. It means giving over to an intuitive probing of regions where stimuli are perceived to be absent; regions, where other forms of perception may sense the traces lost to memory; regions perhaps as refuge from the present, where at this moment we wander beaconless with no permanence in sight.

The Internal Dialogue of an African Film-maker

An edited transcript of the talk presented on the occasion of the "Appropriations" conference. The editors tried to retain the tone of the spoken original as much as possible.

Haile Gerima

I'm a film-maker but not in the traditional sense in which film-makers have become entertainers. I am not an entertainer, but I am a film-maker. I prefer expressing myself using the medium of cinema. But I also feel the film-maker cannot just passively wait and express himself or herself through only film, especially if one is a third-world person. We have to also engage in debates and discourses to make this experience a meaningful and an honest one.

The struggle I live and fight for has a human face. I always want that to be reflected in my vision, in my dream. The superficial, the liberal appropriation of the African cinema is unacceptable to me. Therefore, in my nine years of trying to produce the *Sankofa* film, while conferences and workshops were taking place throughout Europe and America, I was travelling the length and breadth of Europe and America to raise money to do the film.

I especially feel that the people who are in the African criticism orbit have no realistic perspective as to what the reality of African cinema is. They seem to cannibalise just three films that have been made under the most oppressive conditions, and they seem to always mix it up with the reign of Hollywood cinema, the reign of entertainment cinema.

Sitting through these nine years of trying to do this film [Sankofa], whether I was on location in Jamaica or Ghana, I had my own inner monologue with the ghosts of African film critics and African film producers and African film-makers. So at the time I finished the film, I wanted to exorcise myself out this inner debate I had, by writing down my thoughts, some of which I present here. I have not tried to be objective but subjective because I knew the critics, who are writing about African cinema, are objective enough, and I don't like to justify any of my inner thoughts and theories with any footnotes or justifications, because my interest is not to claim territory in film criticism but to agitate and provoke the film-maker, the missing link.

I see African cinema as a Nomadic activity for many reasons. In fact, I coined this tribal name for African film-makers. I call African film-makers Fulanis, the Nomads of the African intelligentsia. While the historians sit at the university and write with pencil and paper, and the painter can do as much, the film-maker has to travel all over the world to find portable resources and put them together and come up with a film.

This is for many reasons. One is the absence of a viable film-production industry, that is technology as well as capital in Africa. There is also the absence of a coherent visionary national cinema policy by any African government. There is the absence of any contributive infrastructure – only the bureaucratic, neocolonial offspring – from the customs agent at immigration all the way to taxation. We have to move round within a country with all the technology and equipment. These are the nuts and bolts that a film-maker faces in the absence of genuine film culture. The fact is that there are no film societies in Africa. I hope this doesn't include South Africa. There is the absence of truly meaningful debate within the African continent on African cinema; there is the absence of non-exploitative, non-Hollywood cinema, including African films, in the distribution circles of most African countries.

Most African films don't show in Africa. It's only recently that even Sembene Ousmane's films showed in Senegal. My film that I made in Ethiopia twenty years ago has not shown there officially. There is no discussion and debate between film-makers and critics within the African continent. Even in Senegal, where most African film-makers are congregated, there is no debate except for the self-destructive, competitive relationship between film-makers. There is the domination of Euro-American exploitation cinema of African film-makers, not only in distribution and exhibition, but in film language.

The dominant African audience, their expectation of what cinema is, their reference point, has an impact on the kind of films that are made, or the films that are given a chance to be shown. These have to be pitted against an exploitation cinema. The different rural audiences and urban audiences are two dynamics for an

African film-maker. Urbanised, dominated, alienated, polluted, corrupted, colonised, African audience versus virgin territories, because in most of Africa, if you travel out of the main cities you will find different societies.

The African film-maker has to consider his accent or her temperament of film-making within the context of the culture of control of the environment that Hollywood has over African society and imperialist control of the distribution of cinema. I think that even South Africa might end up being the main agent of imperialist distribution in the future years to come when South Africa finally amends its relationship with all African countries. This country may be our biggest controller or dominating distribution agents of American culture into the African countries. There is also government control of television and lack of access, etc. All these realities make the African film-maker one of the warriors of African cinema.

Somebody once said that there are more African film critics than there are African films. That's the humour of it. The reason I say it is humorous is because, take me for example. I made *Harvest* twenty years ago and the critics still write about that film, not because they think it is a classic or anything, but it is because there is no other film from Ethiopia. Why is that so? Why are there not enough films being made in Africa?

Do you locate yourself as a critic more to be in the vanguard, an activist to fight, to struggle, rather than becoming an ivory-tower critic sitting up somewhere, expecting some cultural nutrition to be cooked by the so-called entertainers and to be presented on a plate that is brought forth. The critic continues to devour one film and the film-maker benefits nothing because of the absence of the infrastructures I talked about in Africa, which might make the activist and the film-makers unite to struggle within the concrete realities of African cinema.

In fact, one critic once said to me it was about time for me to go and make a film in Ethiopia, and I said to this guy, at least buy me a ticket to Ethiopia and then say that. You claim so much about what African cinema is and you don't even know why films are not made. It is a total isolation; it is a totally separate world. African film-makers don't debate, they chatter about what African cinema is. Wherever our work is being looked at, we are not part of it.

Although the tradition of African cinema when it emerged at the Ouagadougou Film Festival (though I was not one of the participants, but you know from the history of it) was different. It was based on the debate and discussion between film-makers. One of the most attractive features that I read about before I went to Ouagadougou was the fact that film-makers debated and discussed their works and even critics joined the debate and discussions. Those interactions helped transform African cinema to a point.

I talked earlier about how African cinema is so stagnant for many reasons. The first generation of film-makers made films because it was like Nkrumah writing a book or Cabral coming out with a certain theory about culture. Film-makers equally just picked up the camera to express themselves, so this is what the intellectuals had in common – whether it's film, poetry or a novel – the intelligentsia entered the picture as warriors, as struggling visionaries, in quantifying the collective struggle of a people. That was the constant debate that helped many film-makers shape their temperament, accent and their film work in general. But at a certain point, for the many reasons I explained first, including European control of African cinema especially in the Francophone area, the younger generation of African film-makers are more interested in what Europe wants to see about their culture or their society.

Now, you are going to say, what's wrong with this? The problem is finance. If the only place I can get money to make a film is France, then I become a translator and a tour guide, at best a mercenary for France. What it means is that a country called France begins to interfere in the creative process of the mind of an African film-maker; which means I begin to conceive stories and ideas to please the consumers or the financiers, the people who finance my films. That in itself has intruded as a reality in the further development of African cinema. It is even one of the causes why African film-makers don't talk to each other. In most cases African film-makers are individuals, in orbit without reference – without reference to collectively shared experiences.

The film-maker is a researcher in the sense that as you move from film to film you try to find your accent, you try to find your identity in film. Otherwise why even make films? I say this within the African-American struggle. What is the use of being an African-American, who went through changes to make movies, if it is to make movies like Hollywood? Then we might as well leave it to the best technically equipped people to speak about us anyway. The battle is because my identity, my face, my humanity, my grandmother's humanity are totally censored or totally non-existent in motion pictures.

Even in terms of aesthetic criteria of beauty, womanhood, manhood, humanhood, all this is a totally destroyed heritage for most of our people. What is the use of an African film-maker torturing himself, his family, her family, to make a movie if it is to regurgitate Hollywood's films? It disqualifies our inclination to want to be film-makers and to have our own representation. Within this kind of turmoil, the critic does not come to activate a constructive relationship between film-makers. In fact, the critics divide African film-makers. Within the context of Hollywood, you find the critics' interest is not to nurture and transform a film culture; their interest is to commercially push one movie upward, one movie down, to praise this film and to disgrace that one. They don't have to have any responsibility, any social commitment; it's a capitalist venture; it's all entertainment; it's business, so this starts to filter into the African film critics. They are without any constructive purpose and objective to transform the African film-maker and the African film society.

Film language is coined, not by the film editor sitting and hiding in an editing room and shooting movies to people by telegraph, but by completely engaging with audiences and critics to transform a language. Because our purpose is not just to make films, but also to introduce our way of speaking, which is a displaced accent. It's not just making a film, but also asserting our language and our thought processes, although Europe has dislocated them as a barbaric logic. Our sentences and our utterances are all classified as barbarian and savage talk. So to assert our language, which is part of the revolution of the struggle, we have to introduce daily, however imperfect, our own accent, our own temperament, our thought processes, our way of seeing, into cinema. That is why I think most film-makers in the Third World are into film.

What then are the logical relationships that have to be created between all the partners in that presentation? There is this thing that I call a triangular relationship between the audience and the critics and the African film-maker. The three can't be traditionally infected or disfigured by Hollywood's notion of what the critic is, what the film is, what audiences are. Within the Hollywood context, the audience is addicted, hopelessly colonised and there is no active relationship. It's a very passive relationship that Hollywood audiences have. The critic is also a dislocated critic, a sour critic. It's the only time he or she is empowered to cut a film, down or up, it doesn't matter which way.

In African cinema, for us to go around imitating the Hollywood notion of what a film-maker is, contaminates the triangular relationship. The traditional role played by Hollywood has no place in African cinema. It's a waste of our people's money. It's a waste of African people's time. It's joining an exploitative class. The pain and misery of the African people totally contradicts this notion of this kind of cultural relationship.

Why make movies? Why am I making movies? Why do I put my kids (I have four kids) through all the changes? Why don't I put in all the money that I work for and save, beg and steal, towards my kids? My answer always is because there is a struggle. That's how the African film tradition emerges. That's my notion of the Sembene Ousmane tradition – for me it's a struggle in a very liberated, dialectical sense, not loyalistically submitting to a party or a country or a race, but challenging all facets of our society.

There are critics I respect, and I want critical analysis. At the same time, I don't want to say certain people are okay and other people are not. Its not my job to do that. My job is to provoke, to make an intervention.

What is African cinema? That is another part of it. We read a great deal about it. How is it evaluated? I feel film analysis is a very critical weapon. At the same time I feel African film has so far been analysed on the basis of content. I don't want you to think I am pushing no content, just formalistic analysis of just the technique of film-making. But everywhere African films are displayed and exhibited and we read manifestoes and love declarations of the uniqueness of African cinema and African visual identity books. Articles and journals have been written by many scholars using headings such as the Aesthetics of African Cinema, The Griot Cinema, The Bush Cinema. We have seen many paradigms and correlations to other African artistic mediums. While the debate is sound and convincing in appearance, by and large, in my opinion, to this day, African cinema is a victim of fraudulent and false scholarship, a scholarly impersonation. At the end of the day we are left without any clue as to what constitutes an African cinematic language. Again and again, in the name of searching for the film's language, we are given a synopsis of social, political and cultural analysis of the film. What makes this a vicious circle is that since there are not many African films, we are subjected to a re-hashing, again and again, of the content of the same film, rather than the cinematic analysis of the film.

It is even sometimes an embarrassing moment in forums and panel discussions to utter questions dealing with African cinematic language, because African cinematic language, as a concept, is taken by this official creed of critics, to mean the spoken language of the character, that is, the dialogue delivered by the actors and actresses. Incidents such as this and the confusion that is triggered, suggest to me the underdeveloped state of film analysis within the confines of African cinema discourse. Cinema as a medium of sight and sound and a discipline of linguistic film analysis, is the clue to any form of comprehension of what an African cinema is about.

It is an historical fact that non-western societies from Japan to China and India have pushed the limits and boundaries of conventional cinema in order to accommodate their accent, social and cultural temperament. Isn't it an historical task for us to be interested in understanding and quantifying the linguistic aspect of Sembene Cinema? Ousmane Sembene is a Wolof-speaking Senegalese, fed and raised by a specific and particular Afro-Islamic society, a man who cut his teeth thinking, seeing and speaking Wolof within the environmental conditions of his culture.

Against all odds he grabs a medium of sight and sound and establishes himself as one of the leading, most prolific film-makers of Africa. With the great body of works Sembene has been able to accumulate, at no time are we taken to the aesthetic principles of Sembene's style of sight and sound. During all the years of analysis of Ousmane Sembene's work, by and large an injustice is done especially by those who loudly proclaim to have quantified his work in the context of African cinema language. Personally I can only register my dissatisfaction, in order hopefully to provoke the necessary logical dialogue between the critic and the film-maker.

Unbalanced content analysis exists. Yes, we have read the synopsis of the story many times – the political view and messages, the cultural context of the social relationships, the subtexts, the metaphor, the allegory, the state of the church, neo-colonialism – all crucial and critically relevant as far as the content of film is concerned. This is important especially in film dealing with the struggle against neo-colonialism in a way invisible to the ordinary eye.

Equally important is the struggle between opposing aesthetic values, between the coloniser and the colonised. Here I am not trying to separate form from content. It is not a contradictory struggle between form and content. We should be able to study form and content in the way that we understand biologically the complimentary and productive nature of our right and left leg, in order to understand the aesthetic aspect of content and form, in the medium of sight and sound, especially as it relates to the syntax of the cinematic language.

Film analysis as a discipline implies the task of a linguistic examination and an investigation of the aesthetic of sight and sound by breaking down the elements of the film, frame by frame, shot by shot, sequence by sequence and ultimately assembling the qualitative structure of the audiovisual codes and medium of cinema.

Throughout the world film-makers have been inventing, shaping and restructuring the multidimensional non-linear aspect of cinema in order to accommodate their own cultural voice in inventive cinematic tradition. In order to appreciate the film work it will be constructive for those interested in understanding the cinematic language of a given film, to be taken behind the scenes of the film project to see the years of research, the amount of mental and physical work that takes place behind the construction of the film project. Committed and creative film-makers work years in advance, under the most tedious of circumstances, nurturing the cinematic visual concept before imprinting it onto the film celluloid. From pre-production to post-production, in collaboration with different creative talents, they prepare the basics for artistic and creative conditions, in order to unleash the creative process, as well as the artistic process, activating the dynamic narrative of sight and sound around the visual concept.

In the pre-production stage especially, African film-makers not only struggle to raise the finance to undertake the given project, but take years of hard work and research to find and locate a visual concept. It's a period of total immersion, a time of extensive research, combing libraries, conducting popular interviews and surrounding oneself with the paraphernalia and all the materials related directly or indirectly to the subject matter at hand, in order to shape the visual idea and allow the subsequent growth and transformation of a collective creative process. A committed film-maker eats, drinks and sleeps around it. Film-makers who have chosen to neglect this are paying the price.

I feel justified in challenging the African film theoreticians, the self-proclaimed critics. I dare you to read the cultural, social and psychological grammar of my imperfect cinematic expression. I challenge you in the name of honesty and intellectual integrity to excavate a structural narrative of my sight-and-sound language. I dare you to lift the layers and unravel the visual subtext of my dramatic narrative, born sometimes as a result of my conscious effort, at other times sheer subconscious of a creative accident. I dare you to excavate the obvious and the subliminal, the metaphor and the abstract language of the soul, of the non-linear, zigzag imaginative mind. I dare you to break down my visual melody, my sometimes mediocre and at other times smooth rhythmic structure of sight and sound. I dare you to utter and qualify my imperfect sight and sound accent, quantifying to the spectator my primitive vertical image as well as the horizontal sound. Like me, I dare you to journey imperfectly, to explore and research the sight and sound assembly of the sometimes orderly, and other times disorderly, arranged sequences. I dare you to trace your intellectual footprint along the demolished Aristotelian linear narrative, in order to discover the multidimensional narrative concept of the wax and wane of old and of my ancestors. Enough of your rehashing the obvious message under the pretext of searching for the African cinema temperament and language. Roll up your academic buttoned-up sleeves, free yourselves, release first your honest self like the truly committed African film-maker; get down on your knees, submerge yourself inside the legacy of your ancestor storytellers. Dig deep down and idolise the different ingredients that make up the symphony of an African film narrative. Spend a quarter of the time that it took just to do the post-production aspect of the film. Don't forget it's a battle zone – the most decisive battle between the dominant and the dominated worlds. The battle is against the cultural snatchers. Your abstract, exotic headings might impress the foreigner, the academic tourist, the modern missionary, but not the film-maker.

Don't think I'm a very negative person. This is an honest and if possible constructive criticism, so that I as a film-maker can grow and transform from film to film. The African cultural movement, even if it mushroomed, could never amount to anything significant without equally developing a culture of critical analysis, alongside film production.

Two Responses to *Sankofa*

I   David Coplan

Haile Gerima's feature-length film, *Sankofa*, expresses with great visual and iconic power African-American views, both academic and popular, of the Atlantic Slave Trade and its legacy. In this the film is certainly instructive (if not precisely rewarding), and South Africans of all backgrounds would do well to familiarise themselves with the ideological uses of slavery in American discourses on race, colonialism, "multiculturalism", and their representations. Any commentator must first understand, with the most profound reflexive sensitivity, the unhealing wound of slavery and its consequences in African-American constructions of history, an indissoluble mix of self-perception and perceptions of the oppressing, gender subsuming Other: the white man. Slavery, to be painfully brief, is both black Diaspora and Holocaust, both Babylon and Bergen-Belsen. Though auditors of this discourse who are not African-American, do, naturally, often respond differently to it, we must all understand at the outset that black people regard their own representations of slavery, such as this film, as unreproachably moral and beyond the reach of conventional modes of artistic criticism. Before one expresses criticism of this stance itself, one must ask whether a non-Jew could with impunity express artistic dissatisfaction with the Holocaust Museum in Washington to a Jew.

The story of *Sankofa* involves the visit of a self-alienated and corrupt black model to Cape Coast Castle in Ghana for a photo-shoot (complete with peroxide fright wig) with a white (read slave overseer/rapist) photographer. An Akan ritual priest and drummer, who patrols the castle as self-appointed venerator of the spirits of ancestors shipped off to slavery from its underground cells, expresses his disapproval of her desecration of the site in selling herself into shallow media sexual objectification. Fleeing in fright within the castle she is captured by the souls of slave ancestors and transported (pun intended) through the magic of the cinema into her own previous life as a slave on a New World plantation. From there on things get predictably harsh and harshly predictable. The slaves are brutally mistreated and ultimately rise in rebellion. Nonoo, an old spiritualist woman, plays mother to our disoriented model/slave and Mother Courage to the rest. A black overseer cannot live with his contradictions and switches sides. An insouciant, dreadlocked young hero inspired by an advanced political consciousness and the love of our model/heroine, leads the revolt. Our model, now a house slave, is raped repeatedly by her master in an appropriately bestial manner, though the fact that it is always him gives these episodes a kind of regularised, monogamous atmosphere. The son of old Nonoo, a blue-eyed mulatto overseer, held in mental slavery and physical degradation by Catholicism and the local white priest, is at once the most typical and extreme example of Gerima's realisation of character in the film. The product of a rape (of course) of Nonoo by a white man, the young man's infection by Christianity is the ideological parallel to his physical miscegenation by white blood. Despite his mother's expressions of love and encouragement, he is, needless to say, both infused with evil and devoured by self-hatred. He cannot escape the realisation that he is irredeemably a slave among fellow slaves for whom his very existence is an inherent affront. Not surprisingly, he murders the woman who bore him. The inescapable moral seems to be that the sons of such unions are guilty of the sins of their fathers, though by that measure an awful lot of African-Americans would stand self-condemned. That they do not is rather more a tribute to the sophistication of their self-articulation than Gerima would pay them.

But I digress. The point about Nonoo's matricidal son is that neither he nor any of the other characters ever supersedes their iconic, "representational" mode of being adequately to become, for this viewer, real people whose fate one might really care about. Perhaps regrettably, crimes against humanity have to be perpetrated against people who are seen and felt in action to be fully human, if other people against whom these crimes have not been committed are to respond to their enormity with genuine and appropriate emotion. In the same vein, the romantic, socially harmonious, essentialised Garden of Eden image of pre-colonial Africa, that here provides a frame and foil for the antithetical vision of slavery, is not one in which any non-African-American well acquainted with Africa and its history is likely to believe. *Sankofa* may quite understandably inspire African-Americans with a re-newed sense of outrage and solidarity, but is unlikely to inspire in even the most sympathetic Others much more than a polite respect for feelings they have not been moved to share. Admirers of the film may well respond that I do not understand. What I would like to know is: Do they think it is important that this, or any other work, should effect such understanding; or is in-group conscientisation and out-group acquiescence (if, in practice, they get it) enough?

II   Bridget Thompson

This Ghanaian term for a bird which looks into the past as a guide to the future could not be more apt as the title of this gut-wrenching film. Haile Gerima's *Sankofa* exposes the pain in the origins of black American culture at the same time as it releases the viewer into a new and deeper understanding of the utter degradation of the Atlantic Slave Trade and slavery on the plantations. It speaks directly to the haunted souls of Americans and Africans, both black and white, who deny this history. Haile Gerima produced, wrote, directed and edited *Sankofa* in a nine-year quest to tell this story his way and in the short time since he premiered it in Los Angeles to a weeping black and white audience it has been taken up as part of a healing project.

The new culture forged between people from different parts of Africa in response to the collective trauma of slavery still resonates 400 years later. Witness the international response to the Rodney King incident in Los Angeles where black people in ghettos in the United Kingdom and Canada responded with deep-seated anger to the news. Witness too the warmth, strength, resilience and insight of many black women, who hark back to the archetypal mother figure in *Sankofa*, Nonoo. Maya Angelou, Alice Walker and the many, many black women who have nurtured this nation under conditions of terrible personal deprivation, come to mind.

The film is set mainly on a plantation in the Caribbean at the height of the Slave Trade. It opens and closes with contemporary scenes set in a slave fort on the West Coast of Africa – present day Ghana. However, I found these scenes, and the transition from and to them, less cinematically convincing than the core narrative in which diverse characters, each archetypal in their own way, are thrust together by the circumstances of slavery and play out a story of collaboration, solidarity and resistance, which cuts to the essence of what it means to be a human being.

The slave overseer, who in his moment of transition to solidarity with the resistance, evinces what seemed to me to be the proto-lie-smile, the young girl a victim of media rape in the contemporary story becomes the witness in the core story – where her slave persona is repeatedly subjected to rape by the master until, strengthened by the wisdom and strength of Nonoo, she resists. As a "house-nigger" she witnesses the pain and suffering and solidarity culture of the other slaves, but is never accepted by them until she actually resists too.

Nonoo – in real life a Ghanaian princess – a West African princess captured as a slave, inspires love and adoration on the plantation in all but her son – a light-skinned blue-eyed product of rape, who has been nurtured since babyhood by the local Catholic priest into despising his mother. He is tortured by a sense of inferiority so profound that he aspires towards Christianity to sublimate his feelings and deny the oppression he experiences as a slave and perpetuates as an overseer.

The relationship between him and his mother evokes the cultural struggle of our country by highlighting the psychological devastation wreaked by denial of that which we love.

Sankofa is an extraordinary inspiration, but we need South African healing films too.

The Legacy of Suffering
The African Slave Past in
Contemporary West African Literature

Obi Maduakor

Africa my Africa
Africa of proud warriors in ancestral Savannahs
Africa of whom my grandmother sings
On the banks of the distant river
I have never known you
But your blood flows in my veins
Your beautiful black blood that irrigates the fields
The blood of your sweat
The work of your slavery
The slavery of your children
Africa tell me Africa
Is this you this back that is bent
This back that breaks under the weight of humiliation
This back trembling with red scars
And saying yes to the whip under the midday sun.
(Diop 29)

Africa of "proud warriors in ancestral Savannahs" of which the Senegalese poet, David Diop, has hymned a dirge is a continent harassed, brutalised and tortured by history. She has suffered from slavery and from colonialism and is currently attempting to rear her head against the monster of neo-colonialism. The latest phase in the history of oppression manifests itself in the conspiracy of the G-7 nations against the economy of the Third World, which has reduced the paper money of most Third World countries to a worthless trash. The currency of Third World countries has been so devalued that only a basket load of it can match the worth of a single US dollar. Of these three cycles of historical victimisation, slavery is perhaps the most horrifying. It denies the individual of his or her human dignity and treats him or her as a mere commodity. The lot of the slave has been summarised by Suzanne Miers and Igor Kopytoff in their study of the phenomenon:

> He has no control over his destiny, no choice of occupation or employer, no rights to property or marriage and no control over the fate of his children. He can be inherited, moved or sold without regard to his feelings, and may be ill-treated, sometimes even killed, with impunity. Furthermore, his progeny inherit his status. (3)

The Western world's enslavement of the black man is as old as history itself. As far as West Africa is concerned, historians have noted that Portuguese adventurers seeking trade contacts with the West coast of Africa established trading posts on the Gold Coast (modern Ghana), the Congo basin and the island of Sao Thome in the 1430s and 1440s. Elmina Castle in the present day Ghana, the first West African trading post, was built by the Portuguese in 1440. The Portuguese prospected initially for gold, silver, ivory, spices in exchange for salt, copperware and textiles. But soon this legitimate trade was replaced with human trade. Portuguese bandits seized Africans as slaves and transported them to sugar plantations in their home country. Soon they discovered the lucrative trans-Atlantic route and shipped hundreds of thousands of African slaves to the Americas. Between 1450 and 1600 over one million African slaves had been ferried across. In the seventeenth and eighteenth centuries the English, the French, the Dutch and the Spaniards joined the trade which had become a profitable economic business for Europe. By the 1820s, over twelve million African slaves were shipped to the Americas from the West African coast.

But the Europeans were not the only exploiters of the African slave labour. The Arab depredation of Sub-Saharan Africa had been going on since 800 A.D. African slaves built the Byzantine empire and the Egyptian pyramids. By the end of the eighteenth century more than seventeen million African slaves had been transported to the Islamic countries of North Africa, Arabia and India.

Some African historians claim that the exact casualty suffered by Africa from the combined onslaught of slavery and colonialism is yet to be ascertained. Some put the figure to 130 million lives. It is this tradition of plunder and devastation, to which the black African native has been subjected first by the Arab predators and secondly by the white destroyers, that I have designated as the legacy of suffering. How has this tragedy been reflected in our literature?

In the eighteenth century a few emancipated West African slaves had occasion to embody their slave experience in imaginative literature. Phillis Wheatley wrote some religious and secular poetry of outstanding merit. Ignatius Sancho, known then as the foremost man of letters, wrote verse, dramatic pieces, *The Theory of Music*, criticisms and judgement on painting and letters that have been collected and published as *The Letters of Ignatius Sancho*. Ottoba Cugoano and Olaudah Equiano wrote political tracts against slavery. Of these writers Equiano is the best known. His book, retitled *Equiano's Travels* and currently regarded as the beginning of the modern West African novel, narrates the pathetic story of his capture at the tender age of eleven, of the several times he was sold and resold, before he came to the harrowing experience of the middle passage in an execrable slave ship. The overcrowding within the despicable vessel, the suffocation, the perspiration and the loathsome stench on the deck took a huge toll on the human cargo.

Equiano conceived his book as part of the abolitionist literature of the period and wrote with passion and conviction as he sought to expose the trials of the victims of the slave trade. Whipping was the stock-in-trade of the slave masters. Equiano speaks of how he and other slaves were bound hand and foot and flogged severely at the slightest provocation.

Slaves were branded with the initial letters of their master's name and had their necks locked up with a load of heavy iron hooks. The iron muzzle and thumbscrews were familiar instruments of torture and punishment. Female slaves were sexually violated. Families were separated in the endless round of sale and resale during which wives were taken from their husbands and children from their parents. Equiano stresses that slaves preferred death to their condition. During the middle passage many slaves jumped overboard into the sea to be drowned. He appeals to the Christian conscience of a supposedly Christian nation, urging them to realise that slavery brutalises human nature and contravenes God's law:

> Such a tendency has the slave trade to debauch men's mind and harden them to every feeling of humanity! It is the fatality of this mistaken avarice that it corrupts the milk of human kindness and turns it into gall. Surely this traffic cannot be good, which spreads like a pestilence and taints what it touches! Which violates that first natural right of mankind, equality and independence and gives one man a dominion over his fellows which God could never intend! (73)

Paul Lovejoy writes in his book *Transformations in Slavery* that violence is the distinctive hallmark underscoring the relationship between the master and his slave (3). *Equiano's Travels* is replete with several instances of brutal violence. Slave culture is of course nurtured upon violence. David Diop, in the prefatory verse above, responds to the violence of plantation slavery: the sweat and hot blood of forced labour, the tottering back sagging under the weight of heavy burdens, lacerated with bloody scars and cracking with the whips of humiliation. These images tell the story of the inhuman degradation inherent in slavery.

Negritude poets insist on discovering glory even in the gory history of the past. If that past is brutalised by slavery, what the poet does is to defy that brutality. Diop is not allowed by the aesthetic of Negritude ideology to dwell at length on the ignominy of the past or dissociate himself from it. The attempt to do so earns him the mild rebuke: "impetuous son".

> But a grave voice answers me
> Impetuous son that tree young and strong
> That tree there
> In splendid loneliness amidst white and faded flowers
> That is Africa your Africa
> That grows again patiently obstinately
> And its fruit gradually acquire
> The bitter taste of liberty. (29)

The poet has to identify himself with his slave past and must look forward to the regeneration (freedom) that will emerge from that degradation. The impetuous son who tends to shrink from his history must learn to appreciate the heroism of the human spirit rebelling against oppression. Aime Cesaire, who wrote a few decades before Diop, comes to that same conclusion:

> in vain does the captain have the most troublesome nigger hanged from the yard-arm, or overboard, or fed to his mastiffs. In their spilt blood the niggers smelling of fried onion find the bitter taste of freedom. (88)

But it is the very damnation in the slave past that caused Soyinka to question the Negritude poet's glorification of that past. How can there be glory in a past that is damned, the more so as the African himself had contributed to the damnation? In *Equiano's Travels*, the author, while not exonerating the brutality of his European captors, hinted at "the violence of the African slave-dealer". In Soyinka's play, *A Dance of the Forests*, written to commemorate the attainment of nationhood for many African countries in the sixties, Soyinka warned the new independent nations not to be carried away by the euphoria of independence. The characteristic feature of the totem that marks this event is violence. The totem, rooted to the earth (the past) and piercing through to the heavens (future) is an emblem for human bestial and criminal passions. To illustrate the violence of the past, the action of the play unwinds several centuries backwards to the Kingdom of Emperor Mata Kharibu in the eighth century. Mata Kharibu's kingdom is the prototype of such ancient kingdoms as Mali and Songhai celebrated by Negritude. "The accumulated heritage . . . that is what we are celebrating. Mali. Chaka. Songhai. Glory. Empires", intones the Court Orator, Adenibi. But this kingdom is riddled with violence and corruption. The Emperor sentences to slavery a gallant warrior who refused to commit his troops to a war of blame. After the men had been condemned, an unscrupulous slave-dealer makes himself handy to collect the cargo with his rickety vessel to the moral outrage of the court physician:

> I know the man of old, and I know the slight coffin in which he stuffs his victims. He knows how to get them down alive; it is his trade. But until he nears the slave-market, the wretches have gone through twenty torments of hell. (52)

All the African writers that have treated the theme of slavery (from Equiano through Ouologuem to Armah and Ama Ata Aidoo) have implicated the African middlemen in the trade.

In his adaptation of *The Bacchae of Euripedes*, Soyinka returns to the theme of slavery but focusing attention this time on the enslavement of the African during the period of ancient classical civilisations. The slave leader in the play, Soyinka insists, must be played by a character who is "fully negroid". The slaves are used in the play as carriers in the rites of initiation and purification. Old Man, an ancient eunuch in Pentheus' household, was marked out as the sacrificial victim for the New Year cleansing rites. The procedure for such ceremonies was to have the victim sprinkled with ash before he was flogged to death.

The liberation of all those condemned to every form of slavery was the principal purpose of Dionysus' mission to Thebes. The slaves, the helots, the women, waited anxiously for the manifestation of the new god of freedom. The slaves regained their freedom at the death of that symbol of dictatorial authority, Pentheus.

The consciousness of the African slave past is marginal, surprisingly, to the preoccupation of Nigerian literature. When Achebe had documented the history of our colonial past in two major novels set in the past, Nigerian writers felt that the task of engaging the past in an imaginative dialogue had been satisfactorily accomplished. There has been no comparable sortie into the past by any other Nigerian writer since Achebe.

The Malian poet, Yambo Ouologuem, is the first West African writer to attempt what must be regarded as the most comprehensive investigation of the African slave past in fiction. Eight hundred years of oppression and victimisation of the black Africans of the Nakem Empire called the "Niggertrash" were uncovered in his epic novel, *Bound to Violence*, beginning with the reign of the first Nakem dynasty in 1202 and extending to the outbreak of the Second World War.

The Nakem emperors unleashed a reign of violence and terrorism upon the black populace within their Kingdom. Claiming Jewish descent they regarded the black communities as things to be exploited. Under the reign of one of the most wicked of the emperors, Saif al-Haram, an unprecedented orgy of violence ensued throughout the empire and its dependencies. Al-Haram intensified slave trade. Thousands of innocent black children were massacred in the course of the horrendous raids. Captured slaves were roasted alive and eaten. The women's sexual parts for obvious aphrodisiac intent were reserved for the notables as special delicacies. The women prisoners were collectively raped and men were castrated. Under Al-Haram, over 100 million African slaves were carried away, flogged, stockpiled, bound in bundles of six, shorn of all human dignity and flung into dingy ship holds and delivered to the Portuguese, the Spaniards, the Arabs, the French, the Dutch and the English.

In their pursuit of excesses in villainy and sadism the Saifs did not spare themselves. Saif Al-Haram murdered his brother and married his father's four wives among whom was his own mother. He died in the process of indulging himself sexually with the four women at the same time:

> On April 20, 1532, on a night soft as a cloak of moist satin, Saif al-Haram, performing his conjugal "duty" with his four stepmothers seriatim and all together, had the imprudent weakness to over-indulge and in the very midst of his dutiful delights gave up the ghost. (16)

As with their sadistic histrionics, the political acrobatics of the Nakem emperors was truly heroic. The last of the emperors, Saif ben Isaac al-Heit, like his predecessors, master juggler, necromancer and sorcerer, and an adept in the art of deception, duplicity and political expediency, outwitting and out-manoeuvering the French who were duped and poisoned; for in dealing with their victims the Nakem emperors stopped at nothing: they invoked black magic and witchcraft. Muslim to the core, Isaac al-Heit embraced Christianity when it suited his fancy. In order to win favours and privileges from the French he recruited the Niggertrash into the French army at the outbreak of the First World War by evoking their allegiance to the Christian doctrine of immortality and resurrection Saif announced to the soldiers:

> that if they died in battle they would live again in their former tribes, "their souls sevenfold more pure than the dawn at the time of the morning prayers". (117)

In his return to several centuries of African past, Ouologuem is holding up an alternative image of the past to Negritude ideology and Pan-Africanism:

> . . . the legend of Saif Isaac al-Heit still haunts Black romanticism and the political thinking of the notables in a good many republics . . . (8)

Probably because of the continuing physical presence of the Elmina Castle on the Ghanaian coastline, the African slave past is deeply embedded in the subconscious of many Ghanaian writers. The Elmina Castle features in their work even when those works are not primarily devoted to the theme of slavery. In Ayi Kwei Armah's *The Beautyful Ones Are Not Yet Born*, the rulers of the new Ghana are guilty of the same crime perpetrated by the old slave master:

> After a youth spent fighting the white man, why should not the president discover as he grows older that his real desire has been to be like the white governor himself, to live above all blackness in the big old slave castle? (108)

In *Fragments* (1974) Armah evoked also "the white form of the old slave castle which had now become the proud seat of the new rulers" (44), adding that the worst crime might not have been the sins of old but the people's and the rulers' "ignorance of past crime" (44).

Armah's compatriot, Kofi Awoonor, is also haunted by the old slave castle. In his novel, *This Earth, My Brother* the castle is evoked with its historical association with slavery. The Leader slept there, we are told, and is ready to escape if there is a revolution through the same tunnels by which the slaves were shipped in ancient days to the Americas (27). Awoonor's latest novel, *Comes the Voyager at Last*, influenced by Alex Haley's novel, *Roots*, enacts the theme of the return of a Black American voyager to his roots in Africa. The hero, Sheik Lumumba Mandela, was happily reunited with his past in the friendly welcome he received in Awoonor's family back in Africa. Through flashback Awoonor reveals the slave agonies of Lumumba Mandela's ancestors. There was a slave caravan moving laboriously from the desert Savannahs to the sea. Among the chained gang was Lumumba Mandela's ancestors, and an old man possessed with the gift of poetry who died of exhaustion from the tedious march, uttering magical incantations. The gang encountered on its way an ancient mother, sole survivor of a slave raid and symbol of mother Africa. She was hacked to death by the captors.

The dramatist, Ama Ata Aidoo, in her play *Anowa* writes of "Those forts standing at the door/Of the great ocean" which "shall remind our children of our slave past/Of which the sea bear witness" (6). The play is based on the myth of Anowa, a beautiful girl, who refused the suitors approved by her parents and married a man she loved, but who sold his manhood to the devil in exchange for wealth. Ama Ata Aidoo works the theme of slavery into the legend. Anowa objects vehemently to her husband's trafficking with slaves on moral grounds: "I shall not feel happy with slaves around, Kofi. No man made a slave of his friend and came to much himself", she tells Kofi Ako (30). But Kofi Ako, who had stepped into the whiteman's shoes like the new African leaders in Armah and Awoonor's novels, is bent on playing the white man to the full. He is carried in a hammock by his slaves, is bedecked from toe to crown with gold jewellery and is surrounded by attendant slaves. The chorus, functioning as the dramatist's moral consciousness, reinforces Anowa's stand: "There must be something unwholesome about making slaves of other men, something that is against the natural state of man and the purity of his worship of the gods. Those who have observed have remarked that every house is ruined where they take in slaves." (39).

As a child Anowa had heard the story of the big stone house built by the white people to keep slaves. Her childish mind pondered on the role of African middlemen (like Kofi Ako) in the trade:

Did the men of the land sell other men of the land, and women and children to pale
men from beyond the horizon? (46)

The myth of Anowa (spelt Anoa in Armah) is one of the elements of folklore Armah
has appropriated in the construction of the story in *Two Thousand Seasons*. Anoa,
the Seer, the utterer of folk wisdom was a woman, in Armah's tortuous poetry,
"possessed by a spirit hating all servitude so fierce in its hatred it was known to
cause those it possessed to strangle those whose joy it was to force the weaker into
tools of their pleasure" (121). It was Anoa who predicted the coming of the Arab
predators and European destroyers and her people's subjection to one thousand
years of slavery under these two powers as a result of their neglect of their native
way of life, defined in the book as the way of reciprocal care-giving.

In dipping into the past to uncover 1 000 years of Arab and European enslavement
of people of black Africa, Armah is following the example of Ouologuem. And as
in Ouologuem, the two phases of white domination were characterised by violence,
greed, robbery and sexual gluttony. The white destroyers, not content with the
spoliation of native resources, organised a massive transportation of the African
slaves into the plantations in the Americas: "The white men have come here wishing
to buy humans, to buy women among us, to buy men among us, to buy children
among us and take them to unknown lands. In return they will reward the King and
his courtiers with gifts." (129).

Armah is critical of the complicity of the representatives of Islamic and Christian
religions in the politics of exploitation, but he is hardest on those African traitors
that betrayed their own kith and kin by collaborating with the invaders. These
traitors called "zombis", "ostentatious cripples", and "askari zombis", have been
seduced with the attraction of "shiny things" in the form of privilege, gifts or power.

One healthy development in Armah's story of the African tragedy is that his
characters, unlike Ouologuem's, resist oppression so unlike the passive visionaries
of his first two novels. Such characters presage the birth of the "Beautyful" ones,
and are regarded as heroes : Idawa, Abena, the women of the harem, Isanusi and
members of the revolutionary vanguard of "the Way". The women of the harem
were instrumental in the successful overthrow of the first phase of Arab domination,
and the youths of "the Way", staging a successful mid-sea revolt against their
captors, constituted themselves into a revolutionary task force dedicated to the
destruction of the destroyers and their agents.

But this revolutionary task force is by no means less vulnerable to the attraction
of material things than the zombis. They were tricked into the slave ship in the first
instance by greed: "The things it lit [moonlight] stood out in accusation against us,
against our greed, against our blindness, against the ease with which we had let
ourselves slide into doom." (173). Is Armah saying that there is no future for African

revolutionary movements if the core itself is made up of men so greedy, so obtuse and so devoid of foresight, as members of this commando task force? The fact of their success in the act of liberation itself would negate this suspicion.

The African slave past is currently in the news as a result of a modern form of slavery – economic slavery or market colonialism. African nations grappling with the problem of foreign debt and balance of payment difficulties resurrect the ghost of the slave past. African leaders call upon the West to relieve the debt burden by paying reparation in respect of the damage done to the continent during the era of slavery and colonialism. But this call is bedevilled by the present situation of slavery in most African dictatorships. In Soyinka's *A Dance of the Forests*, dictatorship (in the imagery of the triplet with "an overblown head") was one of the plagues predicted in the emerging African nations. The antics of the monster with over-blown head are featured prominently in two studies of dictatorship by Soyinka, *Kongi's Harvest* and *A Play of Giants*. Ghanaian writers juxtapose the past form of slavery with the present mode by emphasising the continuing relevance of the old slave castle in the present Ghanaian polity. Armah insinuates an overt analogy in *Fragments* with the work done by Baako for Ghanavision, *The Root*, which deals with slavery. Rejecting the work, the Director of Ghanavision says: "We're a free, independent people. We're engaged in a glorious culture, and that's what we're here to deal with." (209) This rhetoric recalls the glib oratory of the court orator in *A Dance of the Forests*. Baako's reply to the Director of Ghanavision is that "slavery is a central part of [our inherited] culture" (209).

Literature of the slave past mourns Africa as a doomed continent, plundered and betrayed by human greed. The writer with historic sense recovers the past in its totality, implicating the African himself as a junior partner in the plunder, and juxtaposing the past with the present in an ironic commentary on the recurrent cycle of human violence. Here in South Africa history is repeating itself. Sponsored violence is undermining the current effort to dismantle another form of slavery.

Part Three

FUTURE DIRECTIONS AND CONCLUSIONS

Cultural Identity, Cultural Studies in Africa and the Representation of the Middle Passage

Brenda Cooper

How did the triangle of this paper's title emerge? We ran a conference in the Centre for African Studies in September 1993, in order to deliberate on the question of the nature of cultural studies in an African context, broadly defined, and within the University of Cape Town. What became clear was the lack of a concrete understanding of what constitutes an appropriate methodology and content for African Studies curricula.

Simultaneously, the issue of the representation of slavery developed as another important question in the conference, with the screening of Haile Gerima's film, *Sankofa*, and his presentation on the topic, reproduced earlier in this book. Coincidentally, I was due to visit Ghana in March 1994, where I was part of an expedition to the slave forts at Elmina and Cape Coast. Time renders history's horrors commonplace and habitual. Like the Holocaust, slavery recedes into cliché. The visit to the slave forts was timely, ghastly and moving, foregrounding afresh the terrifying nature of human atrocity. At the same time as remembering and grieving, however, there has to be a way of conceptualising these historical tragedies without doing further damage by misinterpreting them.

Part of the insight into the way to achieve this analysis was to be aware of the differences in response to the slave forts on the part of the African-Americans and

Africans, who were on the expedition. These historical differences led to the question of the nature of cultural identities in the postmodern era of late capitalism. The theoretical foundation of this paper shows that answers to this question of identity cannot be found within ethnic and essentialist definitions of race and culture, but have to be sought within what Colin Bundy called for in chapter two of this book – a reconstituted Marxism.

A bridge between the responses of Africans and African-Americans was Syl Cheney-Coker, a Sierra Leonean Creole, whose novel I had just finished reading before the trip to Ghana, and who was present in Accra. He agreed to being interviewed and he explained, articulately, how for him, and unlike other Africans, the middle passage begins his history. It is primarily by way of his writing that I will be applying the theory under discussion to the representation of slavery.

In this way, this paper is designed to bring together a range of the concerns of this book. I will begin with a few theoretical propositions, apply these to a fictional representation of the middle passage and then conclude with some questions about the nature and scope of African Studies within the African continent in general and at the University of Cape Town specifically.

Totality and national cultural identity

The theoretical argument following will lead from the acceptance of Marxist structures and social determinations, to the rejection of identity politics, precariously positioned within the postmodern labyrinth of innate difference.

When Colin Bundy calls for a reconstituted Marxism, the keyword he uses to describe it is "totality" – "Marxists should be prepared – let me take a deep breath here – to defend the totalising powers of Marxist analysis" (page 38).

In similar vein, Fredric Jameson, in his *Postmodernism or the Cultural Logic of Late Capitalism*, declares his own war on the "war on totality", on the "so many people" who are "scandalized" by his attempts to "map a totality". He insists that

> the positing of global characterizations and hypotheses, the abstraction from the 'blooming, buzzing confusion' of immediacy, was always a radical intervention in the here and now and the promise of resistance to its blind fatalities. (400)

Along with its rejection of totalities of all kinds, postmodernism is often associated with "a logic of difference or differentiation" (342). Both Lovell and Comaroff, in their chapters in this collection, are concerned about, and critical of, this barrage of difference at the expense of any form of unity or organisation (or "totality" as we are conceptualising it here).

There is a perplexing contradiction here within postmodernism. In a cultural style that utterly rejects cores, kernels and hearts, whose metaphors instead are labyrinth, migrancy and layers, there has been a resurgence of asserted intrinsic human essences and identities. If there is indeed a Tower of Babel of multiple babbling tongues, these tongues appear to group together into bigger and smaller formations of absolute, inviolate and indelible core difference.

Perhaps the perplexing contradiction would be better described as an important paradox, what Jameson calls "the paradoxical combination of global decentralization and small-group institutionalization" which "has come to seem an important feature of the postmodern" (408).

Stuart Hall, writing from Britain, has discussed this phenomenon in almost identical terms. Hall has questioned: "What is happening to cultural identity in late-modernity? Specifically, how are national cultural identities being affected or displaced by the process of globalization?" (Hall 1992: 291). He describes the incorrectness of the assumption that, with globalisation, "the sorts of thing which would be 'melted away'", would be "the irrational attachments to the local and the particular, to tradition and roots, to national myths and 'imagined communities'" (314). Instead, with ever more intricate and intertwined networks joining the world together, there is a simultaneous resistance to cultural homogenisation and a revival of interest in the local and the ethnic.

Hall suggests in the same article that the "general impact" of globalisation "remains contradictory":

> Some identities gravitate towards . . . "Tradition", attempting to restore their former purity and recover the unities and certainties which are felt as being lost. Others accept that identity is subject to the play of history, politics, representation and difference, so that they are unlikely ever again to be unitary or "pure" . . . . (309)

There is, then, an uneven development, ranging from the celebration of migration and hybridity, to the "proliferation of new identity-positions" as well as "the strengthening of local identities" (308).

In other words:

> The trend towards "global homogenization", then, is matched by a powerful revival of "ethnicity", sometimes of the more hybrid or symbolic varieties, but also frequently of the exclusive or "essentialist" varieties . . . .(313)

Hall is adamant as to the problematic nature of these more "essentialist varieties". He isolates and discusses five main elements of the "narrative of the national culture", which attempts to forge an essentialist identity via the race and the nation, which I will give in summary (the emphasis in each case is his). There is firstly the *"narrative of the nation"*, by which he means the "stories, images, landscapes, scenarios, historical events, national symbols and rituals which stand for . . . the shared experiences, sorrows, and triumphs and disasters which give meaning to the nation". There is secondly "the emphasis on *origins, continuity, tradition and timelessness"* and thirdly *"the invention of tradition"*. A fourth feature "is that of a *foundational myth"*. Hall explains the use of the term "myth" because "as was the case with many African nations which emerged after decolonization, what preceded colonization was not 'one nation, one people', but many different tribal cultures and societies". Fifthly "national identity is also often symbolically grounded on the idea of a *pure, original people or 'folk'"* (293–5).

Hall's example of new identity positions emerging "grouped around the signifier 'black'", will be relevant to us when we examine the representation of slavery. He describes how this new identity, in the British context, provides a new focus of identification "for *both* Afro-Caribbean and Asian communities" (308). This has also occurred in the United States with a strong resurgence of identification, not only around black, but around African, and a whole new generation of African-Americans clamouring for their "roots". I will suggest that they have forged a variant of the ethnic national cultural phenomenon, whose elements were described by Hall, in order to construct an essentialist, black, ethnic, African-American nation, which stretches back to Africa itself.

The representation of the middle passage

In an earlier 1990 paper (re-printed in a later collection) entitled "Cultural Identity and Diaspora", Hall focuses upon this essentialised identity that searches for lost roots in Africa. He does so in a wonderfully nuanced and compassionate manner, both rejecting this type of identity, but recognising the history and pain and need behind it. This will provide me with a mode of entry into the difficult areas of the nature of the representation of slavery and the appropriate methodology for a cultural studies in Africa.

Interestingly, Hall exemplifies his position through an analysis of "a new cinema of the Caribbean" which is emerging, thereby making his comments especially relevant to our discussion of the film, *Sankofa*. He contrasts "at least two different ways of thinking about 'cultural identity'". Within the terms of the first

> our cultural identities reflect the common historical experiences and shared cultural codes which provide us, as "one people", with stable, unchanging and continuous frames of reference and meaning, beneath the shifting divisions and vicissitudes of our actual history. This "oneness", underlying all the other, more superficial differences, is the truth, the essence, of "Caribbeanness", of the black experience. It is this identity which a Caribbean or black diaspora must discover, excavate, bring to light and express through cinematic representation. (Hall 1993: 393)

In this "oneness" of black experience, an imaginary Africa plays a critical role. Africa is represented "as the mother" of all the different black civilisations:

Africa is the name of the missing term, the great aporia, which lies at the centre of our cultural identity and gives it a meaning which, until recently, it lacked. No one who looks at these textural images now, in the light of the history of transportation, slavery and migration, can fail to understand how the rift of separation, the "loss of identity", which has been integral to the Caribbean experience only begins to be healed when these forgotten connections are once more set in place. (394)

In other words, before rejecting the flaws in this position, Hall stresses that "such a conception of cultural identity played a critical role in all post-colonial struggles which have so profoundly reshaped our world". We should therefore "not, for a moment, underestimate or neglect the importance of the act of imaginative redis-covery which this conception of a rediscovered, essential identity entails". It has "played a critical role in the emergence of many of the most important social movements of our time – feminist, anti-colonial and anti-racist" (393).

Ultimately, however, Hall does reject this essentialist identity, posing a second and contrasting one, with which he clearly identifies. This one recognises significant differences among and between black communities, "since history has intervened" ensuring "ruptures and discontinuities". Unlike essences, which are fixed and unchanging, this second view understands cultural identities as not already existing, "transcending place, time, history and culture" and as such "they undergo constant transformation" and "far from being eternally fixed in some essentialized past, they are subject to the continuous 'play' of history, culture and power" (394).

The contrast between the two positions is summed up as "not an essence but a *positioning*" (395 emphasis in original). This does not simply solve the problem of this complex identity issue and Hall has to question "if identity does not proceed, in a straight unbroken line, from some fixed origin, how are we to understand its formation?" (395). He answers this question by insisting on the simultaneous existence of two axes – one of "similarity and continuity" and another of "difference and rupture" (395). There are experiences, desires and pain in common, there are radical historical changes and differences constantly in the making.

The problem comes when only the one axis, that of "similarity and continuity" is emphasised to the exclusion of "difference and rupture". It is this view of the origins of culture or the nature of identity, within an African Studies programme, that I am resisting here. A good example of this problematic position, as I see it, is that taken by Gates (1988), a powerful, scholarly work that carries tremendous conviction.

The gist of Gates's argument is that "two signal trickster figures, Esu-Elegbara and the Signifying Monkey" are "separate but related" (xx). They are separate in that Esu "figures prominently in the mythologies of Yoruba cultures found in Nigeria, Benin, Brazil, Cuba and Haiti, among others", while the "Signifying

Monkey, it seems, is distinctly Afro-American" (xxi). Nevertheless, Gates is struck
by what he calls their shared "curious tendency" to "reflect on the uses of formal
language". Gates would in a sense have us believe that deeply embedded in black
culture, and surviving the middle passage from Africa, is a postmodern-like tendency to reflect on the form, the techniques, devices and language of its stories,
myths and culture. At the heart of this self-reflexivity is the strategy of play, of mask
and trick, of survival by wit. His book attempts

> to show through their functional equivalency that the two figures are related histori-
> cally and are distinct aspects of a larger, unified phenomenon. Together, the two
> tricksters articulate the black tradition's theory of its literature. (xxi)

Throughout the rest of the book, both theoretically and applied to black writers,
Gates illustrates this fundamental similarity in the black tradition globally. The
common role that Esu plays across all the different cultures in which he is found, is
as a figure of the indeterminacy of meaning, the fickleness of interpretation; he is a
"meta-linguistic device", pondering on the ambiguity and murkiness of all truths:

> Esu's hat is neither black nor white; it is both black and white. The folly depicted
> here is to insist . . . on one determinate meaning. (35)

One of Esu's hats emerges across the seas, originates in slavery and becomes the
Signifying Monkey. To signify is to play consciously with form, language and
performance.

Gates' book is brave and daring. However, the difficulties that I described much
earlier with postmodernism are here again interestingly and contradictorily combined with that of essentialism. Gates depicts as the essence of blackness the fact
that its tradition "is double-voiced". This is "epitomized by Esu's depictions in
sculpture as possessing two mouths" (xxv). In other words, the shifting, masking,
theatrically posing indeterminacy of life stops at the still point of a racial essence
that is ultimately an eternal truth of how blacks, the world over, ponder their being.
Esu's hat turns out after all to be unambiguously black.

Gates is not unsubtle. He is aware that "our [black] canonical texts have complex,
double formal antecedents, the Western and the black" (xxiv). He is aware that "the
degree to which the figure of the Monkey is anthropologically related to the figure
of the Pan-African trickster, Esu-Elegbara, shall most probably remain a matter of
speculation". Nevertheless he insists that they are related as "functional equivalents"
because "both figures function as repositories for a tradition's declarations about
how and why formal literary language departs from ordinary language use" (88).

I reject the existence of one, universal black tradition, given in the singular, and
have a deep distrust of repositories – conserving myths that freeze history into a
mould the shape of a coffin. By being fixated on a universal black tradition, Gates

ultimately refuses both history and the significance of factors such as gender or class.

Stuart Hall was theorising black diaspora identities. What he said applies profoundly to Gates. It applies also, but with more complexity, to the Sierra Leonean Creole novelist and poet, Syl Cheney-Coker, to whose representations of the middle passage I will now turn.

Syl Cheney-Coker, slavery and *The Last Harmattan of Alusine Dunbar*

Sierra Leoneans are, by definition, the syncretic result of cultural mingling between African, American, Caribbean and European cultures. The Creoles of Sierra Leone are descended from "liberated slaves who were racially and, often, culturally akin to the indigenous inhabitants, but who had also been exposed to Western culture" (Spitzer 3). This resulted in "a syncretism of African and European practices" on the part of "the majority of Creole society". And, in fact, says Spitzer, "there can be little doubt that in their everyday life most Creoles retained and mixed elements from traditional African culture with the ways of the West" (138).

This syncretism was not, as it probably never is, a smooth and seamless melting pot. It is this Creole identity crisis that leads Cheney-Coker in his poetry painfully to question:

> but from what plantation
> and from what people my rum
> in my country the Creoles drink only
> Black and White with long sorrows
> hanging from their colonial faces!
> (*Hydropathy* 8)

This cultural crisis leads to what Spitzer has called "defensive Africanization". Desperate for a means whereby they can "regain their self-respect and heal their battered race pride", the Creoles "began to search back in history" seeking "evidence of great deeds and past glories" (120).

Cheney-Coker's poem, Freetown, is a powerful example of the ambiguous recourse, in this search for rooted cultural identity, to a romanticised African cultural nationalism. I quote the first and third verses:

> Africa I have long been away from you wandering like a Fulani cow
> but every night
> amidst the horrors of highway deaths
> and the menace of neon-eyed gods
> I feel the warmth of your arms

centrifugal mother reaching out to your sons
we with our different designs innumerable facets
but all calling you mother womb of the earth
liking your image but hating our differences
because we have become the shame of your race
and now on this third anniversary of my flight
my heart becomes a citadel of disgust
and I am unable to write the poem of your life . . .

there are those who when they come to plead
say make us Black Englishmen decorated Afro-Saxons
Creole masters leading native races
but we wandering African urchins
who will return one day
say oh listen Africa
the tomtoms of the revolution
beat in our hearts at night
(*Freetown* 16)

Here is a cacophony of conflicting emotions. It is a poem about the inability to write
a poem of Africa. It is about being an African, but an "urchin", a wandering lost
child. It is a negritude praise poem to Africa, which follows the conventions of the
myth of the contrast between the horrors of the Western city of neon lights and
dangerous, killing highways and the safe, protective womb of Mother Africa,
encased in the beat of the tomtom and the blood pumped through the heart. There
is the double distance from this mother to whom the relationship is ambiguous – the
urchin is not merely an exile, struggling against the acculturation of being a "Black
Englishman", but is a Creole, struggling against the pressure of being the master of
"native" Africans, a Creole, however, who compares his wanderings to those of the
"Fulani cow". Concealed like a pearl in the misery of the poem's uncertainties is
the celebration of difference – the possibility that Africa is, in fact, a heterogeneous
continent of many parts, given "our different designs innumerable facets". But this
complexity is reduced, romanticised and homogenised within the problematic
image of us all being able to call Africa the "mother womb of the earth", an image
that is particularly problematic in gender terms.

In the enormously complex longer work of fiction, *The Last Harmattan of
Alusine Dunbar*, there is also both the reification and mythologising of Africa, as
well as a contradictorily profound rejection of such distortions. What is attempted
is to create the great tales of heroic deeds and glorious pasts via the story of ex-slaves
who return to Africa, through their difficult and courageous lives.

This is the weighty symbolic significance of the origin of the legend of the
founding families of Cheney-Coker's fictional Sierra Leone, called Malagueta, and

why such a legend is at the heart of the narrative structure. Cheney-Coker said as much in an interview that I conducted with him:

> By telling the history of what slavery produced in Sierra Leone, however fictional it was going to be, but along historical lines, I wanted to show how these remarkable people, in two hundred years (mind you its longer than two hundred years in my novel) did so much, not just for Sierra Leone but for West Africa. It was for me an act of celebration. I think in some ways I was trying to do what in a much larger context Derrick Walcott has done in his poetry. (Cooper 1994: 12)

However, the search for such myths and heroes, whether they are sought within a reified and distorted African past, or within the roots of the Creolisation attendant on slavery, will, in my view, always result in an ethnic type of smokescreen that tends to contaminate enlightened and sophisticated perceptions of class or gender difference, of real histories and complex struggles, struggles that are central to a Marxist analysis. Let us see how this is played out in the novel.

The long ancestral bridge: The middle passage and back to Africa

Like Marquez's *One Hundred Years of Solitude*, which clearly influenced it, *The Last Harmattan* is also a gripping, epic tale taking us through the generations. The long cycle of inhumanity and oppression that is historically re-enacted, is counter-balanced by the elite of strong, morally unwavering families – the founders of Malagueta, such as the Cromantines and the Martins, and later Thomas Bookerman, Phyllis Dundas and the Farmer brothers. For the most part originally slaves, they return to Africa and become the aristocracy of the new African settlement and symbolic of the human urge to justness, righteousness and freedom. They are mystically linked to the god-like Sulaiman the Nubian, otherwise known as Alusine Dunbar, who has supernatural powers and who foresees all the unfolding events of the novel, and to his daughter, also endowed with unnatural powers, Fatmatta, who alternates between fatal temptress and ultimately, her role as protector and keeper of the returnees.

There is a complex interlinking chain of stories within stories, of life histories, which link up in time and space. Parts to be played by various characters are mentioned before we meet them in the language of prediction. As we move through great cycles of repeated cruelty – slavery, colonialism, post-independence corruption, as we move across those "great landscapes of time" through the generations, we have to question whether we are in the mythical time of universal repetition or whether we are in the historical time of the possibility of political intervention. The cycle of greed and degradation is potentially broken with the retribution at the end of it, within the contradictory framework of the inevitability of prediction.

When she is still a slave in America, Fatmatta has the following vision:

> she saw a long ancestral bridge with a lot of people crossing from one end to the other, and suddenly everything was clear to her. Cut off from that coalescence of man and spirits, burdened by servitude, she had merely been fulfilling a destiny circumscribed by fate, by an old animated life rhythm that went round the universe like a great flame and then she knew that she would not die in the land of leeches but that she would return, shed all signs of degradation and abuse. Because by the persistence of its look, by the grave and reverential distance it put between itself and other turkeys, the great bird had come to take her home to that land where her navel string was buried. (67)

This extract presents a plot puzzle and also a summary of the tension in Cheney-Coker's portrayal of the return to Africa on the part of ex-slaves. The puzzle is why does he not allow Fatmatta the Bird-Woman, the character of the above quotation, who had been sold into slavery as a young woman, to return home? What is the symbolic significance of her being made to die on the boat back, to return only in order to be buried herself along with her birth cord in Africa? I think that the answer to that question is that the warning that Cheney-Coker is signalling from the outset is that the return to Africa is not going to be a fairytale of happy endings and ever afters.

At the same time, this complex sense of hard reality reveals its underbelly of essentialism and romanticisation. It is implied, with the approval of the omniscient narrator, that only in Africa is there the "coalescence of man and spirits", a belief that the novel will confirm when describing the events leading up to the birth of a central character, called "Garbage". This combined with the image of ancient life rhythms and the pull of the place where the "navel string was buried", reinforces the mystical view of a place as in the blood, of Africa as teeming with mysteries and spirits, of humanity as overtaken by an inflexible and autonomous blood rhythm.

At the beginning of the novel Sebastian Cromantine, who is still a slave, is haunted by a terrible dream and the voice of his father who is "a rootless man burdened by his inability to find a resting place" (9). He will only be at peace once he is buried in Africa and it becomes Sebastian's sacred mission to return father's bones to their origins. Already here is the tension. Sebastian is appropriately overwhelmed "as he tried to imagine the untried chasm of supposition that he had to cross to understand the world of his father" (14). He gains courage, however, as he evokes

> a lineage that was not defined by time, but by the spirit, by the force of all eternities and the running music of ancestral water that coursed through his blood. (14)

It is this ethnic essentialism that runs through this theme that I find so problematic. This spiritual lineage, the ancestral bridge, is a kind of blood knowledge, unmediated by experience or time. If his father's bones are his "Magic Lantern" gaining him admission to his father's past, then his weapon to protect and arm him for the journey is not "a gun" but "his bloody history" and his hope is "buoyed by the potency of the black man's sperm that had begun to explode and generate its force in the universal womb of woman" (14–15). The reality of the tragic and bloody history and of the separation between Sebastian and his father's knowledge, is radically contaminated by metaphors of blood, sperm and female, universal wombs. Woman, her body, her fertility and mothering as metaphor of the return, of the land, of the nation, problematically recurs entwined with the essentialised myth.

Cheney-Coker veers, however, contradictorily between Stuart Hall's two different versions of identity – the one essentialised and static, and the other historical and kinetic. No sooner does Cheney-Coker passionately espouse this ethnic essentialism than he humorously distances himself from it with the funny image of the passage back and the number of returnees, armed with bags of the bones of their dead,

> which they were hiding under their bunks so that the crew would not find them. During the periodic storms at sea, the rattling of the bones in the bags helped to reassure their owners that they would make it to the shore. (15)

Then again, the meeting between the locals and the returnees is wonderfully wise and subtle. The newcomers are unaware and ignorant of local customs as would obviously be the case, given that they have, for the most part, been born and bred in America. This ignorance becomes clear in their negotiations with the king. Sebastian asks for land "which they were prepared to farm, and pay him back from the harvest" (69). The king has to point out that this is not African custom: "'Here, no one owns anything, not even the stones,' the king replied." (70). He grants them all the land that they need to use, but there is no welcome for lost brothers and sisters. They are warned that this is conditional of their respecting "our laws and the men keep off our women" (70). Hands off our women is the clearest message that these are strangers and that their arrival is a tense one. Again no sooner has Cheney-Coker given this nuanced description than he has Sebastian dream

> that he had been in that country before, and that he knew all its history so that nothing was hidden from him, and he could retell all that had happened before. (70)

In this highly questionable vein, in line with the mythology of the spiritual ancestral bridge, the returnees discover "this dance which was part of a heritage that they had forgotten but was nevertheless in their blood" (97).

Then, again by contrast, Cheney-Coker writes the following wonderfully enlightened conversation between Sebastian and his son, Emmanuel. Sebastian acknowledges the history of distrust between the locals and returnees and the ideal, not yet realised, of the unity possible and desirable between them sometime in the future, when they have developed a shared history. This ideal is symbolised by the marriage of Isatu and Gustavius, a local and a returnee:

> "And why we don't mix too much with the people in the next town?" Emmanuel asked.
>
> "Because some is good, and dey come here and brung us food rice and beans, and before you was born your mother gives 'em lesson in crochet and make puppets for 'em. But the others bad, bad; dey attack us and burn down de first place we build, and sometimes dey come with white men to us, so we gotta fight."
>
> "But Gustavius married one of dem, and I call her auntie?"
>
> "Dat is what we want, son, dat one day we all marry each other, be de same people, speak de same language, and build up de place; because your grandfader told me before he died, he come from dis people and he asked me in a dream to dig up his bones and bring 'em back." (138)

Having said this, there is nowhere in the novel more revealing evidence of its multiple and taut allegiances, than in that marriage between Gustavius and Isatu and the circumstances surrounding the birth of their son, Garbage. Going against the injunction of the king and in the face of the prejudices and superstitions surrounding them, Gustavius and Isatu courageously marry and are deservedly happy. Isatu's knowledge of the local terrain – how to get food, shelter, water and protection from wild animals, of which the newcomers are, of course, ignorant – means that "she had virtually assured the survival of the exiles". Here is a different bridge from the ethnic ancestral one – Gustavius was happy that he had a wife "who respected the supernatural extremes of her world and had bridged theirs together" (188).

However, I take issue with Cheney-Coker when that supernatural world is romanticised as spiritually superior, as that coalescence between mortals and spirits, as the spiritual life-blood of humanity, which is lost away from Africa and can only be restored on returning and, more than that, by ritual cleansing of the impurities contracted in exile. Herein lies the suspect key to why the marriage is, highly symbolically and within the problematic gender metaphor, not blessed with a child. Only after being ritually cleansed of the contamination by the debris of an inferior foreign culture, can "the fecundity of the woman . . . respond to the male-power of the husband" (206). The child that is born is symbolically called Garbage.

This theme of contamination, ritual cleansing and roots is taken up by Haile Gerima in his film, *Sankofa*, about which I cannot go into any detail here, but by reference to which I would like to conclude this section.

David Coplan has summarised the story of *Sankofa* elsewhere in this volume as follows:

> The story of Sankofa involves the visit of a self-alienated and corrupt black model to Cape Coast Castle in Ghana for a photo shoot (complete with peroxide fright wig) with a white (read slave overseer/rapist) photographer. An Akan ritual priest and drummer, who patrols the castle as self-appointed venerator of the spirits of ancestors shipped off to slavery from its underground cells, expresses his disapproval of her desecration of the site in selling herself into shallow media sexual objectification. Fleeing in fright within the castle she is captured by the souls of slave ancestors and transported (pun intended) through the magic of the cinema into her own previous life as a slave on a New World plantation. (page 149)

The theme of the impurities of the diaspora, which have to be purged in Africa itself by way of return to spiritual roots, is the core, and for reasons already given, problematic, theme. The intervention of time, which Stuart Hall sees as an essential component to be acknowledged in a dynamic view of identity, is given in the film only as a degeneration. The insistence that that history should not be forgotten is obviously correct. The problem is that this can only occur once the major character has been reunited with Africa itself and with the African mother, exemplified by the character, Nonoo, who has never lost touch with her African roots. The film is predicated on the ultimate unity and intrinsic oneness of Africans and ex-slaves, a oneness that is lost only at the peril of one's spiritual wholeness.

Coplan, like Hall, acknowledges the terrible history of cruelty and oppression that slaves and their descendants suffered and cautions us with his question as to whether "a non-Jew could with impunity express artistic dissatisfaction with the Holocaust Museum in Washington to a Jew?" (page 149). At the same time, he states categorically, and correctly, that

> the romantic, socially harmonious, essentialised Garden of Eden image of pre-colonial Africa that here provides a frame and foil for the antithetical vision of slavery is not one in which any non-African American well acquainted with Africa and it's history is likely to believe. (page 150)

Gerima is bitterly critical of commentators who concentrate solely on the content of his film. By this I think he means two things. Firstly, film as a medium of sight and sound, demands that the skilled analyst breaks down "the elements of the film, frame by frame, shot by shot, sequence by sequence" and thereby "ultimately assembling the qualitative structure of the audiovisual codes and medium of cinema" (page 147). While this point is unarguably valid, it is also true that there is a fundamentally important core of shared belief in the essentialised "roots" perspective that was contradictorily expressed in Cheney-Coker's Alusine Dunbar and is unambiguously and passionately held in Gerima's film, *Sankofa* and likewise in Henry Louis Gates Jr's *The Signifying Monkey*.

The second aspect to Gerima's point about the limitations of restricting analysis to that of content relates to the issue of language. He makes films in order to construct "our [black] language and our thought processes":

> although Europe has dislocated them as a barbaric logic. Our sentences, and our utterance are all classified as barbarian and savage talk. So to assert our language, which is part of the revolution of the struggle, we have to introduce daily, however imperfect, our own accent, our own temperament, our thought processes, our way of seeing, into cinema. (page 145)

By language, Gerima refers to the deepest cultural expression of black people, who have to search for a voice, seize a space, within a racist and insulting European culture. He is embarrassed when "African cinematic language" is taken to mean simply and superficially "the spoken language of the character, that is, the dialogue delivered by the actors and actresses" (page 146).

Gates would concur with Gerima when he defines "'the speakerly text'" in relation to Zora Neale Hurston's novel, *Their Eyes Were Watching God*, as one that not only deploys rhetorical strategies and is aware of so doing, but, further, one in which these strategies themselves are central to the purpose of the text. In other words, "the narrative strategy signals attention to its own importance". And "Janie's quest for consciousness" in Hurston's novel, is the "very quest to become a speaking black subject" (181). We saw that this play on language, this metaphorical self-consciousness as a trickster device of black resistance, defines for Gates a universal black heritage. Moreover, this is precisely what I understand Gerima to be saying, both in his talk and his film.

For example, Gates notes the difference in the language spoken by Janie, the main character in the novel, and by her grandmother, Nanny:

> Nanny narrates her slave narrative in a linear, or metonymic, manner, with one event following another in chronological order. Janie, by contrast, narrates her tale in a circular, or framed, narrative replete with vivid, startling metaphors. (207)

He refuses, however, the fundamental difference in their histories, and ultimately in the histories of African and American blacks, of men and women, along with whatever fundamental similarities on the grounds of race or of humanity that they might share.

It is Hurston herself in her novel, who annihilates the perennial African grandmothers, the Nonoos of the negritude tradition, endlessly telling their stories around the fireside, the myths that conserve and perpetuate become the stagnant repositories of tradition. Hurston, whose protagonist does not mother children, refuses the metaphor of woman as the receptacle of social and biological reproduction, refuses to endow her own or her grandmother's body with the burden of reproducing the land and the species. She rejects the burden of her misguided granny, and the baggage these women carry of conservatism and essentialised race and gender. Zora Neale Hurston knows a whole lot more than her admiring critics. The revolutionary significance of her powerful and wonderful rejection of her grandmother's very being is radically significant. I must quote this magnificent passage in full:

> She hated her grandmother and had hidden it from herself all these years under a cloak of pity. She had been getting ready for her great journey to the horizons in search of *people*; it was important to all the world that she should find them and they find her. But she had been whipped like a cur dog, and run off down a back road after *things*. It was all according to the way you see things. Some people could look at a mud-puddle and see an ocean with ships. But Nanny belonged to that other kind that loved to deal in scraps. Here Nanny had taken the biggest thing God ever made, the horizon – for no matter how far a person can go the horizon is still way beyond you – and pinched it in to such a little bit of a thing that she could tie it about her granddaughter's neck tight enough to choke her. She hated the old woman who had twisted her so in the name of love. Most humans didn't love one another nohow, and this mis-love was so strong that even common blood couldn't overcome it all the time. She had found a jewel down inside herself and she had wanted to walk where people could see her and gleam it around. But she had been set in the market-place to sell. Been set for still-bait. When God had made The Man, he made him out of stuff that sung all the time and glittered all over. Then after that some angels got jealous and chopped him into millions of pieces, but still he glittered and hummed. So they beat him down to nothing but sparks but each little spark had a shine and a song. So they covered each one over with mud. And the lonesomeness in the sparks make them hunt for one another, but the mud is deaf and dumb. Like all the other tumbling mud-balls, Janie had tried to show her shine. (85–6)

The passion of the rejection is startling. By retaining a slave mentality, her grandmother becomes the oppressor, selling her own granddaughter back into bondage. There is no common blackness bonding them here. Granny becomes slaver. Slavery damaged, slavery changed and scarred human beings not all of whom sang the blues with a deepened insight and romance forged in the fires of pain. Some died, some never recovered their humanity. Such a one was Nanny.

Moreover, history separates the slaves and their descendents from Africans, who never travelled the middle passage. This is why Obi Maduakor should not be so surprised that "the African slave past is marginal . . . to the preoccupation of Nigerian literature" (page 157). Unless we are talking about a Syl Cheney-Coker, the middle passage was not undertaken by these African writers. It is only part of their history in a radically different sense by comparison with a Sierra Leonean Creole or an African American, who themselves are as different as they are similar. They might share fundamental experiences of racism, but these are mediated by the particularities of the societies in which they live, their privileged positions within those societies and their genders.

African studies, culture and some conclusions

If the theory and method that is being proposed for African Studies is this newborn Marxism, where does the nature, focus and scope of African Studies come in? Moreover, what is the appropriateness of centres of African Studies in Africa itself? African Studies arose out of a colonial situation and has its origins in such questionable areas as "Bantu administration". It was predicated on the otherness of so-called primitive societies, which captured the exotic interest of adventurers, colonisers and old style anthropologists. As Terry Lovell puts it in regard to African Studies – and distinguishing it from Woman's or Cultural Studies – "The colonial gaze generated a new discipline" (page 14). Does it not perpetuate a colonial mentality by retaining the area studies model, when your area is your own country and continent? And has a radicalised African Studies been appropriated from that old patronising mould?

I began this paper with a triangle of concerns – the theoretical middle ground, African Studies and the middle passage. I will conclude with a new triangle of issues, centred on the question of African Studies, but incorporating and pulling together all the foregoing strands. The following are starting points of the process of investigation, rather than answers to difficult and on-going questions: firstly, the question of African Studies within debates around the terms "postcolonial" and "the third world"; secondly, multidisciplinarity and the study of culture; thirdly, "standpoint knowledges", Marxism and politics.

It is not only appropriate, but urgent, that in Africa we consider what is distinctive about our continent and what is part of a pattern of Third World or postcolonial discourse. Even the terms themselves are unstable and their appropriateness repeatedly interrogated. We have to participate in this debate. Elsewhere I have written about the question of the use of the term "Third World". It is a contested concept and yet remains current because it serves a necessary descriptive purpose.[1]

I suggested that I am no longer certain that the generalised term "Third World" reflects economic realities. I accepted the powerful arguments of thinkers like Aijaz Ahmad who articulately rejects the way in which "difference between the First world and the Third is absolutized as an Otherness", the way in which "the enormous cultural heterogeneity of social formations within the so-called Third World is submerged". He insists, in relation to Asia, Africa and Latin America, that

> [t]hese various countries, from the three continents, have been assimilated into the global structure of capitalism not as a single cultural ensemble but highly differentially, each establishing its own circuits of (unequal) exchange with the metropolis, each acquiring its own very distinct class formations. (104)

However, I concluded that while in economic terms it is probably no longer possible to talk sweepingly about Third and First Worlds, I do think that the term still has effectivity as a cultural concept, particularly in relation to the urban intellectuals who produce the bulk of the literature and culture of their countries. This is not to accept a separation between issues of development and of culture. Culture still has to be understood in its global contexts, as well as in terms of its own complex specificities.

Their countries are those that have experienced Imperialism and also the racism which accompanied this Imperialism as a weapon of enslavement. In this situation the war of combat against the cultural hegemony of the First World continues not only to dominate the literary strategies, images, languages and forms of Third World intellectuals, who are not white, but in fundamental ways to define them as a grouping. Furthermore, and as I will be suggesting below, I think that it is precisely in the area of culture that African Studies can make its most powerful intervention.

The same objections have been levelled at the term "postcolonial", which I have also discussed elsewhere.[2] I referred to Anne McClintock, for example, who articulately describes what she sees as the pitfalls of an embracing concept of "postcolonialism". For her, it simplifies and distorts those complex differences, reinforcing binary thinking by reorienting "the globe once more around a single, binary opposition: colonial/post-colonial":

> "post-colonialism" . . . is unevenly developed globally. Argentina, formally inde-
> pendent of imperial Spain for over a century and a half, is not "post-colonial" in the
> same way as Hong Kong (destined to be independent of Britain only in 1997). Nor
> is Brazil "post-colonial" in the same way as Zimbabwe. Can most of the world's
> countries be said, in any meaningful or theoretically rigorous sense, to share a single
> "common past", or a single common "condition", called "the post-colonial condi-
> tion", or "post-coloniality"? (294)

The significant historical and cultural differences between countries that were once colonised is fundamental and undeniable. And here a kind of kaleidoscopic thinking emerged. Looked at from one angle, and with a particular set of issues and questions in mind, the pattern that emerges is significant differences between societies that were once colonised. Looked at from another angle, and never forgetting those differences, the pieces rearrange to show the simultaneous existence of similarities.

Again, Stuart Hall expresses this articulately in relation to his native West Indies. He describes how

> [v]isiting the French Caribbean for the first time, I also saw at once how different
> Martinique is from, say, Jamaica: and this is no mere difference of topography or
> climate. It is a profound difference of culture and history. And the difference *matters*.
> It positions Martiniquains and Jamaicans as *both* the same *and* different. (1993: 396)

He continues that "we are very much 'the same'" in that "we belong to the marginal, the underdeveloped, the periphery, the 'Other'". He concludes crucially that

[a]t different places, times, in relation to different questions, the boundaries are re-sited. They become, not only what they have, at times, certainly been – mutually excluding categories, but also what they sometimes are – differential points along a sliding scale. (1993: 396)

Like Hall's study of the West Indies, it is a fundamental task for African Studies to delineate what is unique and distinctive about Africa; it is also imperative to distinguish differences within Africa itself, given how heterogeneous a continent it also is; simultaneously, it is necessary to have a global, international perspective that can also perceive Africa's position within the Third World.

In other words, and in conclusion on this first prong of exploring the nature of African Studies, it is in excavating those similarities and the significant differences among and between African countries and Third World territories, that we can carve out a focus and a terrain. The language of terrains leads to the question of disciplines and territoriality.

African Studies is, by definition, not restricted to any one discipline. At the same time, it cannot simply become a conglomerate of disciplines concerned with Africa, on a kind of "pick and mix" basis.

Interestingly, both Jean Comaroff and Terry Lovell expressed reservations about the jettisoning of disciplinary boundaries, while endorsing the validity of interdisciplinarity. Jean Comaroff says that she has "benefitted from the permissive interdisciplinary climate of the moment" (page 43) but insists that "we still need a division of intellectual labor" but it has to be the kind of division of labor that encourages "openness to multiple discourses" (page 43). However, she is "still anxious, as an anthropologist, to preserve something of the special legacy of my discipline" (page 44).

Terry Lovell, whose paper is entitled "The Burden of the Disciplines" argues "against the burden of my title" in making the point that "the disciplines are less burdensome than they once were; that interdisciplinarity carries its own burdens" (page 26).

African Studies makes no sense if it simply duplicates the work of the Africanist disciplines. Its area of focus has to be those concerns that cannot be studied in any other way than through the insights that cut across the boundaries of the traditional disciplines. It is for this reason, I think, in searching for an appropriate focus, that we in the Centre for African Studies at the University of Cape Town are increasingly moving into the cultural studies area. And by culture I am speaking about the more broadly defined, way of life, as well as, more narrowly, the arts, literature, film and so on.

I cannot go into detail regarding this huge issue of culture and its definitions here, but I think that the necessity for drawing boundaries, albeit within an interdisciplinary framework, is what Lovell was referring to when she mentions "African studies as it has been practiced at the University of Cape Town". She was basing her argument on what she had seen and heard at the conference, which is also reflected in this publication. She perceived the standpoint knowledge commitment exemplified by the dominance of "Marxist oriented historiography" and feminism, but she was concerned about what she saw as an insistence "on the necessity of addressing African literature and art within the same frame as African history, economics, politics" (page 26). The main problem here is that

> [i]n principle, this architectonic structure of theory might include culture, language and gendered subjectivity. But it provided little by way of concepts and theory to guide these inclusions . . . . (page 27)

In other words, a reconstituted Marxism, harnessed to an African cultural studies, has to develop the language and concepts to deal with the specificity of cultural concerns, which are not identical with those of historians or economists.

This leads directly to the third point, which is that Marxism, whether reconstituted, reborn or diehard, has to be a politics as well as a theory of history, society or culture. As Lovell points out in Britain, but also here in South Africa, "radicalised African Studies from the 1960s", (i.e. contrasting with the colonial legacy of earlier variants) became "self-consciously 'standpoint knowledges'". What this means is that "each erected their knowledge-claims from the standpoint of a subordinated and oppressed social category or grouping" (page 14). This has been particularly so in South Africa, where, in my view, the overriding reason for being of Centres for African Studies has been to play an oppositional role – oppositional to colonial mentalities, to racism, to entrenched privilege, and, within the Marxist framework that has been so influential, to essentialised views of race and gender that ignore socio-economic forces.

This search for knowledge from the standpoint of oppressed groupings, moreover, has to cut across the boundaries of any one discipline. Again, as Lovell indicates, oppression takes many guises and appears in many diverse places.

> Standpoint theories, armed with an epistemology which links knowledge to human interests, begins from those interests. But typically, these take the theories across conventional demarcations of the disciplines within the social sciences and humanities, because all of these resources are required in order to understand and confront the multifarious forms and sites of that oppression. (page 19)

A reconstituted Marxism has to find a language in which women, the colonised, the descendents of slaves, the marginalised and the neglected, can frame their questions in a language that is their own. Simultaneously, these many different formations, be they large ones of class, race or gender, or smaller ones opposing nuclear energy or in favour of abortion, have to be understood socially and historically and not in terms of inflexible, even biological, essentialised constants.

This is the reason why I have attached such importance to opposing the ethnic view of rural Africa as the only authentic conception; it is why I have opposed the myth of the soil of Africa running in the blood of black Americans, who can simply return to their "roots". I think we have to continue to fight for an image of Africa that is both urban and rural, hybrid, and heterogeneous.

The African studies that is being proposed here, then, can be summarised as follows: it investigates Africa's position globally; it is both interdisciplinary but also takes as its boundary of investigation a broadly defined cultural studies; it is standpoint knowledge, committed politically to the oppressed; in an African environment where cultural nationalism that relies on myths of origins and essences is very powerful, the history of iniquities of racism has to be formulated in terms of a reconstituted Marxism that can think structurally and historically. It must however, in speaking holistically, deal with global realities and totalities, while not marginalising non-class realities and while recognising and celebrating, humour, magic, the unpredictable and idiosyncratic, all of which holistic thinking demands.

By presenting the case study of the representation of the middle passage, I hoped to demonstrate some of this in practice. Slavery is a powerful reality and an historical symbol for blacks in general and for descendents of slaves in particular. I tried to capture a sense of the similarities and differences within a critique that opposed essentialism, accepted explanations that are historical and social, rather than biological and intrinsic. While the services of history and politics as well as film, literary theory and fiction, were required, the focus was on how slavery has been represented culturally.

Appropriate Appropriations?
Developing cultural studies in South Africa

Laura H. Chrisman

The notion of "appropriation" as the founding dynamic for an African cultural studies leaves the crucial notion of "preservation" to one side, untouched. There is, arguably, an uneasy dialectic between these notions, which needs critical mapping. If the burden of this conference has been "Where and how are new knowledges being created and what do they look like? What role does appropriation play in this process?" (conference introductory statement), it is important to now ask "What happens to 'old' knowledges in this process? What happens to the legacies of South African indigenous scholarship, history and politics? What roles do they play in a new cultural studies?"

How we conceptualise the future directions of cultural studies depends in large part on how we have conceptualised the origins and genealogy of that discipline. In the United Kingdom (UK), two versions of origins have emerged, the textual and the sociological. I want to spend some time on this because I see it as having a strong bearing on the ways in which African cultural studies is to be theorised, analysed and invented. The textual version is probably dominant, at least within British academia: It locates three texts, Richard Hoggart's *The Uses of Literacy*, E. P. Thompson's *The Making of the English Working Class* and Raymond Williams's *Culture and Society*, as the progenitors of what was to become the academic field of cultural studies. It is interesting that Raymond Williams has himself been one of the most energetic critics of this textualist version; in "The Future of Cultural Studies", for instance, he argues forcefully that this textualist account is "only the surface of the real development, and is moreover misleading" (Williams 1989a: 155). Instead, Williams points to diverse adult education activities in the 1940s as the origins of cultural studies. Even if one accepts these three texts as "seminal", but gives a materialist attention to the conditions of their composition, Williams's point is underscored. For those texts were in fact, as Peach has observed, "written while their authors were working outside the mainstream in higher education: Hoggart was employed as a staff tutor in adult education at Hull University, E P Thompson was a staff tutor in the Yorkshire Workers Education Association and Raymond Williams was an Oxford staff tutor in the Sussex WEA and an occasional summer school lecturer in Yorkshire" (6).

As Williams sees it, the core distinguishing characteristic of adult education projects of that period was that

> Academics took out from their institutions university economics, or university English or university philosophy, and the people wanted to know what it was. This exchange didn't collapse into some simple populism: that these were all silly intellectual questions. Yet these new students insisted (1) that the relation of this to their own situation and experience had to be discussed, and (2) that there were areas in which the discipline itself might be unsatisfactory, and therefore they retained as a crucial principle the right to decide their own syllabus. (1989a: 156)

The intellectual significance of these non-university, non-textual contexts and origins for cultural studies, is something that institutional academics often seem have a problem in recognising. It is as if we – I include myself here – are reluctant to address the complexities of the processes of institutionalisation, to perceive and theorise the extent to which our own intellectual formations are dependent on our place within this institution. Instead, institutionalisation as a process is displaced and externalised. Cultural studies may be historically derived from institutions of local adult education, so this version might allow, and the particularity of these local institutions may have determined the forms of knowledge which once passed as "cultural studies", but such institutional contingencies have no intrinsic intellectual/theoretical value or interest, and vanish anyway when the discipline is taken up within the academy, allowed a pure, unmediated articulation, an intellectual authenticity for which textual production is the only sign.

The institutions, the dynamics, of adult education, then, are a matter for history, not theory, in contemporary cultural studies. But what happens if, as Williams suggests, we start seeing these historical, institutional origins of cultural studies as an analytic challenge as well as, or instead of, an empirical observation? What happens if we start analysing the role of our own institutionalisation in the way we conceive and practice the project of cultural studies?

I want to get back to the issues of institutionalisation and history (seen as both a concept and as an academic discipline). But here I want to focus on what all these non-textual, non-academic components of cultural studies might mean for a new

South Africa. Among other things, it might mean that we start allowing for the possibility of African cultural studies as already existing outside the academy, and that furthermore this existence may be historically long-established, preceding any university formulations of the field. It might mean that what South African academics "appropriate" from the UK are not only aspects of its current theoretical capital, but also insights inspired by the UK's social, educational and cultural history.

I do not want to imply by this that there is any direct parallel between the history of South Africa and that of the UK in the 20th century: on the contrary. (Later on I will address what I see as the dangers of application of theoretical paradigms developed in the UK, United States of America (USA) and Europe for, and by, a new academic South Africa.) But I want to argue that the British historical experience of cultural studies – and the conflicting ways in which that experience can be interpreted – are something from which South African academe can learn. I have been struck, since arriving here, by just how massive the non-university sphere of community-led adult education is; I have been equally struck by how huge, diverse and energetic is the range of community arts projects, civics, and so on. What I find exciting is the prospect of developing a cultural studies field, within the academy, which interacts with, taps, is even generated by, these extra-academic demands, formations and dynamics, as once was the case in the UK

A compelling rationale, to my mind, for introducing cultural studies as an academic field in the new South Africa, is as Williams suggests: The project arises because "people's questions are not being answered by the existing distribution of the educational curriculum" (1989a: 160). And a compelling "goal" for such cultural studies is suggested by Green:

> . . . for some while Cultural Studies may be of best use, neither as an academic discipline with its own rigours, nor in the revolutions of intellectual/political para-digms (important as these are), but in its consolidation as a public presence. Not an area of new professional "expertise" with "answers", but a space openly available for thought and analysis . . . Not a vanguard with its own language, but a continuing activity, responsive to short-term pressures and to the longer-term interests of participants. (36)

Cultural studies, indeed, has something particular to offer the rest of the academy here, precisely because of its fluid intellectual boundaries and its newness as a university discipline. More than any other academic field, cultural studies provides the potential for producing new forms of teaching, learning and knowledge which are local-based and people-led. I would go further and suggest that cultural studies also provides the potential forum for new forms of cultural production as well as interpretation, and for new forms of cultural policy too. In other words, one of the

exciting contributions South African cultural studies could make to a new peda-
gogy/knowledge is by providing an institutional matrix in which the traditional
distinctions between (firstly) academic and aesthetic production, and secondly,
between theoretical reflection and practical (policy) intervention, are deliberately
interrogated, challenged and transformed.

The importance of policy-making within a cultural studies agenda is something
that Australian cultural critics and university departments have recently addressed,
with interesting results. Bennett, for example, provocatively argues against current
critical dispositions to view culture as a set of signifying practices and argues instead
that

> Culture is more cogently conceived, I want to suggest, when thought of as a
> historically specific set of institutionally embedded relations of government in which
> the forms of thought and conduct of extended populations are targeted for transfor-
> mation-in part via the extension through the social body of the forms, techniques,
> and regimens of aesthetic and intellectual culture. (26)

From this he argues for a contemporary cultural studies project which foregrounds
policy and governmental engagement in a number of ways. Because it is both
troubling and suggestive, I want to quote his argument in detail:

> It might mean careful and focused work in the service of specific cultural action
> groups. It might mean intellectual work calculated to make more strategic interven-
> tions within the operating procedures and policy agendas of specific cultural institu-
> tions. It might mean hard statistical work calculated to make certain problems visible
> in a manner that will allow them to surface at the level of political debate or to impinge
> on policy-making processes in ways which facilitate the development of administra-
> tive programs capable of addressing them. It might mean providing private corpora-
> tions with such information. One thing is for sure, however: it will mean talking to
> and working with what used to be called the Ideological State Apparatuses rather
> than writing them off from the outset and then, in a self-fulfilling prophecy, criticizing
> them again when they seem to affirm one's direst functionalist predictions. (32)

I am aware that the above might be sheer anathema for a new South African cultural
studies project, situated as it is in a new country which is already perhaps oversatu-
rated in the languages and practices of policy formation. But I take Bennett's final
sentence seriously, as a call for pro-active academic involvement with cultural
policy which could effect a positive intervention in the emergence of a democratic
culture(s) and government.

Questions of theory:
Intellectual paradigms for African cultural studies

The preceding section was concerned with mapping out some of the ways in which African cultural studies could take on dynamics and directions which break from traditional formulations of academic endeavour. In this section I want to return to the practices of academic production as we know them now, and to ask what kinds of critical approaches could be most fruitful for the project of a new African cultural studies. I do not intend to contradict the drift of my previous section altogether, however. I want to continue with some of the questions, and insights, raised most sharply by Raymond Williams, concerning the role of history and of institutionalisation in the formation of cultural studies.

Underlying much of Williams's discussion of cultural studies and theory within the (UK) academy is his concern with the implications of the textualism and "linguistic turn" of UK cultural theory/studies/politics which emerged and became dominant in the 1980s. For a quick definition of formalism and the "linguistic turn" in cultural studies, let me quote Stuart Hall here:

> (a conviction of) the crucial importance of language and of the linguistic metaphor to any study of culture; the expansion of the notion of text and textuality, both as a source of meaning, and as that which escapes and postpones meaning; the recognition of the heterogeneity, of the multiplicity, of meanings, of the struggle to close arbitrarily the infinite semiosis beyond meaning; the acknowledgment of textuality and cultural power, of representation itself, as a site of power and regulation; of the symbolic as a source of identity. (283)

I want to demarcate three, interlinked, areas of concern in Williams's discussion of this theoretical development. One, which I will explore in the next section, concerns the social/political premises and implications of such theory; its relation to existing forms of social, political and economic power. The second concern is the adequacy of this theory as an explanatory and interpretive tool for analysis of contemporary and emergent practices of (aesthetic) cultural production. The third concern is to do with the ways in which such theory's contents articulate with institutional pressures and priorities, including the drive (be it structural or personal) by academics for self-empowerment and legitimation.

The most negative account – which is present in Williams's discussion – of these problematic areas is one which explains such cultural theory as squarely serving the interests of the political, social and academic/institutional *status quo*. As regards political alignments and implications, the post-modern cultural theorists of 1980s Britain stand condemned by Williams for providing "long-term adjustments to short term situations" by rationalising the ostensible triumph of post-industrial capitalism.

As far as such theory's relations to contemporary culture goes, Williams sees this theory as failing in precisely its most crucial role: committed to a theorisation of "the new" developments in cultural production, such theories as were selected for this purpose are "deficient above all in this key area, of the *nature of cultural formations and thus of ongoing agency and practice*" (Williams 1989b: 171; emphasis added). The corollary of a theory which constructs "the text" as the source (as well as the end) of critical/cultural agency is the exclusion of social agency in the production of texts; furthermore, there is no way to account for precisely what is distinctive and materially specific in new cultural expressions. There is no way, that is, of conceptualising the historical meaning of this new culture.

As to the third problem, the role such theories play in institutional academic self-legitimation, let me give an extended quotation of Williams at perhaps his most polemic and exasperated:

> At just this moment (ie, the formalisation of cultural studies in/by UK academe), a body of theory came through which rationalized the situation of this formation on its way to becoming bureaucratized and the home of specialist intellectuals . . . the theories which came – the revival of formalism, the simpler kinds (including Marxist kinds) of structuralism – tended to regard the practical encounters of people in society as having relatively little effect on its general progress, since the main inherent forces of that society were deep in its structures, and – in the simplest forms – the people who operated them were mere "agents". This was precisely the encouragement for people not to look at their own formation, not to look at this new and at once encouraging and problematic situation they were in; at the fact that this kind of education was getting through to new kinds of people, and yet that it was still inside minority institutions, or that the institutions exercised the confining bureaucratic pressures of syllabus and examination, which continually pulled these raw questions back to something manageable within their terms. At just that moment . . . there was . . . a quite uncritical acceptance of a set of theories which in a sense rationalized that situation, which said that this was the way the cultural order worked, this was the way in which the ideology distributed its roles and functions. The whole project was then radically diverted by these new forms of idealist theory. (Williams 1989a: 157)

(For Williams, the problems of formalism, ideological determinism and pessimism present in structuralist cultural theory/studies are repeated in the current dominant academic constructions of post-structuralism and post-modernism.) What I want to ask is: How might Williams's account assist our development and understanding of new cultural studies in South Africa? Is there any danger, in this highly contrasting social, political and economic climate, of the repetition of such theoretical failings? Having witnessed, and enjoyed, this conference, I am inclined to answer myself that there is no such danger, that formalism and textualism will always be tempered by materialism here in South Africa, that critics and academics working today simply could not reinforce, repeat, a theoreticism which marginalises or excludes the dynamics of social agency in producing (and opposing) cultural texts, that neglects the dynamics of history, and overlooks the complex role of contemporary academic institutions in defining the operations of knowledge/power.

Yet at the same time, I cannot rest entirely easy with this affirmation. For it also seems to me all too possible that the problems outlined by Williams could indeed be repeated here. I see this risk as having two sources. One has to do with the very exhilaration caused by the emergence of a new South Africa. As a new nation inclined (as presumably many such are) to celebrate and allegorise itself as the epitome of emancipated society, as epitome of "post-coloniality", perhaps South Africa may fall prone to the idealistic versions of cultural theory, may see itself as having transcended all those structural conditions which generate and require a theoretical emphasis on self-reflectivity, history and materialism.

The other reason I see a risk of theoretical idealism has to do with a scenario rather different from the above. In this scenario (which is perhaps closely if paradoxically tied up with the first scenario, after all) South African academe continues to see itself with colonial eyes, and to place itself as intellectually dependent, for the most part, upon metropolitan values and formulations. This is a colonial version of the problem of agency. The transnational effects of this "travelling theory" are such that just as popular social agency is precluded by the deterministic theorisation of the academy, so too is South African academic agency precluded by the deterministic premisses of the theories themselves; doomed to passively adopt, not transform, them.

This could be intellectually, culturally and politically disastrous. At the very point at which the new South Africa is released from its isolation, is ready to remap its relations to the cultural, intellectual and economic processes of Africa, of the developing world, of transnationality – at this point, why reinforce a colonial axis of theoretical authority? Why adopt a methodology of cultural analysis which favours the micrological over the macrological, which renounces the possibility of there being a social/cultural totality available for critical consideration? Why, at the moment when new forms and processes of transcontinental history and geography can be invented and imagined in South Africa – why embrace a theoretical orientation which eschews historicism and the discipline of history, a discipline which is surely one of South Africa's greatest intellectual assets? Why settle for the insularities and parochialisms of "the text" when "the world" is available for scrutiny?

I want to get back to these questions, and to turn them around, to argue that in fact South Africa has a great deal intellectually to offer "the West" by way of the immensity of its existing cultural, historical and linguistic understandings. But first I want to suggest that in so far as South African cultural studies needs theoretical stimulation from overseas, there are strong reasons why such stimulation could be sought from countries with which it shares certain social and economic features – from these countries, that is, as much if not more than the UK, the USA and Europe. I am thinking here of Latin America and the formidable theoretical developments in cultural studies that have emerged from a number of Latin American countries. I am also thinking of Australia and Canada, whose situations may not be altogether dissimilar from South Africa now. And I am thinking of "Third World"/liberation cultural theories, from Africa, India and the Caribbean.

To finish this section I want to turn around the question "What kinds of (post-structuralist) theoretical paradigms could South African cultural studies deploy?" to something like "What contributions could South Africa make to a theoretical (re)formulation of cultural studies as practised in the UK/USA?" To answer this, I want to return to the notion of the "linguistic turn" in cultural studies/theory.

In his critique of formalism within cultural theory, past and present, Raymond Williams both includes and excludes the "linguistic turn", arguing that

> . . . the "language paradigm" remains a key point of entry, precisely because it was the modernist escape route from what is otherwise the Formalist trap: that an autonomous text, in the very emphasis on its specificity, is . . . a work in a language that is undeniably social. . . . It is then precisely in this real work on language, including the language of works marked as temporarily independent and autonomous, that modern cultural theory can be centred: a systematic and dynamic social language, as distinct from the "language paradigm". (Williams 1989b: 174)

What I want to suggest is that South African cultural critics and theorists are exceptionally well placed to develop this kind of "real work", a (Bakhtinian) cultural studies grounded in the sociality of language. You people, steeped in the knowledge of the complexity and potency of language formations, of the social dynamics embedded and mediated through languages, could use that knowledge to produce textual, theoretical and sociological analyses from which Western academe could learn a huge amount.

Cultural studies and social analysis

I turn, finally, to issues of social and political analysis: What role could a South African cultural studies play in such analyses? What kinds of relations obtain between cultural, political and economic power in the new South Africa? What insights from cultural studies and theory could assist in the understanding – and transformation – of these relations? In particular, I want to look at ways in which the Gramsci-inflected political analyses within British cultural studies may help or hinder South African discussions. Can paradigms appropriated from what may loosely be termed the "subjective turn" in political theory (parallel to the "linguistic turn" in cultural theory) assist in developing a new public sphere, a new civil society, a new understanding of the state in South Africa?

All I can do here is to toss up a few polemical observations. It would not be useful, appropriate nor possible to enter into a full critical discussion of the pros and cons of the British postmodern socialist theory exemplified by recent work by Stuart Hall, by the sadly defunct Communist Party journal Marxism Today and its influential analyses of post-Fordism "New Times", of Thatcherism, and so on. Instead I will focus my observations on a recent article which draws upon some of the main currents of the above theory to advance an argument about the role of cultural and social "difference" in a new South African polity.

Grant Farred's article takes up a number of notions central to British socialist cultural theory: the rejection of economistic Marxism, the conviction of the importance of the sphere of culture/ideology as a material, and constitutive, element, in social relations and organisations, the suspicion of the formal sphere of the state, the belief in the preservation of cultural difference and (dispersed/multiple) identity against the unifying tendencies of government, the advocacy of coalitionist political mobilisations that are local, contingent and predicated on cultural difference and "affinity". Where Farred differs is in the context and the political impetus of his argument. He writes (this is before the 1994 election) as a socialist who is concerned that the African National Congress (ANC) – as opposition and future government – is silencing the voices and the priorities of working-class and socialist movements; his concern is to find a way for progressive and marginalised constituencies to create a politics which challenges the ANC's monopoly.

There is a lot to agree with in Farred's argument, I think. But I am left with a number of anxieties and questions concerning the premisses and the conclusions of his discussion. And these, I think, reflect some problems I have both with the original Western (post)-Marxist theoretical formulations, and with their application to a new South African situation.

There is both a fatalism and an ambiguity in the way the operations of the state and of culture are conceptualised; both an overly pragmatist and an overly idealist perspective, I think.

I want to take the way in which Farred defines South African cultural "difference", its origins, operations and positive uses. Farred devotes a lot of space to Inkatha-gate, to the Third Force, and more generally, to the ways in which apartheid fostered and then exploited "cultural" differences among peoples. At the same time, he devotes an equal amount of space to enumerating the "cultural" differences generated through a variety of anti-apartheid struggles, in the labour movement and the women's movement in particular. This leads him to contend that

> [t]he distinctiveness of Inkatha, the women's struggle, the trade union and commu-
> nity activists, suggests that black South Africa cannot be naturalised into an undi-
> vided cultural entity . . . it will be extremely difficult for the movement to efface not
> only the distinct cultural identities that apartheid has foisted upon black South
> Africans, but also those identities that have been achieved through struggle with the
> apartheid state and within the black community

which then leads to his argument that

> cultural divisions can actually be used by women's groups, leftists within the ANC,
> other left black political organisations, community activists, and trade unionists to
> give voice to political and ideological differences. (223)

It seems crucial on some level to differentiate "difference", to establish a theoretical
political discourse which does not lump together those differences created by
apartheid with those created through struggle against apartheid, but this differentiation seems to be precisely what Farred's analysis cannot pursue. This is, I suspect,
not only because such a differentiation must be exceedingly complicated and
difficult to achieve, but also because the notions of "culture" and of "difference"
with which Farred is working do not readily allow for such a differentiation.

Actually, I am not sure quite how he defines culture, throughout the article; while
at times it is used to denote ethnicity, at other times it is used to denote political
and/or ideological identities, while at others, "culture" seems to be a general word
for the consciousness that attends a certain relation to economic production. This
fuzziness, too, seems to me to be part of the intellectual heritage of a postmodernised
Gramscianism. The reasons Farred cannot creatively differentiate between "difference" as imposed and as produced through struggle are, again, to do with the fact
that the original context in which "difference" was conceptualised was that in which
a free-market hegemony rather than coercion was the method of government. It is
also arguable that the valorisation of "difference" (cultural or otherwise), even
within its original Western European context, was/is, as Raymond Williams suggests, politically problematic, reflecting a critical inability to do more than fatalis-
tically accept, rationalise and adapt to the logics of the market.

A version of such fatalism is clearly indicated when Farred suggests that

> [t]he articulation of their differences will enable these (the above) groups to
> distinguish and distance themselves from the blossoming partnership between the
> ANC and . . . the NP . . . Such a critical platform can also be used to create a space
> for leftist politics within the ranks of black South Africa, a space which is desperately
> needed so that debates about difference can be initiated before the rhetoric of "unity"
> preempts any such critiques. *At this point, the insistence upon difference – cultural,
> political, and ideological – may be all that stands between the masses of exploited
> black South Africans and the triumvirate . . . of a newly embourgeoised and*

entrepreneurial black middle class, the white upper and middle classes, and multi-
national capitalism. (224; emphasis added)

The fatalism inheres in the ways in which the emergent state is conceptualised: The
ANC, by virtue of its very ascendancy to state power, is assumed to be unable to
avoid ideological convergence to the point of identity with the National Party (NP).
As with "difference", however, there is an ambiguity in the way the ANC is
constructed throughout the discussion. On the one hand, Farred seems to argue that
the ANC through its own historical agency has gained political "hegemony", and
now elects to operate centripetally in order to exclude "difference"; on the other
hand, Farred also seems to suggest that the ANC has been placed in its hegemonic
position by the operations of (home and outside) governments and media, and that
its exclusions of difference are not so much voluntary as the result of outside
determination. In other words, the conceptual distinctions between an ANC power
and identity created through resistance to the state and those granted/invented by
the state(s), are fudged. It is not dissimilar to the problematic conceptualisation (or
lack of it) granted to social agency by cultural theory, discussed in the previous
section of this talk.

Within this somewhat circular and deterministic trajectory, in which the state –
whatever its lead government – is seen as necessarily antagonistic to the
"differences" it has worked to create, all that is left to those oppositional
constituencies of "difference" is to provisionally bond together in what Farred calls
a "politics of affinity", to articulate difference within what appears to be an
essentially discursive, ideological and cultural (rather than formally political) space.
Farred certainly does seem committed to a socialist redistribution of wealth, but
there is to me not a clear sense of how the politics of affinity and the preservation
of differences is to achieve such a redistribution. The languages of difference as
evolved and practiced in the UK left, for instance, seem much more linked up with
flows of consumption than production and distribution.

If I am unclear as to how cultural forces are to translate into political and
economic ones in Farred's scheme, I am also unsure whether this is necessary or
altogether desirable; to insist that "cultural difference" is a material fact of post-
apartheid South Africa is one thing, but to suggest that this is a potentially valuable
political resource, and is the only political resource left to underprivileged groups,
are different matters. It seems to me – ignorant as I acknowledge myself to be – that
the South African left and labour movements (in comparison with Western Europe!)
still have the potential for active representation in government power and economic
policy. If such potential is threatened by the dominance of the ANC, why must the
only response be the renunciation of formal ties with the ANC and the development
of a "counter-hegemonic bloc", derived from cultural differences, and situated

somewhere in civil society? This may be a very important project to develop, but it needs supplementation, I think, and it also needs to be constructed as a means to an end, not (as can be the case in UK cultural/socialist formulations) an end in itself.

Ultimately, this is a social analysis which, in applying the insights and theoretical convictions of Western socialist cultural studies/theory, reveals both their promise and their insufficiency for the new South African situation. This is what I hope the new project of cultural studies in South Africa can work beyond.

South African Cultural Studies in the Moment of the 1990s:
"Dominant Voices" and trends in theory

Gary Minkley and Andrew Steyn

> Nelson Mandela's inauguration, with toyi-toying masses saluting Impala jets flying overhead, heralded the semiotic chaos of the new South Africa.

> Symbols no longer have the same meaning, and visual codes have been broken. Within that chaos, and without the old demons to tilt against, South African artists will be forced to imagine themselves all over again. (Karon 30)

> . . . the sense of "post-apartheid" I am invoking here defines a condition that has contradictorily always existed and yet is impossible of full realization: always existed, because apartheid . . . has from the beginning been shadowed by its own transgression . . .; impossible of realization, because the proliferating binaries of apartheid discourse will long outlive any merely political winning of freedom. (Pechey 56).

I

In the post-1990 moment, as South Africa continues its long march to modernity, questions of new directions in intellectual and cultural practice have forcefully emerged. Amidst pronouncements of "post-apartheid" and "new South Africa", with the official shift from resistance to reconstruction now proclaimed, the role and project of South African intellectuals is up for grabs. It is a moment in which individuals, groups and classes are realigned, institutions are re-structured, and both official and oppositional discourses are (re)organised. This paper considers some of the broad contours of this changing intellectual landscape and the particular sets of circumstances in which it is being transformed. Of special interest to us are the various ways in which cultural studies and African studies are being re-defined in the 1990s.[1]

Our starting point is a series of debates around the question of social and cultural imagination. Writing at a time of transition, Albie Sachs (ca. 1990) and Njabulo Ndebele (1989) in separate papers foreground the word "imagination" in their assessments of contemporary South African cultural practice. Both assert that imagination is shaped by consciousness, identity and subjectivity, which in turn is shaped by social life – by the polar opposites of apartheid domination and the struggle for national liberation. In his intervention in these debates Tony Morphet (1990a) asks what the terms of the return of imagination are likely to be in a post-apartheid social context, with its shift from political struggle to social reconstruction.

According to Morphet the history of cultural imagination in South Africa from the 1950s was shaped between two principal forces – local (conditions of oppression) and global (theory from abroad). He argues the dialectic between the two produces three phases in the period 1950 to 1990 which he re-defines as "settlements": the liberal/formalist settlement (1950 - 1970s), the revisionist settlement (1970s – ca. 1986) with the terms of the third phase, which corresponds to the 1990s, still to be "settled" (1990a: 95).

Morphet describes the notion of "settlement" more broadly as:

> a relatively stable, relatively durable formulation of intellectual functions, monopolies, distribution, qualification, and access – a definition of the dominant forms of intellectual work and hence, perhaps most importantly, of authorisation. (1990a: 95)

The revisionist settlement's intellectual project attempted to balance local black oppression, activism and global socialist imagination as an historical force. At the core of this settlement was the fusion of cultural and political authority. Since the collapse of the Soviet Union and of apartheid hegemony, as well as the challenges posed by post-structuralism to Marxist theory, revisionism was forced on the defensive.

Elsewhere, Morphet (1990b) uses the term "moment" to refer to a period of rupture and transition, of social and intellectual ferment, out of which new cultural settlements struggle to emerge. It is such moments, he argues, which signal "a structural shift in the received intellectual patterns of the social world" (1990b: 93). Our paper is premised on the assumption that, broadly speaking, the 1990s in South Africa represent such a "moment". It is one in which the revisionist settlement continues to crack, lines of fissure open, and the old terms of authorisation appear to fragment. It is also importantly both a shift from critique to policy, and a re-thinking of critique.

This period is also integrally tied to a global context of instability and change. The global village South Africa is being reintegrated into – beyond boycotts, exclusions and refusals of apartheid isolation – is characterised by what Arif Dirlik calls "(t)he transnationalization of production (which) is the source at once of unprecedented global unity and of unprecedented fragmentation in the history of capitalism" (349/50). In this context, "culture" is at once homogenising and hetero-genising. Stuart Hall for example identifies three possible consequences of global-isation on cultural identities: 1) the eroding of national identities; 2) the strengthening of local (national) identities as part of resisting globalisation; and 3) the evolution of new hybrid identities (300). It is in this context of the weakening of national identities under the impact of globalisation, and the simultaneous trend towards national autonomy, as well as the growing influence of transnational theory, that South Africa's "new" nation is being imagined.

For our purposes of talking about the 1990s we have appropriated what Neville Alexander has dubbed South Africa's "moment of manoeuvre"[2] (1). He uses this metaphor to describe the historical, post-February 1990 moment of nation-building in South Africa. Alexander locates this "imagining" of the new nation in the context of the possibilities of the new South Africa and the determinate processes and structures of the old South Africa. This introduces into our notion of "moment", the dimension of continuity in the complex relationships between new theorisations and local conditions of oppression – between text and context. It also enables us to raise the important question of unity and fragmentation in the current South African situation.

II

The moment of the 1990s then is about crossing, moving and re-defining boundaries and borders. It is also however, about how these boundaries and borders will be patrolled in the new South Africa, and under what/whose authorisation this will take place. Broadly speaking, we identify two dominant trends in the redefinition of cultural practice and authority. The one harnesses social imagination and social action to the cause of constructing the new nation, the other highlights the closed imaginings of the nation through poststructuralist theory and the social action of critique. These new directions are, inevitably, either re-appropriations from the revisionist settlement or appropriations from outside of and against the grain of this settlement, and are all potential bases for a new cultural settlement.

Many of the papers within this book reflect parallel and inter-connected theoretical and disciplinary shifts. History is replaced by the foregrounding of culture, which is being re-defined in the context of a postmodernist intellectual framework. These definitions of culture are no longer being informed by history but by anthropology and literary studies in particular. George Marcus, in important ways, makes this connection:

> The power of this intervention [in response to profound discontent with existing anthropological frameworks in the mid-1980s] was in critique rather than in defining a new paradigm or setting a new agenda. The critique has legitimated new objects, new styles of research and writing, and a shift in the historic purpose of anthropological research toward its longstanding, but underdeveloped project of cultural critique [and reoriented] interdisciplinary interests . . . back to the humanities [where the] most energetic thinking about culture, especially in cross-cultural and transcultural frameworks, had been coming from among literary scholars . . . The frame of postmodernism, by this time an interdisciplinary focus or sign of radical critique, has merely enhanced and consolidated the radical critical tendencies within anthropology. . . . (5/6)

This new theory can be intellectually rigorous and imaginative. For example, in the hands of David Bunn, Jane Taylor and Martin Hall, in this volume, the emphasis on textuality, difference, identity and the relational and unfixed nature of meaning operates as a powerful critique of totalising theory. Their emphasis on "material culture" and the differing readings they propose, firmly locate culture at the centre of analysis. For Bunn and Taylor culture is essentially textual. While they argue for the need to differentiate between, and trace the complex intersections between "materiality" (material objects, and non-discursive terrains) and textuality, the overall emphasis of cultural critique is one of reading and representation. The reading and ordering of meaning through sign and symbol provides the means to simultaneously track the cross-cutting and mediated human subjectivities within society, and of the society itself and its particular frameworks of meaning. Much of this is seen as politically enabling. Isabel Hofmeyr, however, is concerned that the kind of analysis put forward by Bunn and Taylor is not likely to place the important question of the appropriation and reception of texts on the research agenda. The reason for this she says is that "it reduces all questions – even broader political ones – to questions of reading" (page 115).

Martin Hall's project is also one of reading, but with important differences. Cultural studies as cultural critique is concerned with unpacking both the brackets of time and the cultural boxes of interpretative meaning. Material objects, if they are to be fully understood need to be granted their materiality and their priority over language. The project of cultural studies entails a creative and cross-cutting refusal to be discipline-bound in appropriations for the reading of material objects as primary texts, followed by verbal, visual and written texts (as language). Meaning is embedded in these objects first, and then in the multiple languages of the present and past – as a series of symbols with multiple meanings and signs with many discourses, including current ones making them inherently political.

The concern to trace how at particular times, and in particular contexts, meaning is appropriated and boundaries collapsed into essential and universal categories is of crucial importance for Hall. These need to be both exposed, and disabled and opposed through cultural critique.

Furthermore Bunn, Taylor and Hall can be seen, in an important new sense, to be responding to and providing alternative readings of the experience of material culture. In their engagement with theory and subjectivity in cultural studies, they attempt to explode the myth of an undivided and dominant identity of class, of "race" and of nation.

This emergent framework of cultural critique can be traced as radical in another sense as well. In the tracking of South Africa's complex positioning in a colonial and enlightenment modern world, the ways in which South Africa (and Africa) prefigures the "West", textually and materially, and internalises its forms of power/knowledge, contradicts conceptions of its pre-modernity. South Africa is modern, and increasingly and contemporaneously postmodern. Modernist theoretical frameworks (like Marxism) can be shown, historically, and in its politics of location to be outdated.

In other chapters in this book, Colin Bundy, Terry Lovell and Brenda Cooper all wish in some way to track the new knowledges of critique, generated by postmodernism back into a necessary reconstituted Marxism. This is the challenge in developing a focus and direction for "African cultural studies". All argue that some form of "totalising" under the rubric of the social and historical relations of production remains crucial. The totality can only be read when the sum includes a critique of capitalism, and of imperialism in a "Third World" cultural frame. The project is one which involves the necessary development of new languages and concepts to historicise the relations of class, "race" and gender, and in so-doing de-essentialise their foundational status – their terms as essentialised constants. The frame which returns this to cultural studies is suggestively captured by Brenda Cooper, who argues that while "Third World" is no longer valid in economic terms, it has "effectivity as a cultural concept" within African studies, given the experience of imperialism:

> the war of combat against the cultural hegemony of the First World continues . . . to dominate the literary strategies, images, languages and forms of Third World intellectuals . . . it is precisely in the area of culture that African studies can make its most powerful intervention. (page 180)

In crucial respects this intellectual framework seeks simultaneously to develop a culture of critique within the radical context not only of theory, but also "from the standpoint of oppressed groupings" (page 182) and thus of history. As such, the terms of its potential settlement are those of materialist culture which will draw oppression, history and theory together in a new and reconstituted Marxism. Despite recognising that the post-structuralist and postmodernist concerns call aspects of the very bases of the historical and Marxist projects into question, this framework proposes that cultural studies must also be defined by

> the observation that while people make their own history, they do not do so under circumstances that they have chosen or can control. (Bundy 1994: 28)

III

Writing in the post-election period, we would argue that any discussion of the ways in which culture, cultural practice and cultural studies is being re-defined, needs to address the question of nation and state in post-apartheid South Africa.

The representations of "decolonisation" after the negotiated political settlement in South Africa, creates a context in which this settlement is seen as an event of unexamined good. The power of these representations is based on their capacity to operate a simple reversal from apartheid – what Graham Pechey refers to as the banal definition of post-apartheid (5). These are encapsulated in the Reconstruction and Development Programme (RDP), and in the emergence of the new language - "in the new South Africa" and "as South Africans", and in the language of the needs and wants of "ordinary South Africans" – in "freedom", "peace", "unity", etc.

Morphet has pointed to the rapid emergence of a "liberal pragmatism" as the new defining discourse of the post-1990 negotiated political settlement (1990b: 98). This would, according to Johan Muller and Keyan Tomaselli be seen to variously include a process of enabling "incorporative state rule", the rise of a technical elite and an ideology of "universalist neutrality". It would also seem to signal a shift from the organic intellectuals of the liberation movement who aimed to empower "the People", to the new technical intelligentsia who, Muller and Tomaselli argue, "aim to address and empower the state (314–5). The implication of this for cultural vision is a cultural nationalism capturing the new as South African. The RDP becomes the vehicle and the sign for this, inclusive of both Sachs's "incorporative ANC" and Ndebele's "my people". The "ordinary" shifts to being defined as the everyday and government. It is a process which simultaneously broadens, in that it incorporates all South Africans, but is also one which adopts the position of speaking for, and thus defining, the ordinary – the new, legitimate, democratic South African state authorises itself as representative of the ordinary people and authorises the ordinary as represented through it. The new culture of the ordinary South African will be one that is designed into the RDP geometries of everyday life:

The plenary accepted that the ANC's overwhelming majority in the National Parliament and seven of the Provincial Assemblies, in the context of political democracy,
enabled the movement to take the lead in organising our entire society for change
through the co-ordination of parliament and extra-parliamentary initiatives. The key
component of such co-ordinating will be the mobilisation of all the communities for
their involvement in the implementation of the Reconstruction and Development
Programme.[3]

Through the "ordinary" the state wishes to capture the social imagination of the
everyday and structure it in terms of "needs" and thereby define and set the
boundaries, within which cultural imagination should function. Beyond art for art's
sake and art in the struggle, the arts and culture are to be located "as integral
components of reconstruction and development in keeping with international experience" (National Arts Coalition 1994). Is this art for the RDP's sake?

Pechey has suggested that power in post-apartheid (postcolonial?) South Africa
is not "secured and centrally exercised", but "a moving field of possibilities which
everywhere carry within them the mutually enabling, intimately cohabiting negative
and positive charges of both power and resistance" (5). Although the matter is
complex, one of the crucial factors in making the negotiated political settlement a
possibility, is the fact that there has all along been more common ground "internally"
than was made apparent outwardly. This is the crux of Pechey's re-reading of the
South African Communist Party's "internal colonialism" theory. He says

The "internality" of this colonialism can then be understood metaphorically as a
redescription of "South Africa" that bypasses the grand categories of the geopolitical
and the world-historical in a new emphasis upon the dialogue that underlies all
antagonism, the competing utopias that speak to each other inwardly even as their
narrators outwardly turn laws and guns on each other. The history of South Africa
is less the simple triumph of one such narrative of collective identity over another
than an irreducible plurality of imagined communities that are not as deaf to each
other as their manifest mutual contradiction might give out. (9–10)

The new state, through the RDP, on the other hand, develops a notion of a core
cultural river of need, into, and from which, tributaries of diversity – of South
Africa's multi-culturalism – can flow. Neville Alexander provides a trenchant way
to re-think this – he argues that a "core culture" will be based on the "interaction,
interpenetration or perhaps even interfluence of all the relevant currents. The precise
definition of the core at any given moment depends on the changing social formation." (10). He proposes that

South African cultural history be seen as a mainstreaming through the confluence of three
or four major tributaries as opposed to the conventional image of separate rivers/streams
one of which dominates and eventually absorbs or assimilates the others. (9)

These are all attempts to address the question of unity and diversity in the cultural imagination of South African politics. We would agree that any post-apartheid discourse of universalism which does not acknowledge the complex of imagined communities in South African politics is likely to be as oppressive as the particularism of apartheid. This is one way of looking at the dilemma of unity and plurality in the current phase of building/imagining the "new" South African nation.

The other view says that nowhere is modernity's project of emancipation more justified than in South Africa and that despite its potential problems for some South Africa's oppressed would risk the dangers of a universalist humanism "as an alternative to what they know of the world's most unjust particularisms" (11). In such a case Pechey says "Postmodernist critiques of totality seem to be a metropolitan irrelevance . . ." (11).

To summarise, in this section we have attempted to raise four basic points. Firstly, in talking about culture in post-apartheid South Africa, questions of the state and nation-building are crucial in so far as they are major spheres in which culture and cultural practice are actually specified and formulated in particular ways.

Secondly, talking about the state and nation has enabled us to re-introduce the issues of oppression – not just in terms of the pre-determined binaries of domination and resistance, but as it is being re-defined in new ways by the state in post-apartheid (postmodern) South Africa.

Thirdly, universalisms and essentialist narratives are not just bound by the social constructions of the modernising project of nationing the new state, nor simply contradicted by the principle of new theoretical constructs. They are located within specific historical boundaries. These fall outside of the state/nation, and are constructed as strategic essentialisms necessary to "live" and to transform the conditions of oppression.

Finally, we make the point that if the context of the local is predetermined as the relocation of the revisionist settlement, this will result in a number of shortcomings in re-defining cultural studies in South Africa in the 1990s. Furthermore, if the state is seen as synonomous with the local, then the implication for cultural critique is that it can only be found outside both the state and the local. On the other hand, we argue that the state cannot be seen as either synonomous with the local, or simply be reduced to experience and the local conditions of oppression. Forms of cultural critique do exist within the local and they do so in a state of tension between needs, critique, oppression and theory. To ignore or elide these contexts within the local and the state, in favour of the boundaries of global theory needs to be both highlighted as problematic, and questioned as to whether it can provide the most durable base for a future cultural settlement.

It should be clear by now that we are concerned to locate the debates about future directions for "African cultural studies" at the boundary of local and global forms of knowledge, and to embed local concerns in a transnational (metropolitan) matrix. We would argue that it is in the dialogue, the "working through at the level of theory" (Morphet 1990a: 103) between local and global knowledges and between the various sites of knowledge production that a "theoretical attitude" (94) should be nurtured. This will also entail the crossing of boundaries between theory and the paradoxes, contradictions and ironies of the South African social reality.

IV

Much of the contribution to this book has been about debating, re-drawing and examining disciplinary and theoretical boundaries in cultural studies. At the core of these debates was the relationship between crossing boundaries, disciplined thought and defining new cultural studies away from a temporal to a spatial root metaphor. "Travelling theory", "middle passage" and journey ("From Lydenburg to Mafikeng"), transmission, circulation and movement all affirm this new sense of direction, of migration, circulation and crossing boundaries. With this image in mind we wish to conclude by looking more closely at knowledge production in the context of the debates around new directions for "African cultural studies" referred to in this publication.

If crossing boundaries is integral to the process of knowledge production, Comaroff, Lovell, Bundy and Cooper argue that so too is "patrolling boundaries". Both are acted out literally and figuratively as part of the process of new knowledge production (and for producing "art" for that matter). Johannes Fabian captures this in relation to anthropology (but he could be talking about social historians or cultural critics as well):

> Whenever we do empirical research we must cross boundaries – with our bodies, with our habits of speech, with our habits of thought. . . . But as soon as we return, . . . and begin to formulate knowledge in writing, we turn from crossing boundaries to patrolling them, making sure that our discourse stays legitimised scientifically in form and content. (52)

In the case of "African cultural studies", this concern with crossing boundaries can be translated into disciplined thought, only if its reformulation acknowledges that the global and local conditions in which this is taking place is different from those under which African studies was established. In the 1970s and the 1980s revision-ist/radical history in South Africa shaped and defined key aspects of African studies practised in South Africa. In general this African studies with history as its prime disciplinary agent was more sensitive to the politics of Western academia, and to the distinctiveness of South Africa, than to the social and political challenges faced by and knowledges produced in African societies.

Current debates within Africa and African studies have highlighted both the problematic basis to conceptions of its colonial past and its "inventiveness", but also drawn serious debate back to the attempt to reclaim African history and culture. Attention has also returned to the foundations and crisis of its economic and political structures. The "many modernities" shaping African societies are seen as crucial in shaping the wide range of cultural practices, spatial arrangements and material circumstances and transformations in diverse ways (Comaroff and Comaroff 1993). As Fred Cooper has pointed out though, "the most important changes occurred not in academia but in Africa . . . concerning the most basic political and economic issue of the 1980s and 1990s: development" (188, 195).

At the same time, as the "Empire writes back", postcolonial theory holds that the basic current issue is that of "culture" in its ability to destabilise existing knowledges of imperialism and the essentialised modernity of the "West". It is these two tensions – between culture and political economy in Africa, and between African ("Third World") culture and the global (Western) context – that have shaped recent debate of cultural studies in African studies in South Africa – most notably in the Centre for African Studies at the University of Cape Town.

These points of debate are most explicitly taken up by Cooper, but also by a number of the contributors in their attempt to address the changing boundaries of African studies. What is remarkable at a more general level, however, is the failure to engage African studies beyond two defining aspects. The first is an unquestioned framework of locality, by virtue of the fact that South Africa is geographically part of Africa. South African studies is, simply by extension, African studies. The second is the sense of intellectual and political defence against the exclusion and domination of a continent by imperialism and the West. In this context Africa remains represented as not only materially, but also theoretically impoverished. Its local debates and knowledges were marginal to re-defining cultural studies or centring "African cultural studies" (with the exception of the interventions of postcolonial critics in the West).

This has entailed that two areas have increasingly come to dominate, and define "African cultural studies" in the present. The first is the concentration on colonial discourse theory and the singular (determining) experience of colonialism and imperialism for the study of Africa (and South Africa). The second is a critique of "Third World" and Africanist cultural nationalism which is seen to essentialise African culture and tradition. Anti-imperialist resistance which is legitimated on the basis of authentic voices which emerge exclusively from within this culture and tradition are questioned.

These cross important boundaries, but in the growing tendency to patrol others, the cultural production of non-metropolitan areas is marginalised, and concerns with political economy and development silenced. Attempts to develop and affirm local knowledges as key sites where theoretical indigenisation occurs has been importantly questioned by Isabel Hofmeyr, briefly in this publication, and much more thoroughly elsewhere. She takes as her starting points the histories of orality and literacy – "perhaps the most crucial issue in cultural history in South Africa" (1990: 69) – and argues for the need to "culturalise" and "literalize" areas "traditionally claimed by history and politics" (1990: 70). More generally Hofmeyr's critique provides a different framework (or set of boundaries) for a radical re-thinking of South African history and cultural studies. It is one that poses the sometimes contradictory intersections between memory, tradition and history, and between orality, literacy and "written histories" in the local constructions, representations and mediations of meaning and knowledge. The need to examine "indigenous intellectual traditions" opens up the space for locating the "manifold institutions and forums in which intellectual activity occurs". She also points out how some of these intellectual discourses are encoded in narrative and are integrally connected to "the social relations that control texts and audiences" (1993: 175–81).

Laura Chrisman similarly raises the question of indigenous intellectual traditions and the varied "locations" of knowledge production. She foregrounds "(t)he intellectual significance of . . . non-university, non-textual contexts and origins for cultural studies" which she says "is something institutional academics often seem to have a problem in recognising" (page 185). This boundary between the academic institution and non-academic/non-textual contexts will have to be crossed in new ways. We believe this will have crucial implications for new directions in "African cultural studies". Where do directions and boundaries lie? Does looking to the West provide the balance between local experiences and the integration of new forms of global knowledge, or are there other sources of "theoretical stimulation", as Chrisman suggests, that need to be explored? (pages 190–1).

If the project for intellectuals today, outside of the processes of policy formulation, is to develop and provide critical theory for social actors, as suggested by Andrew Nash for example[4], the complex question remains: what are the relationships between critical distance, critique and positioning in social action? If critical theory is what intellectuals are to offer, how will this be made accessible, and in what contexts should it be "received"? This persists as the crucial question for us. How, for example, is African Studies and "African Cultural Studies" a standpoint knowledge, and what does it do for "the oppressed"? Should "African Cultural Studies" be a "standpoint knowledge"? The debate is not only between different theories, or between local conditions of oppression and metropolitan theories, but also between cultural and intellectual practice and politics. Does poststructuralism move intellectual practice beyond politics – or does it extend politics?

In the moment of the 1990s, theorising about social imagination and cultural practice in the context of the changing conditions of oppression has generated the need for a new language for rephrasing the old binary oppositions in the 1990s. Alexander, for example, attempts to address contemporary social issues by appropriating from quantum theory the idea of the simultaneous duality of particle and wavelength - of overlapping social spaces that are lived as definable entities and as flux and instability. Cooper, in this volume, drawing on Stuart Hall, argues for a kaleidoscopic thinking that includes different angles, which converge as difference and as similarity. It is not one or the other, but both, at the same time (page 180). This sums up a fundamental shift in ideas in the moment of the 1990s in South Africa, making possible the sometimes strange convergences of practitioners and intellectuals who otherwise hold incompatible theoretical, ideological or political "positions". This is an important development as it partly unlocks the necessity of closure through settlement, authorised by a determining or dominant intellectual framework. In this scheme of things cultural studies "would instead be the way of understanding the distinct and yet coinciding temporalities lived by South Africa's communities as they have journeyed together, belatedly but relatively rapidly, towards modernity" (Pechey 9).

Notes and References

Terry Lovell: The Burden of the Disciplines (pages 14 – 30)

Afshar, Haleh and M. Maynard (eds). *The Dynamics of Race and Gender: Some feminist interventions*. Basingstoke: Taylor and Francis, 1994.

Alexander, Sally. "Women, Class and Sexual Differences in the 1830s and 1840s: Some reflections on the writing of feminist history". *History Workshop* 17 (Spring 1984): 125-149 (Rpt in Lovell 1990).

Anthias, Floya and Nira Yuval-Davis. *Racialized Boundaries*. New York and London: Routledge, 1993.

Armstrong, Nancy. *Desire and Domestic Fiction*. New York and Oxford: Oxford University Press, 1987.

Avineri, Shlomo (ed). *Karl Marx on Colonialism and Modernization*. New York: Doubleday Anchor, 1968.

Barrett, Michèle. *The Politics of Truth: From Marx to Foucault*. Oxford: Polity Press, 1991.

Bergonzi, Bernard. *Exploding English*. Oxford: Clarendon Press, 1990.

Bourdieu, Pierre. *Distinction*. London: Routledge, 1984.

Cameron, Deborah and Elizabeth Frazer. *Lust to Kill*. Oxford: Polity, 1987.

Cohen, Nick and Rachel Borrill. "The New Proletariat". *The Independent on Sunday* (16 May 1993): 19.

Cohn, Carol. "Sex and Death in the Rational World of Defence Intellectuals". *Signs* 12.4 (1987): 687-718.

Eagleton, Terry. *Against the Grain*. London: Verso, 1986.

Eley, Geoff. "The Family is a Dangerous Place: Memory, gender and the image of the working class". In Rosenstone, R. (ed). *Revisioning History: Film and the construction of the past*. Princeton: Princeton University Press, 1993: 17-43.

Foucault, Michel."Two Lectures". In *Power/Knowledge*. New York: Pantheon, 1980.

—. *The Order of Things*. London: Tavistock, 1974.

Graham, Hilary. "Do Her Answers Fit His Questions? Women and the survey method". In E. Gamarnikow (ed). *The Public and the Private*. London: Heinemann, 1983: 132-146.

Hall, Stuart. "Minimal Selves". *Identity* ICA Document 6 (1987): 44.

Hollway, Wendy. "Gender Difference and the Production of Subjectivity". In J. Henriques et al. *Changing the Subject*. London: Methuen, 1984: 227-262.

Hooks, Bell."Postmodern Blackness". In Hooks. *Yearning*. Turnaround Press, 1991.

Hull, Gloria et al. (eds). *All the Women are White, all the Men are Black, but Some of us are Brave: Black women's studies*. Old Westbury, New York: Feminist Press, 1982.

Lovell, Terry (ed). *British Feminist Thought*. Oxford: Blackwell, 1990.

Lovibond, Sabina. "Feminism and Postmodernism". *New Left Review* 178 (1989): 5-28 (Rpt in R. Boyne and A. Rattansi (eds). *Postmodernism and Society*. Macmillan, 1990).

Malos, Ellen (ed). *The Politics of Housework*. London: Allison and Busby, 1980.

Martin, Emily. *The Woman in the Body*. Milton Keynes: Open University Press, 1989.

Mitchell, Juliet. *Feminism and Psychoanalysis*. Harmondsworth: Penguin, 1974.

Modleski, Tania. *Feminism Without Women: Culture and criticism in a "postfeminist" age*. London: Routledge, 1991.

Said, Edward. *Culture and Imperialism*. London: Chatto and Windus, 1993.

Said, Edward. *Orientalism*. New York: Pantheon, 1978.

Sartre, Jean Paul, *What is Literature? And other essays*. Cambridge Mass.: Harvard University Press, 1988.

Smart, Carol. *Feminism and the Power of Law*. London: Routledge, 1989.

Soper, Kate. "Postmodernism, Subjectivity and the Question of Value". *New Left Review* 186 (1991): 120-128.

Spelman, Elizabeth. *Inessential Woman*. London: Women's Press, 1990.

Spivak, Giyatri Chakravorty. In *Other Worlds: Essays in cultural politics*. New York and London: Routledge, 1988.

Weedon, Chris. *Feminist Practice and Postmodernist Theory*. Oxford: Blackwell, 1987.

Woolf, Virginia. *A Room of One's Own*. London: Chatto and Windus, 1984.

Colin Bundy: Sharing the Burden? (pages 31 – 38)

Anderson, Perry. *In the Tracks of Historical Materialism*. London: Verso, 1983.

Best, Steven and Douglas Kellner. *Postmodern Theory*. New York: The Guildford Press, 1991.

Cooper, Frederick. "Postscript: Africa and the world economy". In Cooper, F., A. F. Isaacman, F. E. Mallon, W. Roseberry and S. J. Stern. *Confronting Historical Paradigms*. Madison: University of Wisconsin Press, 1993: 187-201.

Geras, Norman. "Althusser". In Bottomore, T., L. Harris, V. G. Kiernan and R. Miliband (eds). *A Dictionary of Marxist Thought*. 2nd ed. Oxford: Basil Blackwell, 1991: 16-19.

Hassan, Ihab. *The Postmodern Turn: Essays in postmodern theory and culture*. Columbus: University of Ohio Press, 1987.

Jameson, Fredric. *The Political Unconscious*. New York: Cornell University Press, 1981.

Jewsiewicki, Bogumil. "African Historical Studies: Academic knowledge as 'usable past' and radical scholarship". *African Studies Review* 32.3 (1989): 1-76.

Leys, Colin. "On the Relevance of Marxism". In Berman, B. and P. Dutkiewicz (eds). *Africa and Eastern Europe: Crises and transformations*. Kingston, Ont.: Queens University Centre for International Relations, 1993: 173-176.

Mudimbe, V. I. *The Invention of Africa*. Bloomington: Indiana University Press, 1988.

Ross, George. "Intellectuals against the Left: The case of France". In Miliband, R. and L. Panitch (eds). *The Retreat of the Intellectuals: Socialist register*, 1990: 201-27.

Said, Edward W. "Travelling Theory". In *The World, the Text and the Critic*. London: Vintage, 1991 (orig. 1983): 226-247.

Stern, Steve J. "Africa, Latin America and the Splintering of Historical Knowledge: From fragmentation to reverberation". In Cooper et al. *Confronting Historical Paradigms*, Madison: University of Wisconsin Press, 1993: 3-20.

Jean Comaroff: Late 20th Century Social Science (pages 39 – 56)

Bourdieu, Pierre. *Outline of a Theory of Practice*. Transl. Richard Nice. New York: Cambridge University Press, 1977.

Comaroff, John L. "Chiefship in a South African 'homeland': A case study of the Tshidi chiefdom of Bophuthatswana". *Journal of South African Studies* 1 (1974): 36-51.

Hebdige, Dick. *Subculture: The meaning of style*. London: Methuen, 1979.

—. *Hiding in the Light: On images and things*. London: Routledge, 1988.

Frederiksen, Bodil Folke. *Living in the Neighbourhood of One's Dreams: The role of popular writing in the creation of the ordinary*. Ms. n.d.

Hall, Stuart and Tony Jefferson (eds). *Resistance Through Rituals: Youth subcultures in postwar Brit-*

ain. New York: Holmes & Meier Publishers Inc., 1976.

Miner, Horace. "Body Ritual Among the Nacerima". *American Anthropologist* 58 (1956): 503-507.

Ndebele, Njabulo S. *Rediscovery of the Ordinary: Essays on South African literature and culture*. Johannesburg: Congress of South African Writers, 1991.

David Bunn: The Brown Serpent of the Rock (pages 58 – 85)

NOTES

[1] Acknowledgements: With such a broad topic, and the limited time available to me, I would not have been able to complete this initial report without the help of the following individuals and institutions, to whom I am deeply grateful. First, the staff at the Welcome Institute Medical History Library in London, the staff at the British Museum and African Studies at UCT all tolerated my frantic research efforts, while Richard Hanson and Linda Mowat at the Pitt Rivers Museum offered me more information than I was able to use. Martin Hall, Brenda Cooper and members of the Critical Views of the Material World seminar group helped to convince me that poison is a *thing*, and Hylton White and Lynn Lawrence gave me considerable practical assistance.

[2] Porter is one of the most important modern historians of the body, of medicine and of the history of consumer society. He is, moreover, a researcher at the Wellcome. See also the monumental Brewer (ed.), *Consumption and the World of Goods*.

[3] *Kaapsche Plakkaat Boek, Deel II*, 1707-1753. Cited in Searle 47.

[4] See Noli 27 for a useful survey of the history.

[5] Both Deacon and de la Harpe comment on the uncertain history of Bushman arrowhead technology.

[6] See Newton-King, "The Enemy Within". I am relying here on Martin Legassick's characterisation of this part of her argument. Legassick 340.

[7] The standard reference work on poisonous plants is Watt and Breyer-Brandwyk, in which is contained a spectacular range of reports, some of them quite fantastical, about African use of organic poisons.

[8] For a detailed study of *Diamphotoxin* see Shaw et al., and de la Harpe. I would suggest that this reference to detachable barbs is characteristic of eye-witness reporting, as it is not the sort of detail normally transmitted intertextually.

[9] As is probably evident, my discussion in this section has been considerably influenced by the work of Arjun Appadurai.

[10] For a discussion of Barrow and cartography see Nigel Penn (1993).

[11] This is a complex ideological process, best described in Alan Liu 103-113.

[12] Both the critique of structure and the principle of supplementarity are implicit in the early "Structure, Sign, and Play in the Discourse of the Human Sciences".

[13] Alert readers will see an echo here of Spivak's claim that the central mechanism of colonial ideology is intervention on behalf of local comprador classes, with the excuse that "brown women" are being protected from "brown men". See "Can the Subaltern Speak?" 296.

[14] On the Anglicisation of Roman Dutch law see Fine 257-285 as well as Dooling, Crais, Newton-King, Trapido and Legassick, amongst others, who all deal extensively with the contradictions around politics and identity embodied by the "Janus faced" form of liberal justice that served the interests of racist settlers in the Eastern Cape.

[15] Lewis-Williams 121.

[16] See Silberbauer 76/77, de la Harpe, and Lee.

[17] Though the description is confused, and despite the fact that Lewis-Williams identifies the invertebrate as a "bagworm", it seems conceivable that elements of arrow grub usage are also being alluded to. For instance, in the case of the observation that the larva can bite, or that "Bechuana natives believe that it is very venomous", it is possible that the Lebistina parasite is being referred to, which was always held to be more dangerous and deserving of careful handling. (Shaw et al.)

[18] What I am saying here is a far cry, of course, from the descriptions of missionary colonialism common some years ago. For commentary on the history of the debate, see Comaroff and Comaroff 9-11.

[19] When I speak about the "brutality"of Fontana's experiments, I am thinking of the ghastly but quite standard nineteenth-century practice of vivisection. Large numbers of rabbits, cats and guinea pigs were dismembered and tortured in the cause of his curare research.

[20] The brief history is based on a variety of sources, including articles in the *Philosophical Transactions* themselves. The most reliable guide to the topic is McIntyre, and I have made extensive use of his discussion, pages 1-19.

[21] Given the geographical location, I am presuming that this is the genus. For a discussion of Diamphidia simplex see Silberbauer 75-76.

[22] Lewis-Williams 121-122.

REFERENCES

Anon (ed.). *Prestwich's Dissertation on Mineral, Animal, and Vegetable Poisons; Containing a Description of Poisons in General, their Manner of Action, Effects on the Human Body, and Respective Antidotes*. London: F. Newberry, 1775.

Adams, Joseph, M.D. *Observations on Morbid Poisons, Chronic and Acute*. London: W. Smith & Son, 1807.

Arbousset, T. and F. Daumas. *Narrative of an Exploratory Tour to the North-East of the Colony of the Cape of Good Hope*. 1846. Rpt Cape Town: Struik, 1968.

"Dr. Allen". *Synopsis Medicinae, Or a Brief and General Collection of the Whole Practice of Physick*. London: J. Pemberton, 1730.

Bancroft, Edward. *Essay on the Natural History of Guiana and South America*. London: T. Beckel and P. A. De Hont, 1769.

Barrow, Sir John. *An Account of Travels Into the Interior of Southern Africa in the Years 1797 and 1798*. London: T. Cadell, 1801.

Bhabha, Homi. "The Other Question". *Screen* 24 (December 1983): 18-36.

Bisset, N. G. "Arrow and Dart Poisons". *Journal of Ethnopharmacology* 25 (1989): 1-41.

Blackwood, Beatrice. "The Origin and Development of the Pitt Rivers Museum". *Occasional Papers on Technology* 11, 1970.

Bourdieu, Pierre. *Outline of a Theory of Practice*. Trans. R. Nice. Cambridge: Cambridge University Press, 1977.

Breckenridge, Carol A. "The Aesthetics and Politics of Colonial Collecting: India at world fairs". *Comparative Studies in Society and History* 32.2 (April 1989): 195-216.

Brink, Yvonne. "Critical Views in Historical Architecture: Cape Dutch architecture as a body of works". Unpublished seminar paper. Critical Views of the Material World Seminar Series, University of Cape Town, May 1993.

Brodie, B. C. "Experiments and Observations on the different Modes in which Death is produced by certain Vegetable Poisons". *Edinburgh Review*, Vol. xviii (August 1811): 370-379.

Burke, Edmund. *A Philosophical Enquiry into the Origins of Our Ideas of the Sublime and Beautiful*. Notre Dame: University of Notre Dame Press, 1980.

Burke, Peter (ed.). *New Perspectives on Historical Writing*. Cambridge: Polity Press, 1991.

Burton, Sir Richard. *The Lake Regions of Central Africa*. London: Sidgwick and Jackson, 1961.

Campbell, James. *Travels in the Interior of South Africa, 1849-1863*. 2 vols. Rpt Cape Town: A. A. Balkema, 1971.

Cape Archives. Court of Justice. CJ 816. Craddock Circuit Court. Sentence in the Criminal Case of A. Stockenstrom *contra* Vrolyk, a Boschesman.

Clark, J. Desmond. "Prehistoric arrow forms in Africa as shown by surviving examples of the traditional arrows of the San Bushmen". *Paleorient* 3 (1977): 127-150.

Clifford, James. *The Predicament of Culture*. Cambridge, Mass: Harvard University Press, 1988.

Comaroff, Jean. *Body of Power, Spirit of Resistance*. Chicago: University of Chicago Press, 1985.

—, and John Comaroff. *Ethnography and the Historical Imagination*. Boulder: Westview Press, 1992.

—, and John Comaroff. *Of Revelation and Revolution*. Volume I. Chicago: University of Chicago Press, 1991.

Crais, Clifton. *The Making of the Colonial Order: white supremacy and black resistance in the Eastern Cape, 1770-1865*. Cambridge: Cambridge University Press, 1992.

Deacon, Janette. "Arrows as Agents of Belief Amongst the /Xam Bushmen". Margaret Shaw Lecture 1992. Cape Town: South African Museum, 1992.

de la Harpe, Jonathan. "*Diamphotoxin*: The arrow poison of the !Kung Bushmen". Unpublished doctoral dissertation, University of Cape Town, 1980.

Derrida, Jacques. "Structure, Sign, and Play in the Discourse of the Human Sciences". Macksey (ed.), 247-272.

—. *Writing and Difference*. Trans. Alan Bass. London: Routledge,1978.

Dooling, Wayne. "Law and Community in a Slave Society: Stellenbosch District, South Africa, c. 1760-1820". University of Cape Town, Centre for African Studies, *Communications* 23, 1992.

Elbourne, Elizabeth. "'To Colonize the Mind': Evangelical missionaries in Britain and the Eastern Cape, 1790- 1837". Unpublished doctoral dissertation. University of Oxford, 1991.

Fine, Hilton Basil. "The Administration of Criminal Justice at the Cape of Good Hope 1795-1828". Unpublished doctoral dissertation. University of Cape Town, August 1991. 2 vols.

Fontana, Felix. *Treatise on the Venom of the Viper, on the American Poison; and on the Cherry Laurel*. Trans. Joseph Skinner. London: John Cuthell, 1795.

Forbes, Vernon S. and John Rourke (eds). *Paterson's Cape Travels, 1777-1779*. Johannesburg: Brenthurst, 1980.

Foucault, Michel. *Discipline and Punish*. Harmondsworth: Penguin, 1979.

—. *The Order of Things* (*Les Mots et les choses*). Anon. trans. New York: Vintage, 1970.

Gilman, Sander. "Black Bodies, White Bodies" in "*Race*", *Writing, and Difference*. Ed. Henry Louis Gates, Jr., Chicago, University of Chicago Press, 1986.

Godlonton, Robert. *Narrative of the Irruption of the Kaffir Hordes*. Grahamstown: Meurant & Godlonton, 1835. Rpt Cape Town: Struik, 1965.

Gordon, Robert J. *The Bushman Myth: The making of a Namibian underclass*. Boulder: Westview Press, 1992.

Kaapsche Plakkaat Boek, Deel II, 1707-1753.

Kolb, Peter. *The Present State of the Cape of Good Hope*. Trans. Mr Medley. London: W. Innys, 1733.

Knight, Richard Payne. *An Inquiry into the Symbolical Language of Ancient Art and Mythology*. London, 1818.

Lacquer, Thomas and C. Gallagher (eds). *The Making of the Modern Body*. Berkeley and Los Angeles: University of California Press, 1987.

Laidler, P. W. and M. Gelfand. *South Africa: Its medical history, 1652-1898*. Cape Town: Struik, 1971.

Lee, Richard B. *The !Kung San*. Cambridge University Press, 1979.

Legassick, Martin. "The State, Racism and the Rise of Capitalism in the Nineteenth Century Cape Colony". *South African Historical Journal* 28 (1993): 329-368.

Lewis-Williams, J. David. *Believing and Seeing*. London: Academic Press, 1981.

Lichtenstein, H. *Travels in Southern Africa*. Trans. A. Plumptree. Rpt Cape Town: 1928-1930. 2 vols.

Liu, Alan. *Wordsworth: The sense of history*. Stanford: Stanford University Press, 1989.

Macksey, R. and Eugenio Donato (eds). *The Structuralist Controversy*. Baltimore: Johns Hopkins University Press, 1972.

McKeon, Michael. *The Origins of the English Novel, 1600-1740*. Baltimore: Johns Hopkins, 1987.

Mead, Richard. *A Mechanical Account of Poisons in Several Essays*. London: Ralph South, 1702.

Meiners, Cristoph. *Allgemeine kritische Geschichte der Religionen*. 2 vols, Hannover, 1805-7.

Mitchell, W. J. T. *Iconology*. Chicago: University of Chicago Press, 1986.

Newton-King, Sue. "The Enemy Within": The Struggle for ascendendancy on the Cape Eastern frontier, 1760-1799." Unpublished Ph.D. dissertation.

Noli, Hans Dieter. "A Technical Investigation into the Material Evidence for Archery in the Archaeological and Ethnographic Record of Southern Africa". Unpublished Ph.D. dissertation. University of Cape Town, 1993.

Orpen, Joseph Millard. *Reminiscences of Life in South Africa. From 1846 to the Present Day*. 1908. 2 vols. Rpt Cape Town: Struik, 1964.

Paterson, Lieutenant William. *A Narrative of Four Journeys in to the Country of the Hottentots and Caffraria in the Years 1777, 1778 and 1779*. London: J. Johnson, 1790.

Penn, Nigel. "Mapping the Cape: John Barrow and the first British occupation of the colony, 1795-1803". *Pretexts* 4.2 (Summer 1993): 20-43.

Porter, Roy. "History of the Body". In Burke (ed.): 193-205.

Pratt, Marie Louise. *Imperial Eyes: Travel writing and transculturation*. London and New York: Routledge, 1992.

Pringle, Thomas. *African Sketches*. London: Edward Moxon, 1834.

—. *Narrative of a Residence in South Africa*. 1835. Rpt Cape Town: Struik: 1966.

Samuel, Raphael. "Reading the Signs II: Fact-grubbers and mind-readers". *History Workshop Journal* 33 (1992): 220-251.

Searle, C. *The History of the Development of Nursing in South Africa, 1652-1960*. Cape Town: Struik, 1960.

Shapera, Isaac "Bushman Arrow Poisons". *Bantu Studies* 2.3, 1924.

Silberbauer, George. *Hunter and Habitat in the Central Kalahari Desert*. Cambridge: Cambridge University Press, 1981.

Simpson, David. *Fetishism and Imagination*. Baltimore: Johns Hopkins University Press, 1982.

Sparrman, Anders. *A Voyage to the Cape of Good Hope towards the Antarctic Polar Circle, Round the World and to the Country of the Hottentots from the Year 1772-1776*. London: G. J. & J. Robinson, 1785.

Spivak, Gayatri C. "Can the Subaltern Speak?" *Wedge* 7/8 (Winter/Spring 1985).

Stanley, Henry M. *In Darkest Africa*. New York: Scribner's 1890.

Steedman, Andrew. *Wanderings and Adventures in the Interior of Southern Africa*. Two Volumes. London: Longman and Co., 1835.

Thomas, K. B. *Curare: Its history and usage*. London: Pitman, n.d.

Thunberg, Carl Peter. *Travels at the Cape of Good Hope, 1772-1775*. London, 1793. Rpt Cape Town: Van Riebeeck Society, 1986.

Vaughan, Megan. *Curing Their Ills*. Cambridge: Polity Press, 1991.

"Issues in the Medical Anthropology and History of Africa". Unpublished seminar paper. Institute of Commonwealth Studies, University of London, June 1993.

Watt, J. M. and M. G. Breyer-Brandwyk. *Medical and Poisonous Plants of Southern and Eastern Africa*. Edinburgh: E. S. Livingstone, 1962.

White, Hylton. "To Live With the /Ai: A Case Study of the 'Traditional' Hunter-Gatherer Identity of the Kagga Kamma Bushmen". Unpublished honours thesis. University of Cape Town,1992.

Jane Taylor: The Poison Pen (pages 86 – 113)
NOTES

[1]   "The Second Coming of the British" is actually the title of her chapter XV, in *The History of South Africa*.

[2]   For a discussion of the way in which South African medical discourses in the early twentieth century have tried to locate gendered identity in biology, see Zackie Achmat, "'A Cape Coloured, a Botha, as Well as a Lesbian': Carl Buckle, Louis Freed and the Psychiatrisation of Male Homosexuality." Centre for African Studies, University of Cape Town, August 1993.

[3]   There is an illuminating, though quite different, discussion of "English Speech and French Writing" in Chapter Five of W. J. T. Mitchell's *Iconology*. Mitchell examines Burke's distrust of the French model of a written constitution.

[4]   This and all subsequent references to the Sherlock Holmes canon are from *The Annotated Sherlock Holmes* edited by Baring-Gould.

[5]   See, for example, Thomas, *Curare: Its history and usage* and "Experiments on Vegetable Poisons", *The Edinburgh Review*, vol xviii (August 1811): 370-379.

[6]   Doyle's medical background is substantially, if somewhat too reverently, documented by Rodin and Key, whose *Medical Casebook of Doctor Arthur Conan Doyle* seeks to recuperate Doyle by demonstrating his medical savvy.

[7]   By invoking the concept "orientalism" I refer to the familiar work of Said.

[8]   Commentary on Holmes has been split over the identity of this pathology: Some have argued that it does not exist; others that it is in fact scrub typhus or tsutsugamushi fever, "an infectious disease transmitted by mites and found, among other places, in Japan, Formosa, the Pescadores, Sumatra, New Guinea, Northern Australia and the Philippines" (Baring-Gould 441).

[9]   Quoted in Davison, "Human Subjects as Museum Objects".

[10] *Standard and Mail*, 3 October 1872. Page 2, Column e.

[11] *Standard and Mail*, 19 April 1873. Page 3, Column c.

[12] Cape Archives. CSC. 1/2/1/73. 12 (1863).

[13] Cape Archives. CSC. 1/2/1/80. 38;39 (1865).

[14] Cape Archives. CSC. 1/1/1/17. 12 (1857).

[15] From *Provincial Medical Journal and Retrospect of the Medical Sciences 1842*, 35-36. Cited in Peter Bartrip, "A 'Pennurth of Arsenic for Rat Poison': The Arsenic Act, 1851 and the Prevention of Secret Poisoning".

[16] The debate can be more fully tracked through Gilman's now famous article, "Black Bodies, White Bodies", and in the work of Steven J. Gould.

[17] See my paper, "Mark's Signs/Twain's Twins" in *Journal of Literary Studies* 8 (1/2) (June 1992): 70-86.

[18] See, for example, her "Can the Subaltern Speak?"

[19] For a discussion of early criminal investigation in South Africa see the *Standard Encyclopaedia of Southern Africa* entry for "Police". See also A. F. Hattersley, *The First South African Detectives*.

[20] Both of the basic definitions of "poison" given here are from *Chamber's Dictionary*.

[21] For a discussion of this shift see *SESA*, 634ff.

REFERENCES

Achmat, Zackie. "'A Cape Coloured, a Botha, as well as a Lesbian': Carl Buckle, Louis Freed and the Psychiatrisation of Male Homosexuality". Unpublished paper, Centre for African Studies, University of Cape Town (August) 1993.

Bartrip, Peter. "A 'Pennurth of Arsenic for Rat Poison': The Arsenic Act, 1851 and the Prevention of Secret Poisoning". *Medical History* 36.1 (Jan. 1992): 53-61.

Brodie, B. C. "Experiments and Observations on the different Modes in which Death is produced by certain Vegetable Poisons". *Edinburgh Review*, Vol. xviii (August 1811): 370-379.

Burton, Sir Richard. *The Lake Regions of Central Africa*. London: Sidgwick and Jackson, 1961.

Cape Archives. CSC. 1/2/1/73. 12 (Murraysburg. Attempted poisoning by 3 women).

—. CSC. 1/2/1/80 (Beaufort. Attempted poisoning by Aquillus Adolph).

—. CSC. 1/1/1/17. 12 (Attempted poisoning by Othello).

Davison, Patricia. "Human Subjects as Museum Objects. A Project to Make Life-Casts of 'Bushmen' and 'Hottentots', 1907-1924". *Annals of the South African Museum* 102.5 (February 1993): 165-183.

Doyle, Sir Arthur Conan. *Our African Winter*. London: John Murray, 1929.

—. *Songs of Action*. London: Smith, Elder & Co., 1898.

—. *The Great Boer War*. London: George Bell, 1900.

—. *The Annotated Sherlock Holmes*. Ed. W. S. Baring-Gould. New York: Wings, 1967.

Encyclopedia Brittanica. Chicago: University of Chicago Press, 1986.

Fairbridge, Dorothea. *A History of South Africa*. Oxford: Oxford University Press, 1917.

Farini, G. A. *Through the Kalahari Desert: A narrative of a journey with gun, camera, and note-book to Lake N'gami and back*. Cape Town: Struik, 1973.

Forbes, T. R. "Early Forensic Medicine in England: The Angus murder trial". *Journal of the History of Medicine and Allied Sciences*, Vol. xxxvi (1981): 296-309.

Galton, Francis. *Narrative of an Explorer in Tropical South Africa*. London: Ward, Lock and Co., 1891.

—. *Decipherment of Blurred Finger Prints*. London: Macmillan, 1893.

Gilman, Sander. "Black Bodies, White Bodies" in Henry Louis Gates, Jr. (ed.). *"Race", Writing, and Difference*. Chicago, University of Chicago Press, 1986.

Ginzburg, Carlo. "Morelli, Freud and Sherlock Holmes: Clues and scientific method". *History Workshop* 9 (Spring 1980): 5-36.

Hattersley, Alan F. *The First South African Detectives*. Cape Town: Howard Timmins, 1960.

Jager, Adonis (Pseud.). "The Diary of an Idle Hottentot". *Cape Monthly Magazine*, n.s. Vol. xiv, (Jan.-June 1877): 159-166.

Kolb, Peter. *The Present State of the Cape of Good Hope*. Trans. Mr Medley. London: W. Innys, 1731.

Laidler, P. W. and M. Gelfand. *South Africa: Its medical history*, 1652-1898. Cape Town: Struik, 1971.

McKeon, Michael. *The Origins of the English Novel, 1600-1740*. Baltimore: Johns Hopkins, 1987.

Mitchell, W. J. T. *Iconology*. Chicago: University of Chicago Press, 1986.

Noli, Hans Dieter. "A Technical Investigation into the Material Evidence for Archery in the Archaeological and Ethnographic Record of Southern Africa". Unpublished Ph.D. dissertation. University of Cape Town, 1993.

Paterson, Lieutenant William. *A Narrative of Five Journeys into the Country of the Hottentots and Caffraria in the Years 1777, 1778 and 1779*. London: J. Johnson, 1790.

Pearson, Hesketh. *Conan Doyle*. London: Methuen, 1943, 1946.

Pratt, Marie Loiuse. *Imperial Eyes: Travel writing and transculturation*. London and New York: Routledge, 1992.

Rodin, A. E. and J. D. Key. *The Medical Casebook of Doctor Arthur Conan Doyle*. Malabar, Florida: Robert E. Krieger, 1984.

Searle, C. *The History of the Development of Nursing in South Africa, 1652-1960*. Cape Town: Struik, 1960.

Schiebinger, Londa. "Why Mammals Are Called Mammals: Gender politics in eighteenth-century natural history". *American Historical Review* 98.2 (April 1993): 382-411.

Shakespeare, William. *Hamlet*. Oxford: Oxford University Press, 1987.

Spivak, Gayatri C. "Can the Subaltern Speak?" *Wedge* 7/8 (Winter/Spring), 1985.

Sprat, Thomas. *History of the Royal Society*. Ed. Jackson I. Cope and H. W. Jones. London: Routledge and Kegan Paul, 1959.

Standard and Mail. "Atrocious attempt to poison a mistress". 3 October 1872. Page 2, Column e.

—. "A Bushman girl, who was scolded by her mistress". 19 April 1873. Page 3, Column c.

Standard Encyclopaedia of Southern Africa. Cape Town: Nasionale Boekhandel, 1973.

Stanley, Henry M. *In Darkest Africa*. New York: Scribner's, 1890.

Swift, Jonathan. *Gulliver's Travels*. New York: Norton, 1970.

Taylor, C. Jane. "Mark's Signs/Twain's Twins". *Journal of Literary Studies* 8.1/2 (June 1992): 70-86.

Thomas, K. B. *Curare: Its history and usage*. London: Pitman, n.d.

Twain, Mark. *Pudd'nhead Wilson*. New York: Norton, 1980.

van der Westhuizen, Jacob and H. Oosthuizen, *Portents of Violence?* Pretoria: Unisa Institute for Criminology, 1983.

Martin Hall: From Lydenburg to Mafikeng (pages 116 – 133)
NOTES

[1] This seems to have been an informal decision. There is no record of a decision to adopt a logo in the papers of the Board of African Studies. The first public use of the logo was on the cover of the Centre's first publication. (Twentyman-Jones 1979) The logo first appeared on the Centre's *Newsletter* in May 1980 but has not been used since July 1992.

[2] Bob Molloy, "Head in the Clouds". *Cape Times*, 10 May 1979.

[3] "Famous Lydenburg Heads now on View". *Cape Times*, 23 May 1979.

[4] *Cape Times*, 23 May 1979.

[5] This essay builds on two prior papers which approach the same problem from different directions: A critique of Sol Kerzner's Lost City of Bophuthatswana which, I have argued, appropriates a master narrative of the African past which precedes the experience of the continent by European colonial settlers, and a narrative on the Lydenburg Heads which is part of a project with Malcolm Payne and Patricia Davison, and which contemplates the meaning of the heads and the manner in which they can serve as a point of departure for understanding material things and their representations (Hall 1993; 1995).

[6] It has recently been argued that the heads were made later, probably in the mid-eighth century (Whitelaw 1992).

[7] Inskeep and Maggs titled their paper "Unique Art Objects in the Iron Age of the Transvaal" and speculated that the heads were "a unique experiment which we shall not find repeated". (Inskeep and Maggs 1975: 136) As Evers (1982) pointed out, this claim for uniqueness has proved unjustified, as fragments of terracotta sculptures have been found from other Early Iron Age sites in South Africa.

[8] Examples are discussed in Hall (1987). This tradition of interpretation continues today. In the most recent re-analysis, it has been suggested that the Lydenburg site was occupied in three phases, and that the heads were part of the last occupation, sometime in the mid-eighth century. In turn, this periodisation offers a new approach to assessing competing models for Early Iron Age dispersal patterns: the "Kulundu Tradition" (indicating movement into South Africa through Botswana and Zimbabwe) or the "Urewe Tradition" (tracing southward movement along, and close to, the eastern seaboard); Whitelaw (1992).

[9] Marx (1974). Nick Shepherd (UCT Department of Archaeology) is completing an important Ph.D. dissertation which will make a major contribution towards reintegrating Marx's seminal work into archaeological interpretations.

[10] For "contextual archaeologists" meaning is not appropriated by a claim of objectivity, but emerges

from the totality of context. "It is . . . by looking for significant patterning along dimensions of variation that the relevant dimensions are defined. The symbolic meaning of an object is an abstraction from the totality of these cross-references. The meaning of an object is derived from the totality of its similarities and differences, associations and contrasts." (Hodder 1986: 138) Hodder's first delineation of Contextual Archaeology was his "Symbolic and Structural Archaeology" (1982).

[11] This list repeats the subjects of five successive essays in "Reading Material Culture". (Tilley 1990a) The Preface announces that "this book is an exploration of a number of important contemporary positions in the human sciences which appear to have great relevance to material-culture studies". (Tilley 1990a: vii) The slippage in the use of the positivist term "human sciences" anticipates many of the ambiguities to be found in the essays that follow. It is, of course, ironic that archaeologists should be turning to "authorities" who themselves come from a tradition that denies the possibility of authority.

[12] "Much, if not all, material culture production can be described as a process in which different interest groups and individuals try to set up authoritative or established meanings in the face of the inherent ability of individuals to create their own, shifting, foot-loose schemes . . . All aspects of cultural production . . . can be seen to play a part in the negotiation and 'fixing' of meaning by individuals and interest groups within society . . ." (Hodder 1986: 151).

[13] ". . . each individual act of material culture production and use has to be regarded as a contextualized social act involving the relocation of signs along axes defining the relationship between signs and other signs which reach out beyond themselves and towards others becoming amplified or subdued in specific contexts" (Tilley 1989: 188-189).

[14] These confusions continue in a later paper. Tilley argues that "any writing of material culture is transformative . . . The associations made between artifacts and their context occur as much in the linguistic medium of the text as they do in that which the text may attempt to describe and discuss." (Tilley 1990b: 332) But at the same time the text is not "a free-floating medium, an endless play of meaning which can only refer back to itself". Why? Because the artefact is always a "discursive object" which is "transcribed" in the process of study. Therefore the text "mediates" – it has a dual meaning in its own organisation and syntax, and in its "relation to the world", although these dual meanings cannot be "separated out" (Tilley 1990b: 332).

[15] "The meaning of material culture is created in the text. From the beginning to the end meaning resides in what the text does to material culture. Meaning is internal to the text and its language use." (Tilley 1990b: 332-333).

[16] This debate was the focal point of the Theoretical Archaeology Group Conference in Southampton in December 1992. Despite its esoteric title, this annual meeting has become one of the most important conference series in European archaeology.

[17] Payne 1989, 1990, 1992. "Market Forces" was an exhibition in the Long Cell, Graduate School of Business, University of Cape Town, June 1992; Pippa Skotnes, opening address to the exhibition "Market Forces", Graduate School of Business, University of Cape Town, 2 June 1992.

[18] Skotnes, opening address, June 1992.

[19] Both Hodder and Tilley worry fitfully about the "materiality" of material culture. Hodder, for instance, sees the inadequacy of structuralism as its focus of relationships, rather than on objects: "there is little interest in the 'thing' itself . . . We dig up material as much as we dig up ideas. And we wish to see each object *both* as an object, the result of processes of production and action, *and* as a sign, since the object . . . can itself be a signifier for other concepts . . .". (Hodder 1986: 47, original emphasis) Tilley becomes confused about the concrete properties of his artefacts. On the one hand he tries to collapse materiality and discourse into one another; "the notion of materiality needs to be extended so as to properly include discourse". (Tilley 1990a: 333) But later, on the same page: "material culture is non-discursive in the limited sense that it is a set of objects".

[20] Molino (1992: 22). But this material existence is only one aspect of the sign – in addition, the sign has an "aesthetic" existence, in that it is received by someone. Thus the sign is reference, as well as object, and the object is only a trace of the full sign. This partiality denies the possibility of "ob-

jective", positivist study, since all archaeology has are the traces of meaning.
[21] To avoid a discussion of what constitutes an academic discipline, here is the full entry in Collins English Dictionary. These eight aspects of discipline all seem to have some relevance to the codes of academic practice. "1. training or conditions imposed for the improvement of physical powers, self-control etc. 2. systematic training in obedience to regulations and authority. 3. the state of improved behaviour, etc., resulting from such training or conditions. 4. punishment or chastisement. 5. a system of rules for behaviour, methods of practice, etc. 6. a branch of learning or instruction. 7. the laws governing members of a Church. 8. a scourge of knotted cords."

REFERENCES

Cooper, Brenda. "Let's give the boot to the Lydenburg Head". Centre for African Studies, University of Cape Town. *Newsletter* 2 (March 1988).

Evers, T. M "Excavations at the Lydenburg heads site, eastern Transvaal, South Africa". *South African Archaeological Bulletin* 37 (1982): 16-30.

Hall, Martin. *The Changing Past: Farmers, kings and traders in southern Africa, 200-1860.* Cape Town: David Philip, 1987.

—. "The legend of the Lost City; Or, the man with golden balls". Journal of Southern Africa Studies 21 (2) (1995): 179-199.

—. "Tales and Heads: Bodies and landscapes". In Payne, Malcolm. *Face Value: Old heads in modern masks*. Cape Town: Axeage, 1993.

Hodder, Ian. *Symbolic and Structural Archaeology.* Cambridge: Cambridge University Press, 1982.

—. *Reading the Past. Current approaches to interpretation in archaeology.* Cambridge: Cambridge University Press, 1986.

—. "Post-Modernism, Post-Structuralism and Post-Processual Archaeology". In Hodder, Ian (ed.). *The Meanings of Things. Material culture and symbolic expression.* London: Harper Collins, 1986: 64-78.

Inskeep, R. R. and T. Maggs. "Unique Art Objects in the Iron Age of the Transvaal, South Africa." *South African Archaeological Bulletin* 30 (1985): 114-138.

Jaume, Damia, Guillem Pons, Miquel Palmer, Miquel McMinn, Josep Antoni Alcover and Gustavo Politis. "Racism, Archaeology and Museums: The strange case of the stuffed African male in the Darder Museum, Banyoles (Catalonia), Spain." *World Archaeological Bulletin* 6 (1992): 113-118.

Maggs, T. and P. Davison. "The Lydenburg Heads." *African Arts* 14 (2) (1981): 28-33.

Marx, Karl. *Capital. A critical analysis of capitalist production.* (ed. Frederick Engels). Volume 1. London: Lawrence and Wishart, 1974.

Miller, Daniel. *Material Culture and Mass Consumption.* Oxford: Basil Blackwell, 1987.

Molino, Jean. "Archaeology and Symbol Systems". In Gardin, Jean-Claude and Christopher Peebles (eds.). *Representations in Archaeology.* Bloomington: Indiana University Press, 1992: 15-29.

Olsen, Bjornar. "Roland Barthes: From sign to text". In Tilley, C. (ed.). *Reading Material Culture. Structuralism, hermeneutics and post-structuralism.* Oxford: Basil Blackwell, 1990: 163-205.

Payne, Malcolm. "From Lydenburg to Witbank", *Artworks in Progress. The Yearbook of the Staff of the Michaelis School of Fine Art,* University of Cape Town, 1 (1989), 36-41.

—. Untitled. *Artworks in Progress collection,* 2 (1990): 20-23.

—. "Form and the Picturing of Mining. An epistemology of form with special reference to the explication of iconography." Unpublished MFA thesis, University of Cape Town, 1992.

Skotnes, Pippa. "Letter to the editor". Centre for African Studies, University of Cape Town. *Newsletter* 3, May 1988.

Smit, Louis Almaro. "The Lydenburg Museum". *Overvaal Museanuus* 18 (1) 1992: 4-6.

Tilley, Christopher. "Interpreting Material Culture". In Hodder, Ian (ed.). *The Meanings of Things. Material culture and symbolic expression.* London: Harper Collins, 1989: 185-194.

—. (ed.) *Reading Material Culture*. Blackwell: Oxford, 1990a.

Tilley, Christopher. "Michel Foucault: Towards an archaeology of archaeology". In Tilley, C. (ed.). *Reading Material Culture. Structuralism, hermeneutics and post-structuralism*. Oxford: Basil Blackwell, 1990b: 281-347.

Twentyman-Jones, Leone. *Research Resources in Cape Town. A guide*. Centre for African Studies Occasional Papers No. 1, 1979.

Van der Merwe, N. J. "Letter to the editor". Centre for African Studies, University of Cape Town. *Newsletter* 3, May 1988.

Von Bezing, K. L. and R. R. Inskeep. "Modelled Terracotta Heads from Lydenburg, South Africa". *Man* 1 (1), 1966: 102.

Whitelaw, Gavin. "Lydenburg Revisited: Another look at the Eastern Transvaal Early Iron Age sequence". Paper presented at the Conference of the Southern African Association of Archaeologists, Cape Town, 1992.

Malcolm Payne: Face Value (pages 136 – 140)
NOTES

[1] A designation coined by Archille Bonito Oliva in describing his curatorial vision for the XXIV Venice Biennale of 1993.

[2] Institute of New International Visual Arts (INIVA). A British Arts Council initiative to create an institute of new international art in support of culturally diverse visual arts.

[3] Artists on the other hand, tired of the academism of the salons, were delighted by the transformative and regenerative potential of these new formal conceptions. They were used as revisionist tools to invigorate early modernism.

[4] Morphet suggests "the goal which the book works towards is a demonstration of a cornerstone of the project – that the Lydenburg Heads are 'empty'." (Morphet, Anthony. "Continental Drift". *Southern African Review of Books* 6.3.31 (May/June 1994): 3-5.

REFERENCE

Bhabha, Homi K. *The Location of Culture*. London: Routledge, 1994.

Obi Maduakor: The Legacy of Suffering (pages 153 – 161)

Aidoo, Ama Ata. *Prologue to Anowa*. London: Longmans, 1970.

Armah, Ayi Kwei. *The Beautyful Ones Are Not Yet Born*. London: Heinemann, 1969.

Armah, Ayi Kwei. *Two Thousand Seasons*. Lusaka: East African Publishing House, 1973.

Armah, Ayi Kwei. *Fragments*. London: Heinemann, 1974.

Awoonor, Kofi. *This Earth, My Brother*. London: Heinemann, 1971.

Awoonor, Kofi. *Comes the Voyager at Last*. Trenton: Africa World Press, 1992.

Cesaire, Aime. Return to my Native Land. Harmondsworth: Penguin, 1969.

Diop, David. "Africa". In Reed, John and Clive Wake (eds). *A Book of African Verse*. London: Heinemann, 1964.

Equiano, Olaudah. *Equiano's Travels: An autobiography*. Ed. and abridged by Paul Edwards. London: Heinemann, 1969.

Lovejoy, Paul E. *Transformations in Slavery*. Cambridge: Cambridge University Press, 1983.

Miers, Suzanne and Igor Kopytoff (eds). *Slavery in Africa: Historical and anthropological perspectives*. Madison: The University of Wisconsin Press, 1977.

Ouologuem, Yambo. *Bound to Violence*. Translated from the French by Ralph Manheim. London: Martin

Secker and Warburg, 1971.

Soyinka, Wole. "A Dance of the Forests" In Soyinka. *Collected Plays 1*. Oxford: Oxford University Press, 1973.

Brenda Cooper: Cultural Identity, Cultural Studies in Africa and the Representation of the Middle Passage (pages 164 – 183)

NOTES

[1]   Forthcoming 1995, "Postcolonialism Against the 'Empire of the Discipline'". Fincham, Gail and Myrtle Hooper (eds). Under Postcolonial Eyes: Joseph Conrad after empire, University of Cape Town Press.

[2]   Ibid.

REFERENCES

Ahmad, Aijaz. *In Theory*. Verso, 1992.

Bhabha, Homi K. *The Location of Culture*. Routledge, 1994.

Bundy, Colin. "Sharing the Burden". In Cooper, B. and A. Steyn (eds). *Transgressing Boundaries*, Cape Town: UCT Press, 1996.

Comaroff, Jean. "Late 20th Century Social Science: A conversation". In Cooper, B. and A. Steyn (eds). *Transgressing Boundaries*, Cape Town: UCT Press, 1996.

Cheney-Coker, Syl. *The Last Harmattan of Alusine Dunbar*. Heinemann African Writers Series, 1990.

Cooper, Brenda. "Does Marxism Allow for the Magical Side of Things? Magical realism and a comparison between *One Hundred Years of Solitude* and *The House of the Spirits*". *Social Dynamics* 17.2 (1991): 126-154.

—. "Syl Cheney-Coker: *The Last Harmattan of Alusine Dunbar and an Interview*". *ALA Bulletin*, vol. 28.3 (Summer 1994): 3-17

—. "The Two-Faced Ogun: postcolonial intellectuals and the positioning of Wole Soyinka". *English in Africa*, October 1995.

Gates Jr., Henry Louis. *The Signifying Monkey*. Oxford University Press, 1988.

Hall, Stuart. "The Question of Cultural Identity". In Hall, S., D. Held and T. McGrew (eds). *Modernity and its Futures*. Polity/Blackwell/Open University, 1992: 273-325.

—. "Cultural Identity and Diaspora". In Williams, Patrick and Laura Chrisman (eds). *Colonial Discourse and Post-Colonial Theory. A reader*. Harvester Wheatsheaf, 1993: 392-403.

Hurston, Zora Neale. *Their Eyes were Watching God*. Perennial Library, 1990 (orig.1937).

Jameson, Fredric. *Postmodernism or, The Cultural Logic of Late Capitalism*. Verso, 1991.

Lovell, Terry. "The Burden of the Disciplines". In Cooper, B. and A. Steyn (eds). *Transgressing Boundaries*, Cape Town: UCT Press, 1996.

McClintock, Anne. "The Angel of Progress: Pitfalls of the term 'Post-colonialism'". In Williams, P. (ed.). *Colonial Discourse and Post-Colonial Theory. A reader*. Harvester Wheatsheaf, 1993: 291-304.

Spitzer, Leo. *The Creoles of Sierra Leone*. University of Wisconsin Press, 1974.

Laura H. Chrisman: Appropriate Appropriations? (pages 184 – 195)

ACKNOWLEDGEMENT

With thanks to Bob Matthews and Leon Robinson for their generous assistance in preparing the final version of this paper.

REFERENCES

Bennett, Tony. "Putting Policy into Cultural Studies". In Grossberg, L., C. Nelson and P. Treichler (eds).

Cultural Studies. London: Routledge, 1992: 23-34.

Conference brochure "Appropriations: New Directions in the Study of Culture in Africa". Centre for African Studies, University of Cape Town (September 1993): 1.

Farred, Grant. "Unity and Difference in Black South Africa". *Social Text* 110.2/3.31/32 (1992): 217-234.

Green, Michael. "'Cultural Studies!', Said the Magistrate". *News from Nowhere, Journal of Cultural Materialism* 8 (Autumn 1990): 28-37.

Hall, Stuart. "Cultural Studies and its Theoretical Legacies". In Grossberg et al. (eds). *Cultural Studies*, 1992: 277-286.

Peach, Linden. "Yorkshire and the Origins of Cultural Politics". *Red Letters* 27 (Autumn 1990): 6-7.

Williams, Raymond. "The Future of Cultural Studies". In Pinkey, T. (ed.). *The Politics of Modernism. Against the new conformists*. London: Verso, 1989a: 151-62.

—. "The Uses of Cultural Theory". In Pinkey, T. (ed.). *The Politics of Modernism. Against the new conformists*. London: Verso, 1989b: 163-176.

Gary Minkley/Andrew Steyn: South African Cultural Studies in the Moment of the 1990s (pages 196 – 207)

NOTES

1. It needs to be mentioned at the outset that South Africa does not have the kind of institutionalised "cultural studies" project associated with Britain, for example. There are rather numerous, more or less connected "spaces", concerned with the study of culture. We therefore use the term cultural studies in a more general sense, to refer to a range of approaches to these studies of culture. In South Africa, these have been variously defined in history, literary studies, African studies, anthropology and the Centre for Cultural and Media Studies, as well as by practitioners, intellectuals and policy formulators. The theory, practice and scope of cultural studies also varies according to "location". The academy is only one site, and it has significant relationships with cultural critique and production beyond its "borders".

2. Alexander has borrowed the term from Chatterjee. (1993: 110-111)

3. Statement by the National Executive Committee of the African National Congress. ANC Department of Information. Internet, 29/8/1994.

4. See Morphet, 1990b: 98.

REFERENCES

Alexander, Neville. "'The Moment of Manoeuvre': 'Race', ethnicity and nation in post-apartheid South Africa". Unpublished paper presented at the International Sociological Association XIII International Congress in Bielefeld, Germany, 1994.

Bundy, Colin. "The Art of Writing History". *Southern African Review of Books* 6.1 (issue 29) 1994.

—. "Sharing the Burden? A response to Terry Lovell". In Cooper, B. and A. Steyn (eds). *Transgressing Boundaries*. Cape Town: UCT Press, 1996.

Bunn, David. "'The Brown Serpent of the Rocks': Bushman arrow toxins in the Dutch and British imagination, 1735 - 1850": In Cooper, B. and A. Steyn (eds). *Transgressing Boundaries*. Cape Town: UCT Press, 1996.

Chatterjee, Partha. *Nationalist Thought and the Colonial World. A derivative discourse*. London: Zed Books, 1993.

Chrisman, Laura. "Appropriate Appropriations? Developing cultural studies in South Africa". In Cooper, B. and A. Steyn (eds). *Transgressing Boundaries*. Cape Town: UCT Press, 1996.

Comaroff, Jean. "Late 20th Century Social Science: A conversation". In Cooper, B. and A. Steyn (eds). *Transgressing Boundaries*. Cape Town: UCT Press, 1996.

—, and John Comaroff. *Modernity and its Malcontents: Ritual and power in postcolonial Africa.* Chicago: University of Chicago Press, 1993.

Cooper, Brenda. "Cultural Identity, Cultural Studies in Africa and the Representation of the Middle Passage". In Cooper, B. and A. Steyn (eds). *Transgressing Boundaries.* Cape Town: UCT Press, 1996.

—, and Andrew Steyn (eds). *Transgressing Boundaries. New directions in the study of culture in Africa.* Cape Town: UCT Press, 1996.

Cooper, Frederick. "Postscript: Africa and the world economy". In Cooper, F. et al. (eds). *Confronting Historical Paradigms.* Madison, Wisc.: University of Wisconsin Press, 1993: 187-201.

Dirlik, Arif. "The Postcolonial Aura: third world criticism in the age of global capitalism". *Critical Inquiry,* 20.2 (Winter 1994): 328-356.

Fabian, Johannes. "Crossing and Patrolling: Thoughts on anthropology and boundaries". *Culture* 13.1 (1993): 49-53.

Hall, Martin. "Decapitation – Recapitulation. From Lydenburg to Mafikeng: Appropriations of images of the past". In Cooper, B. and A. Steyn (eds). *Transgressing Boundaries.* Cape Town: UCT Press, 1996.

Hall, Stuart, "The Question of Cultural Identity". In Hall, S., D. Held and T. McGrew (eds). *Modernity and its Futures.* Cambridge: Polity in association with the Open University, 1992: 274-316.

Hofmeyr, Isabel. "Introduction to History Workshop Positions". *Pretexts* 2.2 (Summer 1990): 61-71.

—. "Response to Taylor and Bunn". In Cooper, B. and A. Steyn (eds). *Transgressing Boundaries.* Cape Town: UCT Press, 1996.

—. *We Spend our Years as a Tale that is Told: Oral historical narrative in a South African chiefdom.* Johannesburg: Witwatersrand University Press, 1993.

Karon, Tony. "SA artists in Havana: Close, but no cigar". *Weekly Mail & Guardian* 10.25 (24 - 30 June), 1994.

Lovell, Terry. "The Burden of the Disciplines: African studies, women's studies, cultural studies". In Cooper, B. and A. Steyn (eds). *Transgressing Boundaries.* Cape Town: UCT Press, 1996.

Marcus, George. "Possibilities for Critical Anthropology: What comes (just) after 'post'? The Case of Ethnography". Unpublished paper, Centre for African Studies, University of Cape Town, October 1993.

Morphet, Tony. "Cultural settlement: Albie Sachs, Njabulo Ndebele and the question of social and cultural imagination". *Pretexts* 2.1 (Winter 1990a): 94-103.

—. "Brushing History Against the Grain: Oppositional discourse in South Africa". *Theoria* 76 (October 1990b): 89-99.

Muller, Johan and Keyan Tomaselli. "Becoming appropriately modern: Towards a genealogy of cultural studies in South Africa". In Mouton, J. et al. (eds). *Knowledge and Method in the Human Sciences.* Pretoria: Human Sciences Research Council, 1990: 301-319.

National Arts Coalition. Flyer advertising their conference "Bringing Cinderella to the Ball: Arts and culture in the new South Africa". Johannesburg, September 1994.

Ndebele, Njabulo. "Redefining Relevance". *Pretexts* 1.1 (Winter 1989): 40-51.

Pechey, Graham. "Post-Apartheid Narratives". In Barker, F. et al. (eds). *Colonial Discourse, Postcolonial Theory.* New York: Manchester University Press, 1993.

Sachs, Albie. "Preparing Ourselves for Freedom". ANC in-house seminar on culture. Mimeo. No date, ca. 1990.

Taylor, C. Jane. "The Poison Pen". In Cooper, B. and A. Steyn (eds). *Transgressing Boundaries.* Cape Town: UCT Press, 1996.

Index